SYDNEY
NOVEMBER 2006

LIFE AND WORK

£5-

7|4t.

gen

Life and Work is co-authored by scientist Charles Birch and business change-management specialist Dr David Paul. **Charles Birch**, Emeritus Professor of the University of Sydney and winner of the prestigious Templeton Prize, has published many books on ecology and the philosophy of biology – the latest is *Biology and the Riddle of Life* (also by UNSW Press). Quality of life is a recurrent theme in his writings. **David Paul** has worked with banks and government organisations and has been an adjunct lecturer at the University of Technology Sydney Graduate School of Business. His business interests include people management, cultural change and quality of life in the workplace.

To Elizabeth More

LIFE AND WORK

CHALLENGING ECONOMIC MAN

Charles Birch and David Paul

UNSW
PRESS

A UNSW Press book

Published by
University of New South Wales Press Ltd
University of New South Wales
Sydney NSW 2052
AUSTRALIA
www.unswpress.com.au

National Library of Australia
Cataloguing-in-Publication entry

Birch, Charles.
  Life and work : challenging economic man.

  Includes index.
  ISBN 0 86840 670 8.

  1. Work and family. 2. Quality of life. 3. Quality of
  work life. I. Paul, David (David Victor Emmanuel).
  II. Title.

  306.36

Printer BPA
Cover design Di Quick
Cover image Mysterious Dialogue (*Dialogo Misterioso*, 1973),
© Georgio de Chirico, Licensed to VISCOPY, Sydney, 2003

CONTENTS

FOREWORD

While in Italy recently I was in a travel agency booking seats for a train trip. My conversation with the Italian travel agent turned to our children, and she mentioned she had a daughter living in the United States, married to an American. 'My daughter wants to return to Italy', the agent said. 'She says that in America people only live to work while in Italy we work to live.'

Birch and Paul take up this theme in their thought-provoking book. They pose the blunt question: 'What's the point of working?' Work plays an increasingly important part in most of our lives. For some of us it seems all-consuming. For many the 'forty-hour week', aspired to and fought for by the union movement for decades, is a joke. In the 1980s, futurists were fond of telling us that modern labour-saving devices would free us from the drudgery of work at home and in factories and offices — the problem for all of us would be how to spend the newly found leisure time. But many families today are working longer hours to pay for burgeoning new technologies that feature in our homes and offices, and they hardly have time to pause and ask: 'What went wrong? Are the new technologies really serving our needs?' Yet again, for others in our society, the possibility of finding paid work at all is a forgotten dream and much of this new technology is inaccessible.

In this century, two philosophies vie for our allegiance. One is economic rationalism (also known as 'neoconservatism' in North American and 'neoliberalism' in Europe), which reduces human nature to 'economic man' and supports a morality based on a belief in market forces and the pursuit of short-term profit. Economic rationalists view work as necessary for productivity and productivity as necessary for profit. Economic rationalists seldom ask, let alone answer the question: 'Profit for whom?' They ignore the increasing contribution that their policies make to social inequality and impending ecological disaster.

The other philosophy is sustainability, which sees humans as one of many diverse species on the planet and strives to revise economics to include social relationships and ecology. Its advocates are redefining economic activity to create social justice, and redesigning production systems to support planetary life systems. In this philosophy, work supports the ongoing survival of all Earth's diverse species, creates a global society worth living in, and provides meaning and significance to our lives. Economic rationalists argue that this way of viewing the world is idealistic and impractical. However, there is increasing evidence that this is a better way of doing business — even in traditional business terms.

Birch and Paul enter this debate on the sustainability side. They write clearly in a straightforward style free of jargon and cant, and the book is a handy review of current thinking in the area of life and work. But the authors go well beyond this to put forward fresh and original ideas and a clear charter for change — ten core principles for increasing quality of life in the workplace.

I would like to see the book as required reading for students in MBA and Commerce programs. But it will also be a useful guide for senior executives increasingly concerned about making their organisation an 'employer of choice'. Demographic changes are reducing the number of future workforce entrants, so sensible executives are trying to build corporate cultures that will attract the best and brightest to their organisation. Newer generations are looking for more than just financial rewards from work. Most also want work to provide meaning and support their quality of life. Whatever our role in the workplace, however, this is a book that challenges us to contribute to the transformation of the workplace so that it supports genuine productivity and the needs of humanity and the Earth.

Dexter Dunphy
Distinguished Professor
University of Technology, Sydney

PREFACE

The theme of this book is the relation between life and work. Its central focus is the quality of our lives and how that is influenced, for good and for bad, by work. Likewise we consider how our non-working lives influence our work.

This is a new theme for organisations whose one bottom line is profits and the contribution work makes to profits. Theirs is an ideology which pretends that those values which can be measured in terms of money are the only ones that ought to count. In this scheme of things there are big winners and there are big losers. There are heads that are bloodied and hearts that are broken. That is because too many organisations are careless of the dignity of the individual and show an insensitivity to real values.

There is another way. It sees not just a bottom line of profits, but a triple bottom line that includes also social and environmental responsibility. It can put back into the making of the world a richer set of values that can be transforming.

This book deals with the two bottom lines of social responsibility and profits. It claims indeed that when organisations get relationships with employees and customers right, profits follow as a matter of course. Central to this theme is that people matter. To know in what way they matter we need to be clear about what are real human needs, as distinct from manufactured wants. We see a red flag of warning. It leads us to seek a light at the end of the tunnel.

This book is relevant to large corporations, CEOs, senior executives, students and those who are fundamentally concerned with both lifting profit margins and also the quality of life of their employees in the long run. We give many examples of how managing people well leads to increased productivity, efficiency and improved profits. By managing the people side of business, senior executives and managers not only add value to their organisations but also help to create a society that in its turn respects and values its organisations. This is an important element in creating a civil society. The room for progress here is practically limitless.

We suggest each reader ask how he or she could argue for his or her own organisation that social responsibility together with profits offers a low-risk strategy that will deliver value and enthusiasm to shareholders with enhanced quality of life for employees and the community.

'There is a tide in the affairs of men' wrote Shakespeare (*Julius Caesar* IV: iii) 'Which, taken at the flood, leads on to fortune'. On such a flood tide of opportunity we are now afloat. The evidence, we show, is all around us.

ACKNOWLEDGMENTS

We gratefully dedicate this book to Elizabeth More, one-time director of the Macquarie Graduate School of Management, during which time (2002) this school was *The Economist*'s top management school in Australia. She is now the deputy vice-chancellor of the University of Canberra. She has been an inspiration to many, including ourselves.

We are grateful to Bill Ford of the University of New South Wales, who read an early version of the manuscript and made many helpful suggestions. Mary Schmidt and her staff greatly facilitated our use of the excellent library of the New South Wales Teachers' Federation, and to them we are most grateful. To Baden Offord of the Southern Cross University we are indebted for sending us a number of papers, which we could otherwise have easily missed. We thank Sid Birch for providing us with important articles from various sources. Barbara Sanders helped us with internet searches, journal articles and solving computer problems. We also thank Anne Ross-Smith for her help with books on women and management. James Lytton-Hitchens kept us up-to-date with trends in management, and Marissa Crawford helped us to discover 'slow towns'. Library staff of the ACTU in Melbourne were most helpful in giving us access to reports.

Part 1

QUALITY OF LIFE

Quality of life has to do with the sense of fulfilment, worth-whileness and purpose. People are the heart of any living organisation. People matter, both for themselves and for the organisation they serve.

We approach this subject by recognising the common needs of all people, and the implications of this for both employer and employee. From this preliminary understanding we derive a tentative set of ethics (Chapter 2) for the organisation and all those in it. From this basis we make judgments about the role of work, profits, health, technology and culture of the organisation, and of the culture of society. Profit becomes a worthy goal when it is seen as part of the triple bottom line that also includes human and environmental responsibility. The final chapter deals with attempts to quantify the quality of life of societies and its relation to their material standard of living.

1

WORK TO LIVE

What I see happening is that Human Resource professionals are starting to manage the 'people' side of their organizations in such a way as to create value for the organization as well as for the employee. Ultimately, of course, this will also create value for society as a whole.
Jac Fitz-enz, *Human Value Management*, 1990, p xiii.

Capital and machinery make it possible — people make it happen.
Jeffery Pfeffer, *The Human Equation*, 1998, p 305.

'Business searches for a soul', 'Superwoman dies from overwork', 'The sheer misery of more money', 'Wheels of progress fall off the Protestant work ethic', 'Pity the boss: he's working harder', 'Too much to do, not enough staff', 'Life in the balance for workers', 'The overworked Australian', 'Unhappy homes a work hazard', 'Working overtime at keeping a job', 'Slaves to work', 'Distressing news of stress in the workplace', 'Top executives: why they're drop outs', 'Teachers working longer hours than ever', 'Universities slash jobs', 'Student support too little to live on'.

These are not chapters of a book. They are recent newspaper headlines. What they tell us is that all is not well in the workplace. This book identifies the human costs of such a situation. Ours is an outcry that reveals the real state of affairs. It is a call for a more generous, more compassionate and a more humane working life than most people now experience.

As we begin the twenty-first century, Kelly (2001) makes the unhappy judgment that Australia confronts the brutal realisation that, after 20 years of economic reform, it has a weak dollar, devalued assets, a brain drain, and is seeing its best companies fall to foreign control. However, this is not a time to retreat. Rather it is a time to implement a radical strategy of change in our corporate cultures and business environments. One dissatisfaction in the workplace is a feature of life in the world in general. Business reputations have sunk so low that a study in the United States in 2002 found that 'Americans thought more highly of politicians than they did of business executives' (Gettler 2002, p 3). We need a new paradigm, a new model and a new way of thinking and working that will catch the tide that leads on to fortune.

Live to work or work to live? That is the question. Our answer in this book is that simply making a living is less important than living a life, which involves living a fulfilled life.

One of us asked a Brazilian man standing on a languid street corner in the tropical capital of Mato Grosso, 'What do you do here?' — meaning what work do you do in this town.

'Why,' he replied, 'I live here'.

Instead of asking a person what useful things they do, it is indeed appropriate to ask: What is there in your life to make you glad to be alive? What have you done to justify your existence? Have you known love and friendship? Have you been lifted by Bach's 'Mass in B minor'? These questions have to do not with instrumental value but with intrinsic value; not with means but with ends.

'Why, I *live* here' could have rich meaning.

We live to work when work serves the purpose of giving us an income with which to hopefully enjoy life beyond working hours. Work itself is perceived as a necessary burden which people must bear while they long for the weekend and holidays, and exult when the week ends proclaiming 'Thank God it's Friday!' This seems to be true for many people, certainly in the developed world. Richard Reeves' book *Happy Mondays* (2001, p 17) quotes American transcendentalist Henry David Thoreau (1817-62) as saying 'Americans know more about how to make a living than how to live'. These words are probably as true today as when first uttered.

When Americans were asked in the early 1980s whether they would retire from working if they had enough money to live on comfortably, oddly enough some 80 per cent said they would not. Their lives had been spent living to work. When the time came to retire they didn't know how to live or what to do, and they were fearful of the consequences (Yankelovich 1981). This is deplorable. We work to live when work is fulfilling, meaningful, useful, creative and presents us with a level of challenges matching our skills. So we ask in this book: What impedes such work and what promotes it today?

During the first half of the twentieth century, 'Beauty of Work' was an idea in several industrial countries in Europe. It combined ideas of quality of life together with the aims of the garden city movement. But little had come of these endeavours until surprisingly in Nazi Germany Albert Speer took charge of the 'Beauty of Work' office. Eventually his efforts provided better hygiene, better lighting and aesthetic conditions in the workplace. Speer applied himself with zeal to his mission, especially improving industrial safety and better factory architecture. The new drive was promoted under slogans 'German everyday-life must be more beautiful', 'Let nature into your factories,' and 'Clean workers in clean factories'. Companies that distinguished themselves were awarded the title 'National Socialist Model Enterprise' (Fest 2002, pp 45-46). It seemed to be one of the few bright spots in the Nazi programme.

Far more radical is businessman Ricardo Semler's (2003) challenge to the whole idea of a five-day working week with a two-day weekend. Instead he advocates a 'seven-day weekend'.

PROFITS, PEOPLE, PLANET

How do we know when work is contributing to life and bringing joy to the worker? One indication is when work is more than making money, first enough to live on and then enough for other needs. Making money does not constitute a life, either for the individual worker or for business. The good news is that business is beginning to recognise the so-called triple bottom line of wealth creation, social responsibility, and concern for the environment. The door to organisational well-being has three locks, not just one. So it needs three keys. The real success of a business enterprise is measured by its three-fold impact on profits, people and planet. This is evident in some corporations in the United States, Britain, Australia and Scandinavia (Elkington 1997). As yet, the observance is more in the rhetoric than in action. We give examples of both.

In this book we are primarily concerned with the two bottom lines of profits and social responsibility. The bottom line of organisations' environmental responsibility has received concern by others. Profits and environmental responsibility is the theme of a remarkable book by Gretchen Daily and Katherine Ellison, *The New Economy of Nature: The Quest to Make Conservation Profitable* (2002). Here is a recognition of the full value of natural ecological systems and the profit in protecting them. They give the economist Adam Smith's 'invisible hand' a 'green thumb'. Also relating profit and planet is CERES, the Coalition for Environmentally Responsible Economies (www.ceres.org). Formed in 1989 in the United States, it has now 70 members including General Motors, Ford Motor Company, Bank of America and Nike. Our book, on the other hand, presents the thesis that a proper evaluation of people leads to more profitable enterprises.

People are the central element of the triple bottom line. This is a new meaning of responsibility: when a corporation's mission statement contains just the one goal of profits, two essential ingredients have been lost. The new paradigm, however, is a win–win situation for workers, investors and society. The coming together of ethical business and capitalism with a conscience should increasingly be an ambition in business (Knowles 2000).

The Lend Lease Group in Australia, for example, based its success on the philosophy that 'everyone should win', and used this to govern relationships between employees, customers, suppliers, shareholders and the community. Its community activities included funding of more than A$8 million for the Australian Council of Trade Unions–Lend Lease Foundation, which has created more than 50 000 jobs, trained more than 100 000 people, provided employment for thousands of young apprentices, and run programmes for Aborigines and other disadvantaged groups (Knowles 2000, p 6).

There is to be a new focus on employees. This has been well put by Christopher Bartlett of the Harvard Business School:

> In the 1920s people were a cost to the business, they were seen as inputs. They were termed human resources, then they were assets on a balance sheet. But they're not a balance sheet asset. You can't screw them to the floor (Head 2002, p 51).

Bartlett goes on to recommend that it is time to recast staff as 'volunteer investors', people who are voluntarily investing their time and talents in your project.

The concept of the triple bottom line has been tied by some to the concept of 'sustainability', no doubt because of the ecological context in which this word is currently used. Sustainability has come to have a variety of meanings. Its initial use was in connection with the discussion of limits to growth in 1974 (Birch 1993b, pp 113-114). The phrase then promoted was the 'ecologically sustainable society'. This is a society that would last indefinitely into the future because of its sound ecological roots. The term changed to 'sustainable development' in the report of the World Commission of Environment and Development, *Our Common Future* (WCED 1987). This report served as the basis of the famous UN conference on environment and development in Rio de Janeiro. The report dropped the phrase 'ecologically sustainable society' for 'sustainable development' to incorporate economic growth into the phrase, but — as others argued — you cannot grow into sustainability. Some proponents of the triple bottom line also use the original ecological meaning in relation to the third bottom line.

When sustainability is used in relation to the bottom line of social responsibility its meaning is different. For example Dunphy and Benveniste (2000, p 3) write about the 'sustainable corporation' meaning 'commitment to finding a way to involve corporations in increasingly adopting practices that contribute to sustaining and renewing the quality of life of the work forces and the community'. The objective is fine and is similar to ours. But we question whether the word 'sustainable' is appropriate in this context. Maybe we need a new word for Dunphy and Benveniste's definition of quality of work practices. We incline to the view of Diesendorf (2000, p 35) that 'corporations are not appropriately described as sustainable as such but that the practice of corporations may or may not lead to ecological sustainability and increased quality of life'. This is what Elkington appropriately refers to, at least on one page of his book, as 'sustainability/social responsibility considerations' (2001, p 9). It is highly desirable to have the double concept and not subsume both under the one heading of sustainability, especially when that one word (taken out of its ecological origin) is given a number of meanings.

There is at least one organisation in the world which puts the bottom line of social responsibility first, especially to its customers. Moreover, it is a bank — the Grameen Bank. In 1976 Professor Muhammad Yunus, a young economist and university teacher, had the idea of investing in people trapped in extreme poverty by extending to them tiny loans for self-employment. The bank he created is a remarkable example of how an organisation can serve the poor while maintaining its viability and profitability.

The first person to borrow from the bank worked seven days a week making wooden bamboo stools. She had no working capital and a trader sold her raw material on credit and bought the final product at a price that barely covered the cost. She lived in abject poverty. With a loan of the equivalent of a few dollars from Yunus, she was able to become self-employed. Within a few months she had increased her income seven-fold and repaid the loan with interest.

Yunus initially lent a total of about US$27 to 42 landless poor artisans who previously had to borrow this small working capital from money-lenders at 10 per cent per day to capitalise self-employment. Today the bank lends more than the equivalent of US$500 million in 4 million tiny loans each year to the 'poorest of the poor'. Its 12 800 barefoot bankers serve 40 000 villages in Bangladesh. In this conservative Islamic country the bank has managed to extend 94 per cent of its loans to women. Its contribution to the GDP of the country is between 1.1 and 1.5 per cent a year, which is more than half the contribution of the entire formal financial sector in Bangladesh. On the basis of its experience in Bangladesh, and that of its 300 replications in 62 countries, the bank firmly dismisses the notion that the economically poor are skill-poor and need training before they can take the first step out of poverty (Knowles 2000).

In the late 1980s the bank initiated ways in which it could build on the network of its borrowers to take steps towards a poverty-free world. It became involved in leasing under-utilised fishing ponds, irrigation pumps for deep wells and providing training to people who wanted to adapt the methods of the Grameen bank. Its fisheries project became the Grameen Fisheries Foundation. The irrigation project became the Grameen Krishi Foundation. The international replication and a health programme became the Grameen Trust. The bank became involved in venture capital, the textile industry, an internet service provider and much more.

The Grameen Bank did not set out primarily as a profit-making organisation. It set out to help the poorest of the poor. It reversed conventional banking practice by doing away with the need for collateral, and created a banking system based on mutual trust, accountability, participation and creativity. The repayment of loans, which now average US$160 is over 95 per cent. More than 4000 people from 100 countries have participated in Grameen training over the last ten years. Together all their activities have resulted in 222 Grameen programmes in 58 countries providing several hundred thousand poor borrowers with credit (Grameen Bank 2000; 2001).

The concept of the triple bottom line has caught on sufficiently that the *Sydney Morning Herald* and *The Age* produce an annual report called the 'Good Reputation Index' for Australia's 100 biggest companies (Gettler 2002). The index is based on six categories:

- employee management
- ethics and corporate governance
- social impact
- financial performance
- environmental performance
- management and market focus.

The company that heads the top 100 list of the Good Reputation Index for 2002 is Westpac Banking Corporation. Its CEO, Dr David Morgan, said that it was a 'moment of truth' in 1999 when he announced a record profit, but at a time when 'we never had the community more dissatisfied with us, we never had our customers more dissatisfied and staff morale was never where it should have been' (Gettler 2002, p 3). Dr Morgan recognised that even though the share price may increase and record profits are made, the people factor is still a critical element that cannot be ignored.

With Dr Morgan at the helm, Westpac has begun to work on the 'soft issues', which are invariably people issues and often the most difficult. Westpac still has quite a way to go. For example, in the 'employee management' category, Westpac came seventh compared with Australia Post coming first, followed by Queensland Rail, Mitsubishi Motors, Ford, Energex and Woolworths (Gettler 2002, p 4).

In another category, Westpac achieved its top ranking on the Good Reputation Index by paying close attention to its 'ethics and corporate governance' rising from 18th in 2001 to second in 2002. Due to the influence of its CEO, Westpac is Australia's only bank and one of only five worldwide to deliver a triple bottom line report conforming to the standards of the United Nations-sponsored Global Reporting Initiative (Gettler 2002, p 3).

Another example of initiatives by business is the movement for corporate social responsibility, promoted by the World Business Council for Sustainable Development. It defines corporate social responsibility as 'the commitment of business to contribute to sustainable economic development, working with employees, their families, the local community and society at large to improve their *quality of life*' (Holliday, Schmidheiny and Watts 2002, p 102). Corporate social responsibility is not regarded as philanthropy—it is good business. It has become an increasing concern of business during the 1990s and beyond.

PEOPLE MATTER

In organisations in Australia, and elsewhere in the developed world, people are working longer and harder than ever before (Chapter 4), but there is very little to say that the work force is a happy one. The tragedy is that the human factor has been downgraded. People, who are a critical factor in creating profits, are treated as expendable variables. They are valued as means to ends only, and not as ends in themselves. As a consequence quality of life has dropped.

Senior management, in pursuing with zeal the one bottom line of profits, has lost the drive and creativity to tackle the challenging questions concerning quality of life in the workplace. Later we present data showing that in fact enhancing the quality of life contributes to the bottom line of profits. Indeed the case can be made stronger: Catherine Livingstone, former CEO of Cochlear, says 'I believe you've got to come back to your customers and your employees. If you get those two right, shareholder value follows as a matter of course' (Walsh 2000, p 27).

In this book we examine how that can happen and what can be done in Australia and elsewhere. So first we look at how people fit into organisations and what is at present lacking in the people factor.

Organisations, be they financial, telecommunications or other corporations, consist of people who have chosen to spend many of their hours and days working for the organisation. Indeed, most of us will spend more time in work than we spend with our families or elsewhere. Work occupies much of our life. The organisation provides an environment, which influences the quality of life of its members in the workplace. And that, in turn, influences the quality of life of the employees at home and wherever else they may happen to be. The reverse is also true: a happy home life is reflected in the quality of life in the workplace. We consider it is important for any organisation that employs people to ask itself: To what extent does life in the organisation affect the quality of life of the people who work in it? This calls for the leaders of corporations, companies and enterprises to become champions of a management philosophy that is deeply rooted in human values, for this is a debate about values.

Such a debate is beginning to happen in various countries around the world, in those places where there is a growing recognition of the dehumanising character of much of the labour required in modern business and industry. A wholistic life somehow has to combine work and personal life, but many find this hard to achieve in the modern world, largely due to the demands of their employment. Many are too tired to even contemplate a life after work, let alone giving the best part of themselves to their partners and families. The management of organisations has a big role to play if change regarding the quality of life is to take place. For some change is already on the way. According to *US News and World Report*, 'fast-trackers who floored it to the finish line, hyper achievers who slept, ate, and breathed work, now ... are taking weekends off and muttering about personal fulfilment and quality of life' (Salzman 1990, p 57).

Research undertaken in the United States in 1997 identified four key factors that were contributing to the decline in loyalty among employees. They were:

- restructuring (74 per cent)

- re-engineering (48 per cent)

- downsizing (63 per cent)
- outsourcing (44 per cent).

Twelve core factors were identified as those that attracted and retained employees (Read 2000):

- knowing what was expected of one
- having the materials and equipment to do the work properly
- having the opportunity to do what one can do best every day
- receiving recognition or praise for good work
- being cared for as a person
- being encouraged in one's development
- finding that one's opinions count
- finding that the mission of the company makes it feel that one's work is important
- having co-workers committed to doing work of good quality
- having a good friend at work
- talking with someone about one's progress in the past six months
- having the opportunity at work to work and grow.

Most of these factors have to do with the quality of life in the workplace. Interestingly enough, pay was not in the list. High-performing professional workers take it for granted that they will be well paid; working relationships are what count.

Failure to provide such a working environment results in cynicism and poor productivity. Read (2000) makes a point about human nature by drawing a parallel between technological modernism and science fiction movies. Both share a common theme: technology is breathtakingly precise and powerful, glittering and stupendous, but in this exotic future people still relate to each other in exactly the same way as they do now. There is the same duplicity, superficiality, hostility and competition. No improvement whatsoever! Science fiction movie titles are appropriately named *Star Wars*. No matter how streamlined and seemingly efficient an organisation may be it is still dependent upon the human beings in it, with all their quirks and aspirations. Unless consideration is given to these variables in the personal factor, trouble looms. (This can be taken into account in various ways, which is the subject of Chapter 9.)

A survey by the Australian Commonwealth Department of Industrial Relations, released in 1995, gave a picture of views of employees on their relationships to their work over the previous twelve months. Overall employees had experienced a decline over a range of issues. They reported lower levels of satisfaction with management, a sense of job insecurity, increase in stress on the job, and dissatisfaction with a lack of balance between work and home life. They reported working harder and longer hours (Golan 2000). A similar 1995 investigation also of Australian workers in their past twelve months showed that 59 per cent had increased their effort, 50 per cent had been subjected to increased stress, and 46 per cent had increased the pace at which they had worked (Morehead et al 1997). When employees doubt there is reciprocity and fairness, their motivation and work-ethic suffers.

Golan (2000) identified five deficiencies in present practice. First, consultation and involvement of employees is weak and needs reinforcing. They need to have a say in the work being done. Second, there is lack of investment in knowledge and a continuous learning process. Studies in the United States and in Europe show a strong correlation between increased budgets devoted to learning and larger profits. Companies that devote resources to the development of their work, force out competitors. This involves opportunities to learn new skills (see Chapter 11). Third, there is lack of balance between work and life beyond work. The present generation is demanding a better balance as they come to realise that life is more than work. Furthermore the brain cannot function at an optimal level for eight to ten hours a day. This is a physiological fact of life. Fourth is the failure to make adequate organisational change than simply downsizing the work force. Fifth is the need for reform of workplace institutions and systems of employment that are bound to the traditional model of working 40 hours a week for 40 years. People who work for less than 40 hours and for less than 40 years are regarded as peripheral to the main core. An alternative is flexible working hours in a more temporary labour market. People themselves could be responsible for their working patterns, their education and training (Golan 2000). (These matters are considered further in Chapters 5, 7 and 11.)

WHY IS QUALITY OF LIFE SO IMPORTANT?

There are two reasons why quality of life is important. There is the very practical reason that the contented and fulfilled employee is a better worker. He or she adds value to the organisation. Such a person is more likely to contribute both to increased productivity, efficiency and creativity compared with a person who is dissatisfied, unhappy, frustrated and stressed. Secondly, there is the ethical reason that the life of every individual matters and each of us has some responsibility to those others whose lives will be influenced by our decisions and activities. To put this another way, the employer and those in authority contribute either positively or negatively to the quality of life of the employee. This influence should be recognised and directed to creative and fulfilling ends.

When the value of persons is measured solely in terms of their usefulness, we are measuring what is called their instrumental value. It is to treat that person as an object, devoid of feeling and sentience. However, each person has value in and for oneself, which is quite independent of any usefulness the person may have to the organisation. Such value is known as intrinsic value (this is explored further in Chapters 2 and 9).

The organisation has some responsibility for recognising the intrinsic value of its employees. We acknowledge that the safety and health of employees have a value beyond making employees more useful. Our proposition is for that concern to be extended to the whole area of quality of life. There should also be a recognition of differences between people. The Wall Street stockbroker measures quality of life to a large extent by his or her income. The poet and the scientist do not. What satisfies each will not necessarily be the same; a musician must make music, a poet must write, an artist must paint, a scientist must create. Jane Addams found her fulfilment in working with the poor. Mother Teresa found hers in caring for the dying. Albert Schweitzer found his as musician in Europe and as a healer in Africa. Alfred P Sloan found his in the automotive industry. Socrates found his in being a teacher.

In her book *Living Strategy*, Lynda Gratton (2000) of the London Business School says that corporations know more about their customers than they know about their employees. One exception, Richard Branson, who founded Virgin Airways and many other enterprises, has said that in his organisations the staff come first, the customers second and the shareholders third. He elaborated this statement by adding that satisfaction of customers depends upon high standards of service from staff, high standards of service depend upon having staff who are proud of the company. That is why interests of staff come first (Pfeffer 1998, p 293). This kind of thinking is contrary to most management practice today, where shareholders are treated as if they are to have priority.

People are therefore the most important asset of a corporation, yet for many people the reality of life in an organisation is that they do not feel they are treated as such. People, says Lynda Gratton (2000), should be put in the centre, not at the periphery. Furthermore, she sees a need to change the dominant metaphors of humans in organisations. She recognises two dominant metaphors: the person as a machine, and the person as '*Homo economicus*'.

As a machine, employees are interchangeable parts that will perform equally well across a wide range of conditions. As *Homo economicus,* the employee is seen as a rational economic maximiser who will behave in a rational manner to maximise the results of his or her labour. Both views, she argues, fail to capture the complexity of individuals and ignore two important needs: the need for meaning in human life, and the part played by emotions, values, hopes and dreams. So she speaks of the need for the organisation to have a 'soul', by which she means the organisation's commitment to the fostering of qualities of trust, loyalty, caring, inspiration, allowing individuals to have a voice, integrity, justice and whatever characterises the human-ness of people.

From more than half the companies Lynda Gratton has surveyed in Britain and Europe, less than 30 per cent of the employees believe that management cares about their needs and morale. Of six highly successful companies, reported in some detail in her book, less than 20 per cent of employees (the average would be closer to 10 per cent) said that their company 'inspired the best in me'. But, asks the CEO: What difference does all this make to profits? Her answer is a lot. Over the past five years a series of studies in Europe and the United States reveal how the employees' quality of life makes an impact on financial performance. Lynda Gratton's (2000) book is replete with examples of how this works in practice.

There are many aspects of how work impinges on quality of life. In the developed nations both partners may work outside the home, so there is growing need for child-care and other social betterments. Work is no longer the top priority in many people's lives. In a study of 1000 workers each in Japan, Britain and the United States, the subjects were asked to indicate how work ranked on a scale of 1 (high) to 10 (low) against nine other factors in terms of 'life-satisfaction' (Table 1.1).

TABLE 1.1 The importance and satisfaction of work

	Japan	Britain	US
How important is work?	2	4	8
Where does work rank in terms of satisfaction?	4	6	7

NOTE   1 is 'high'; 10 is 'low'.
SOURCE   Fitz-enz, *Human Value Management*, 1990, p 13.

Work is important for the Japanese worker but not so much for the US worker. Likewise the Japanese worker claims to get more satisfaction from work than the US worker. Workers in Britain are in between.

A study by the Australian Council of Trade Unions (ACTU 1999) found that 47 per cent of Australian workers had suffered health and personal problems, such as stress, because of their work. One question that arises from this sort of information is: How can work, for those who find their work unfulfilling and unhealthy, be made more fulfilling? A second question that arises is: How important should work be in one's life anyway? We respond to these questions in Chapter 2.

2

FULLY HUMAN

Corporations are human.
Jack Welch, *Jack*, 2001, p 284.

We get up, and go to the office, and come home again,
have dinner with the family, sit around in the evening
... But sometimes there comes a question: is this all
my life is good for? Shouldn't I be doing some thing
courageous for the good of humanity?
Charles Ives, quoted in K Kemp, 'Charles Ives', 2001, p 1.

To herald hope for a more humane world, one in which
poets might have as powerful a voice as bankers.
Vaclev Havel, President of the Czech Republic, 'Farewell to
politics', 2002, p 1.

The much vaunted phrase 'standard of living' has come to mean
the amount of physical goods and services an individual commands. Gross
national product (GNP) per capita is a typical measure of standard of living.
Quality of life is something different. Quality of life is measured by one's feelings, where potentialities for creative work and creative relationships with
others are being fulfilled. The phrase 'quality of life' also refers to the idea of
human excellence, as does the older term from Nicolai Hartmann's (1932,
p 205) classical ethics 'richness of experience', or the more contemporary
term 'human flourishing'. Together these phrases imply an idea of human
nature which points to what it is to be fully human (see Chapter 9).

A society that has an increasing numbers of suicides, of people opting out
of life by depending on drugs and alcohol, and of stress-induced illnesses and

depression, is a society whose quality of life is falling. Likewise people who are out of work for a long period suffer not just in terms of income loss but also psychologically. They feel isolated within society and start losing the capacity to do things and initiate new activities. To live apathetically amid abundance is nothing short of evil.

The basic questions which this chapter asks are: What conditions of work, what kinds of work, what kinds management and what kinds of reward help people to fulfil their human nature to its fullest stature?

HUMAN NEEDS

To believe that there is such a thing as human nature is to pose the question of what people need universally. There is evidence that the basic things that people need as human beings are quite few in number.

In their study of the universal needs of human beings Boyden et al (1990), of the Australian National University, drew up a list. Here is an abbreviation of their list of non-material needs:

- opportunities and incentives for personal creative behaviour, usually with clear goals

- an immediate sense of purpose associated with the main activities of the day

- an awareness of one's role and usefulness in the community

- general opportunities for self-expression and self-fulfilment.

This set of human values includes social acceptance and self-esteem that lead to self-actualisation. Common human needs imply a common human nature, which we explore in more detail in Chapter 9. What is it to be a fulfilled human being? We could ask the same general question of any living creature. Take a pine tree for example. We could compare the present state of the tree with its potentialities. We could call it poor or sick or a mutilated exemplar of what a pine tree could be. So it is with individual human beings. They can be good exemplars or bad exemplars of what a human being can be. We could even make a list of those human beings we consider to be the best examples of fulfilled human beings. These are not necessarily the same as those who have exercised great influence (for instance Hitler).

We can be more specific and ask why people commit themselves to an organisation and what motivates them to perform at their best? Psychologists Emery and Thorsrud (in Dunphy et al 2000, p 104) consider that there are six psychological requirements for work to be meaningful. It must:

- be challenging
- provide the opportunity to learn
- allow for a certain degree of decision-making
- provide social support and recognition
- be work that the individual can relate to their social life
- be work that the individual feels leads to a desirable future.

People want their work to be meaningful and to be relevant to the society in which they live. Work should meet individual needs and also those of the community.

During the 1980s, Peter Lynch worked 14 hours a day and built the Fidelity Magellan mutual fund into a $13 billion giant. At the age of 46, he startled his colleagues by quitting. Why? Because he asked himself: 'What in the hell are we doing this for?' In answering he was moved to the thought 'I don't know anyone who wished on his deathbed that he had spent more time in the office' (Singer 1993, p 11).

Canadian environmentalist David Suzuki (2000, p 1) asked a Sydney audience:

> When you lie on your deathbed what memories will fill you with happiness, pride and satisfaction? I suspect it will not be the latest designer clothing, a huge house, a sport utility vehicle or a Sony entertainment centre. What makes life worthwhile and joyful is not 'stuff' that can be bought with money. The most important things are family, friends, community and the sharing that enhances the quality of all our lives.

Further examples, together with the underlying psychology, are given by Clive Hamilton (2003) in his challenging book *Growth Fetish*.

But what constitutes quality of life? There is a diversity of views amongst philosophers as to what constitutes quality of life (see Nussbaum and Sen 1993) that goes back to ancient times. For example, Aristotle made a list of ten human experiences, to each of which he attached a virtue. Fear of danger, for example, led to the appropriate virtue of courage (Nussbaum and Sen 1993, p 246).

We are not primarily concerned to pursue these philosophical issues here but to take a more pragmatic approach. Quality of life has a number of components: physical, mental, social and spiritual. These impinge on individual experience in terms of joy, contentment, satisfaction and purpose. Work itself is much more than a source of income. It contributes to one's quality of life.

It forms one's character and contributes to a range of human attributes such as co-operativeness, self-confidence, intellectual capacity and flexibility. Unfortunately, not all work does this and some does the opposite, contributing to stress and low morale (Richardson 1998).

There have been varying attitudes to work, which we now explore under the rubric of work ethics.

THE WORK ETHIC

'Work ethics', or 'business ethics', has a two-fold meaning. One is the actual ethics deemed worthy of people in business, such as is promoted in Quaker circles by *Quaker Business Ethics* (Smith 2001). This booklet is described in its subtitle as 'a plumb-line guide to practical applications in business and industry'. A good deal of what we have to say in what follows has implicit in it these sorts of values to guide individual and corporate activities. That is needed, if what the *Economist* says is true that 'For every corporate crook there are at least ten corporate deceivers' (Anon 2000b, p 7).

The 2002 collapse of Enron and WorldCom are examples. It is not too cynical to have as a working assumption that people today will get away with what they can. But there is nothing particularly new about deception and its consequences. Sir Walter Scott wrote in 1808 in *Marmion*:

> O what a tangled web we weave,
> When first we practice to deceive.

Some people strongly adhere to a code of personal ethics. Some give the minimum adherence to it that they can get away with. Some not even that. Those who infringe it generally give lip service to a code. As Groucho Marx is reputed to have said, 'The secret of life is honesty and fair dealing; if you can fake that you've got it made'. And as for truthfulness, cartoonist Tom Peters (1999, p 134) tells us 'fact is, truth telling is not all that common in Dilbert-ville. And conscientious corporate truth-tellers are a rather rare breed. Thence, truthfulness is a competitive advantage.' (Criteria for making ethical personal choices, ethical options of organisations, are discussed below.)

A second meaning to work ethics is the answer to the question: What is work for? Work was not always regarded as a good thing, and sometimes this is the case now. A change happened about the time of the Protestant revolution with a revaluation of work. The new conception of work became know as the work ethic. It is this meaning we now pursue, following Sharon Beder's (2000) splendid book on the work ethic.

Work has not always been regarded as a major component of life. In ancient Greece the educated held work in low regard. Aristotle and Socrates, like many Greek thinkers, viewed work as interfering with the duties of citizens, distracting them from the important pursuits of politics, art, philosophy and what they called leisure. Significantly the Greek word for leisure is *skhole* from which we derive the word *school*. For the Greeks leisure was not just sitting around doing nothing in particular, it was going to school! The only good purpose of work was to earn enough to have leisure to contemplate noble pursuits. As Greek culture spread to other parts of the world, so did this attitude to work.

The Romans of the Republic period adopted a similar attitude. The Latin word for 'work', *labor*, means 'extreme effort associated with pain'. It comes from the same root as *labare*, which means 'to stumble under a burden'. For the Romans honourable pursuits were politics and war. The ancient Jews also thought of work as a painful necessity. In the book of Genesis, Adam and Eve did not have to work in the Garden of Eden until work was imposed upon them as punishment: 'In the sweat of your face shall you eat bread' (Genesis 3:18). Early Christians had a similar attitude to that of early Judaism. It was much later that work became imbued with a moral quality in what became known as the work ethic.

At the heart of the work ethic is the idea that work is worthwhile for reasons other than the rewards its brings in terms of pay and profits. 'Work is meant to make life more human' said ethicist Ronald Preston (2000b p 268) when summarising the encyclical *Laborem exercens* of Pope John Paul II. 'True there is an element of toil in it. Toil nevertheless brings out human fulfilment … work is meant for man not man for work.' Work is a positive value in itself.

Both the Catholic and Protestant churches imbued work with religious value. Martin Luther and John Calvin helped to baptise the emergent capitalist work ethic by declaring labour to be a sacred calling, not as the medievals thought a divine punishment for sin. This new view of work became known as the 'Protestant work ethic'. The idea of the moral value of work spread from Europe to England where the Puritans in particular embraced the gospel of work. They became know for their industry and frugal lifestyles. From England the Puritans took this idea to America where the gospel of work quickly took root and spread. Poverty became a sign of sin, whereas wealth and profits were a sign of God's blessing.

This idea was a major factor in the rise of capitalism according to the arguments of Max Weber 1904 in *The Protestant Ethic and the Spirit of Capitalism* (1904), and R H Tawney's *Religion and the Rise of Capitalism* (1926). Maybe they overstated their case. Capitalism existed well before the

Protestant revolution. Probably many factors contributed to its rise. But with the rise of capitalism, work came to be valued according to its productivity. Success was measured in terms of profits. Wealth became a measure of a person's worth. The emphasis on work as a religious calling became superseded by a quest for materialistic success.

For many people in the Western world, work no longer offers intrinsic satisfaction (see for instance Table 1.1, page 14). Many jobs are boring or tedious. Quality of life has disappeared. A major problem in an industrial society, and one of the most difficult, is that of making work interesting in the sense of being no longer merely a means to wages. Various attempts were made in the 1970s to promote 'job enrichment', but on the whole they did not work. 'I never felt enriched' said one worker, 'I just felt knackered' (Beder 2000, p 109).

For many the work ethic no longer works. Yet, for some, it is still applied. For example, employers have attempted to foster a sense of belonging by workers. They have encouraged total devotion to work by higher-level employees that goes far beyond normal working hours. They have ensured that work is central and all time-consuming.

The work ethic is also a factor in modern sport. In the lead up to the Sydney Olympic Games in the year 2000, advertisements were placed in the *Sydney Morning Herald*. One said 'I used to swim for fun. Then I heard Sam Riley [Olympic Gold medal winner] speak at school. Now I swim for gold' (quoted in Beder 2000, p 199).

Work has become so central in people's lives that they have difficulty in knowing what to do with themselves without it. This applies not only to retirees and those made redundant, but also to those with chosen or imposed workaholism. It is a factor in reducing the ability to find meaning in anything else. If we are to pass from a culture in which work is seen as the purpose of life to a fulfilling culture, in which living wisely and fully is the object, we shall do so only by deliberately making room in each day for an enhanced quality of life.

A good work ethic would see work as valuable when it provides a service to the community and at the same time is fulfilling and satisfying for the worker. A dysfunctional work ethic is one that values work as an end in itself and which is, at the same time, unfulfilling and stressful for the worker. It is time we concentrated more on judging work by its effect on the quality of life of both the worker and the community. Here is an example.

In addition to making his company a customer-oriented company, and taking it from one highly in debt to one of the greatest and most successful airlines, Jan Carlzon (1987), the highly successful CEO of Scandinavian Airline System, attributes the turn-around to two essential components. One was an overall vision that penetrated all levels in the organisation. The other was the decentralising of decision-making so that every one of the 20 000 employees had some part in decisions, especially those at their particular level in the organisation. (Unfortunately the initiative was not sustained beyond Carlzon's administration.)

Concerning an overall vision, Carlzon tells the story of two stone masons. When asked what his job was the first said he was cutting blocks of stone into different shapes. The second said he was in a team building a cathedral. He was the one who felt part of a vision. Carlzon said of his airline that it communicated a vision of what the company could be, and the employees were willing to take responsibility. He added that by communicating the vision to all employees and by diffusing responsibility they were making more demands upon their employees but that these were accepted enthusiastically. The changes involved flattening the organisational pyramid and therefore increasing responsibilities of middle management and front-line employees. He emphasised that for a company that flattens the pyramid it becomes particularly important to reinforce the self-worth of individual employees. Virgin Airlines is another airline that is known for its 'people first' philosophy. Richard Branson applies the principle that happy employees mean happy customers, which means better returns. 'Our people are the heart and soul of all our business and they come first whenever we make a decision' (*Human Capital* 2002a, p 10).

The hierarchical structure places too much emphasis on the trappings of power, such as office, titles and salaries. Many highly competent employees end up merely passing on decisions made by higher-ranking executives. Empowering employees with real responsibilities and authority requires a radically different organisational structure. The model is horizontal and the work roles are redefined. Everyone needs to know and feel that he or she is needed and appreciated. And each needs to be given freedom to take responsibility, thus releasing personal resources and creativity that would otherwise remain undeveloped. Individual decisions are made at the point of responsibility, not far up the organisational hierarchy. People at the front line of the Scandinavian Airline System were not only given greater responsibility but a secure atmosphere was created in which they dared to use their new authority in this corporate democracy.

The job of the leader in Scandinavian Airline System was to create the right environment for business to be done. The model is a game of football. The coach is the leader whose job is to select the right players. He must ensure that the team goes onto the field full of enthusiasm and zest. On the field there is the captain, analogous to the manager, with the authority to issue orders on the field and to change the play during the course of the game. But most important are the individual players, each of whom becomes his or her own boss during the game. The details of his actions depend upon his own initiative and cannot be referred back to the coach. There is little doubt that Carlzon's team at Scandinavian Airline System operated as in a game of football. From his account, the quality of life of the employees was paramount (Carlzon 1987).

The quality of life in the workplace depends, amongst other things, on the ethics practised there (Lagan 2000). About half of the employees in the United States have done something unethical at work: stealing property, lying about what they did or did not, or using sick days inappropriately. At management level, half of the top executives admitted that they were willing to fudge figures to look good, and as many as 75 per cent of MBA students said they would be willing to distort the facts to make company profits look better. What about a course in ethics for all MBA students? It should be part of the core curriculum but as yet this is not the case in most business and management schools.

Of great influence on ethical behaviour in the workplace is the role of the behaviour of management to set a standard. The personal values that managers and employees bring to work are critical. What top management does can be a role model for what is considered to be acceptable work practices. Many business analysts in the United States warn that the relentless pressures to build profits, outsource, cut costs and provide the minimum in safety standards and a healthy workplace results in low morale among employees. This in turn provides a context for unethical practices in the workplace to flourish.

WEALTH AND QUALITY OF LIFE

Wealth turns out to be a poor predictor of a person's sense of well-being or quality of life. Even very rich Americans are only slightly happier than the average American. Although Americans on average in 1996, earned twice as much as they did in 1957, the proportion saying they were 'very happy' declined from 35 per cent in 1957 to 30 per cent in 1996. People who win the lottery are no happier the year after the event than they were before (Myers and Diener 1996). In Australia, real income per person has doubled in the past 30 years. There is no evidence that happiness has doubled in that time. People in Asia's wealthiest countries, particularly Japan and Taiwan, are routinely ranked as the highest proportion of unhappy people (Diesendorf and Hamilton 1997). As Semler (2003) points out, a list of names of the happiest people would have no-one from the one listing the wealthiest.

Only in the poorer countries, such as Bangladesh, is income a good indicator of a sense of human well-being. If we were to draw a graph of quality of life on the vertical axis and material standard of living on the horizontal axis, the quality of life would be seen to rise with increase in standard of living. That is true to the point where basic needs are provided for such as food, clothing, shelter and education. After a certain peak the quality of life falls with further increase in standard of living. Bigger is no longer better (Birch 1993a, p 15). This relationship between wealth and quality of life was discovered in 300 BC by the Greek philosopher Epicurus, but is a fairly recent discovery by us. (The quantitative relationship between standard of living and quality of life is pursued further in Chapter 3.)

HAPPINESS AND QUALITY OF LIFE

Happiness is, to some degree, an indicator of quality of life. In a 1996 survey, 30 per cent of Americans said they were happy with life. Only 1 per cent chose the most negative description 'not happy' (Myers and Diener 1996). The majority of Australians are happy — at least they say they are.

Happiness is related to a wide range of activities. In many of these activities Australians are well satisfied. In 1997, some 39 per cent of Australians said they were very satisfied with their life (Eckersley 1998a). However, studies show that they are relatively dissatisfied with the amount of free time they have, their physical fitness, physical safety, and with governments in their various forms (Wearing and Headey 1998). Yet there is a special problem of quality of life among today's Australian youth. There have been worsening trends in psychosocial problems leading to depression, delinquency, drug abuse, youth suicide, crime and unemployment. The suicide rate in males' aged 15-19 was 13 per 100 000 in 1986, rising to 17 per 100 000 in 1996. The rate for males aged 24 was higher. The rise in youth suicide peaked in 1988 and appears to have reached a plateau after trebling since the 1950s (Eckersley 1998a; 1998b).

Amongst significant causes of the deterioration of the quality of life of youth, Eckersley sees a major one as being the failure of Western society to provide an adequate cultural framework of values, hope, meaning, purpose and belonging, both socially and spiritually (see also the last section of this chapter).

PROFITS AND QUALITY OF LIFE

Sharing a sense of vision of the purpose of the organisation can have both inspirational effects and practical ones. Such people work more effectively, and as they do, their levels of satisfaction, enthusiasm and contribution goes up. People want to be excited, challenged and stimulated in their work. Like the football team, they want to win.

The Saratoga Institute in California studied factors such as commitment and productivity in 1335 employees in three companies. The institute identified five factors that closely correlated with high commitment and high productivity:

- self-esteem obtained from the job
- the chance to accomplish something worthwhile (as opposed to endless data entering and processing)
- matching workers with appropriate jobs
- the chance to learn new procedures and new skills
- delegation by the organisation, which gives the employee a strong sense of responsibility (Fitz–enz 1990, p 117).

(Further examples of increased productivity resulting from improved human relationships and vision for employees are given by Fitz-enz, 1990, pp 326-33.)

And when companies get these things right, the results can be surprising. Pfeffer (1998, p 34) reports a study based on 968 responses to a survey of senior human resource professionals from all major industries in the United States. The study assessed the effects of the management of human resources on productivity. The increase in productivity of firms that had put greater effort into enhancing the quality of life and work of staff was substantial. An increase in such practices of one standard deviation is associated, on a per employee basis, with a US$27 044 increase in sales, US$18 641 increase in market value, and US$3814 more in profits. Similar results were obtained in a study of more than one hundred German companies operating in ten different industrial sectors.

HEALTH AND QUALITY OF LIFE

Investment in health care to improve the quality of life results in a more productive work force. This investment includes programmes to restrain drug, alcohol and tobacco abuse. There is evidence that now, and for some time in the past, the workplace has had a negative affect on health through stress. One prime cause of stress-related illness is the increasing number of hours of work (which we discuss in Chapter 7). Another aspect of workers' health and illness has to do with workplace hazards, usually referred to as occupational health and safety (Chapter 6). In this section we give a brief historical perspective of the relationship between work and health.

The relationship has been known for a long time, though the particular agencies have only recently been elucidated. For instance, the chief causes of death in Europe in the nineteenth century were not cancer and cardiovascular diseases, but infectious diseases. The most important killers were diphtheria, smallpox, tuberculosis, bronchitis, pneumonia, and measles in children. From about the 1830s the death rates from all of these diseases were decreasing. By the beginning of World War I, 90 per cent of the decrease had already occurred. What was the reason for this dramatic change? It was not the discovery of the germ theory of disease in 1876, for there was no observable effect on death rates after that. It was not the effect of modern drug treatments because these were not introduced until after World War II. It was not improvements of sanitation, since all the principal killers were airborne, not waterborne, diseases. The most plausible explanation is that during the nineteenth century there was an increase in the real wage of workers, a decrease in the number of hours worked, and an increase in the quality of nutrition. As people became better nourished, better clothed and had more time for rest to recover from taxing labour, their bodies reached a less stressed physiological state, and were better able to recover from the further stress of infection (Lewontin 2000).

Nearly 200 years later, stress is one of the major problems for organisations. But stress in the twenty-first-century workplace is different from what it was in earlier times, manifesting itself in different forms affecting the quality of both the work and the life of the worker (Chapter 7).

The twenty-first century also confronts the world with three major global epidemics that cause untold suffering and have an enormous effect on reducing productivity. They are AIDS, tuberculosis and malaria. The United Nations has established a UN Global Fund for these three diseases, estimating the financial need at US$10 billion per year.

TECHNOLOGY AND QUALITY OF LIFE

With the rise of technology, also in the nineteenth century, an initial fear was what came to be called the threat of 'technological unemployment'. Hence the 'machine breakers' or Luddites (named after their leader Ned Ludd) in the early textile factories in England. This was a serious business. Some workers were hanged for their activities, 215 others were amongst the last convicts transported to Australia. (Bix 2000, provides an intriguing history of this debate on 'technological unemployment' in the twentieth century.)

John Maynard Keynes in his 1930 essay 'Economic possibilities for our grandchildren' saw it all:

> We are being afflicted with a new disease of which
> some readers may not yet have heard the name, but of
> which they will hear a great deal in the years to
> come—namely *technological unemployment*. This
> means unemployment due to our discovery of means
> of economising the use of labour outrunning the pace
> at which we can find new uses for labour ... This means
> that the economic problem is not, if we look into the
> future, the permanent problem of the human race
> (Handy 1998, p 59).

Keynes went on to say that once the economic problem is solved, humanity will be deprived of its traditional purpose and will be faced with the real problem how to live wisely, agreeably and well. One of the first manufacturers to recognise this before Keynes was Robert Owen, when machines overtook the weavers in his own factory in Lanark Scotland. He repudiated entirely the Luddite solution to the problem, and tried to work out a relation between men and machines that was creative and profitable, even setting up his own utopian community, in the American state of Indiana, which he called New Harmony. He was later forced to abandon this initiative. However, he was responsible for setting an agenda for the future and could be regarded as a founder of the trade union movement (Bronowski and Mazlish 1960, p 459).

There is a modern problem when technologies make an impact on our sense of self. A study has been made of a large number of young men and women who spend much of their time on the internet. There is evidence that they are developing multiple personalities in which the sense of self becomes somewhat shattered (Elkington 2001, p 138). Others become addicted to the internet. The problem is not in the technology, but in the way it is used.

Another widespread fear of science and technology is that it would dehumanise people and turn them into numbers. That is false. What turns people into numbers is arrogance, dogma and becoming as gods. That happened at Auschwitz. Everyone there had a number tattooed on one arm. In the finale of Bronowski's television programme 'The Ascent of Man' he is seen kneeling in a pond at Auschwitz with his hands in the mud. He says 'This is where people were turned into numbers. Into this pond were flushed the ashes of some four million people. And this was not done by gas. It was done by dogma ... We have to close the distance between the push-button order and the human act. We have to touch people' (Bronowski 1973, p 187). There is a message here. The real problems of regulating technology are human and not technical (see also 'Mechanistic man' in Chapter 9).

We know now that in the twentieth century the engine contributed to the liberation of some 25 per cent of the world's population from hard labour, opening up for them possibilities of a better education and the pleasure of free time (McNeill 2000). Technology has meant that we no longer need the same work force on the land or in factories to do the same amount of work. But advancing technology has meant that new fields of work open, for example in the realm of information transfer.

The main concern today is different from what it was early in the industrial revolution. Instead of science and technology ushering in a promised age of shorter working hours and lots of leisure time for all, they have perplexingly brought with them an increase in working hours for many, with its attendant problems which we discuss. In Australia, less than two workers in five work 'standard hours'. We also face the paradoxical situation of one lot of workers having increasing working hours while for others there is increasing joblessness. This raises the question of whether there can be a better sharing of jobs (which we discuss in Chapter 4).

Many progressive enterprises in the United States and Britain are committed to programmes designed to improve the Quality of Worklife (QWL), particularly in relation to new innovative technologies. That there is a community of interest between management and labour on these matters has largely been learned. But the transformation of practice to conform to the new appreciation is slow. Annual reports on QWL in Britain show little, if any, improvement (Anon 2000b; Worrall and Cooper 1999).

ORGANISATIONS AND QUALITY OF LIFE

Everyone employed in an organisation needs to ask himself or herself from time to time: what is this organisation for? A common answer from commercial organisations is: To make a profit for shareholders. Indeed it is the only answer of many. The dean of Yale University's School of Management, Jeffrey Garten, interviewed 40 of the chief executives of the world's largest companies. They included the heads of AOL, Time Warner, General Electric, and Toyota. Garten concluded that none of these chief executives fully grasped the responsibilities they have, even though they control so much of what goes on in the world. In particular, many considered their mission solely as the maximisation of profits. Rupert Murdoch told Garten 'Its dishonest to pretend otherwise' (Garten 2001).

Some business leaders, when asked this question, go one step further and add: The provision of services to the community. David Packard, co-founder of Hewlett Packard put it this way:

> Why are we here? I think many people assume, wrong-
> ly, that a company exists solely to make money.
> Money is an important part of a company's existence,
> if the company is any good. But a result is not a cause.
> We have to go deeper and find the real reason for our
> being. As we investigate this, we inevitably come to
> the conclusion that a group of people get together and
> exist as an institution we call a company, so that they
> are able to accomplish something collectively that
> they could not accomplish separately—they make a
> contribution to society, a phrase which sounds trite
> but is fundamental (Handy 1998, p 77).

The only real justification for a business is to create and add value to the community. The Stanford University Business School tried to identify the characteristics of highly successful 'visionary companies'. They had core values and ideologies that drove the companies. For example, Johnson & Johnson exists to alleviate pain and disease: customers come first, employees second, society third and shareholders fourth. Another example is Merck, the goal of which is 'preserving and improving human life'. Walt Disney's is 'to make people happy'. All the organisations' activities are measured by their success in achieving their goal. The visionary companies were 15 times more profitable than the general market, even though they claimed that profit was not their primary motive (Olson and Toyne 2000).

Other examples include Boeing, which was committed to building the best planes that flew furthest, fastest and safest. In 1960 Boeing bet the entire value of the company on conferring on the world the jumbo jet. It nearly made the company bankrupt, but it achieved its vision. Regrettably the vision didn't last. Thirty years later it lost the vision of a company dedicated to engineering excellence and committed itself to maximising profits. By contrast innovation passed to Airbus, which was not just a profit maximiser. When Unilever was founded in the 1880s it put at its core its vision — to build the best everyday things for everyday people — and not the maximisation of profits. They still do (Hutton 2002).

Organisations consist of people who have chosen to spend much of their lives there. What about the quality of the lives of those committed to an organisation? What is their current quality of life? Does that count at all?

One group looking for answers to these questions was the Caux Round Table, consisting of a group of international executives who met in Caux Switzerland. The group shared a belief that business organisations can be a powerful force for positive change in the quality of life for the world. They produced the Caux Principles in the conviction that we can all live together and act for the common good. The following is the Caux Principle on employees:

> We believe in the dignity of every employee and in taking employee interests seriously. We therefore have a responsibility to provide jobs and compensation that improve workers' living conditions; provide working conditions that respect each employee's health and dignity; be honest in communications with employees and open in sharing information, limited only by legal and competitive restraints; listen to and, where possible, act on employee suggestions, ideas, requests and complaints: engage in good faith negotiations when conflict arises; avoid discriminatory practices and guarantee equal treatment and opportunity in areas such as gender age race and religion; promote in the business itself the employment of differently abled people in places of work where they can be genuinely useful; protect employees from avoidable injury and illness in the workplace; encourage and assist employees in developing relevant and transferable skills and knowledge; and be sensitive to serious employment problems frequently associated with business decisions and work with governments, employee groups, other agencies and each other in addressing these dislocations (Hartman 1998, p 724).

WHY PROMOTE QUALITY OF LIFE OF EMPLOYEES?

We might ask: What value is it for an organisation to promote quality of life of its employees? There are two sorts of value that ethics recognises: instrumental value and intrinsic value. For example, if an employee has skills that will help the organisation to be productive and efficient, that employee is of instrumental value to the organisation. It will usually be of interest to the organisation that the employee's usefulness increases. So employees may be encouraged to pursue further studies or acquire specialised skills in technology. The employee so described is a means to an end. That is fine in itself. However, an ethical principle, long ago established, is that it is unethical to use a person only as a means to an end, for that is to recognise him or her only as an object. This is to thing–ify the person.

People are more than things. They are more than means to ends. This is because every person has another sort of value which is called his or her intrinsic value. This is the value an individual person has quite independent of his or her usefulness. Intrinsic value is the value of an individual in oneself, for oneself, and some would add also for God. What gives a person intrinsic value is his or her capacity for feeling and evaluating experiences. That is not to say no other creature has intrinsic value. On the contrary, whoever feels, that is suffers and enjoys, has intrinsic value. The lives of animals that enter into our lives should be our concerns as well as the lives of other humans (Birch and Vischer 1997). We have to make the transition from a dominantly thing-oriented society to a person-oriented society that recognises intrinsic value wherever it exists.

HOW SHOULD WE LIVE?

There are two components of the quality of human life, which have to do with intrinsic value. They are harmony and zest. Harmony is accord, congruity and a sense of oneness between our ideas and our experience. Zest is energetic vitality exemplified in feelings of creativity, enthusiasm and passion. It is good to be passionate about one's work. It is good to have work that one can be passionate about.

Social analyst John Gardner, in an address to staff of a large consulting firm, said that boredom is the secret ailment of large organisations. Someone remarked to him 'How can I be so bored when I'm so busy?' (Gardner 1991). We should ask *why* can this be, and how the job can be made interesting and exciting? It is as well to remind ourselves that evil is not only conflict, it is also monotony.

An ethical principle is that we should recognise the intrinsic value of every person, and in so doing promote the fulfilment of their lives. That is what quality of life is all about. All relationships that a person has feeds into that aspect of life. They include our relationship to all those we meet: our friends and family, and our work colleagues. They also include our relations to recreation, hobbies and the world of nature. It is little appreciated that people are constituted by their relationships. In this world there is no such thing as a person apart from his or her relationship with other people and other things. These relationships change the face of corporations, indeed of history.

Daly and Cobb (1989) have written a book that contrasts *Homo economicus* with the concept of the 'person in community' in which relationships define our identity. This is an important principle. To treat persons as self-contained individuals falsifies the real situation. We are members one of another. As the poet Alfred Lord Tennyson wrote in *Ulysses* 'I am a part of all that I have met'. Relationships are what matter because they make us.

The question to organisations is: To what extent are they responsible for promoting the values of 'person in community' in their employees? To what extent should an organisation promote the quality of life of its staff? In answering these questions we discover that there is a relationship between intrinsic value and instrumental value. Considerable evidence is given in Chapters 5 and 7 to indicate that the well-being of employees and recognition of their intrinsic value contributes to their usefulness. Employees who feel stressed, overworked, unappreciated and who experience low morale are less productive and less efficient. Stress and overwork lead to stress-related illness, and as a result work-time is less useful, and more time is taken off. It is a job of managers to recognise tell-tale symptoms of this sort, and deal with such problems humanely.

Mechanistic ways of talking about commerce involve a loss of some degree of human-ness. Workers become mere cogs in the machinery. Covey (1989) puts an emphasis on personal qualities that tend to get second place in organisations. He deplores that so little is said of the personal needs and characteristics of people who work in organisations. It is good to promote worthwhileness anywhere. It is better to promote human-ness than mechanical properties. It is better that people are happy and enjoy their work, have creative opportunities, feel wanted, are encouraged and are compassionate to one another. People are ends as well as means and should be valued as such.

But what are these ends? One way of considering this question is to put it another way, by asking an ethical question: What are the concerns that matter in our lives? It is helpful to make a distinction between ultimate concerns and secondary concerns. An ultimate concern is one that leads to the fulfilment of life. The chief executive who asked 'What the hell am I doing this for?' was facing the reality in his life that what he was doing was not leading to a fulfilled life. It was leaving him with a certain emptiness. His concerns were mainly what we call secondary, not ultimate.

There is a classic story that makes this distinction clearly. It is the story of Mary and Martha. Martha was troubled and anxious about many things as she went about her household chores in preparing for a meal for the visitor who had just arrived on her doorstep. In so doing she missed the one thing needful at that particular moment. Mary chose the one thing needful at that moment, which was her total response to the visitor who happened to be Jesus. The one thing needful was to appreciate and enjoy his presence, and is so doing to discover self-fulfilment both of self and of the other.

Every passing hour we are confronted with choices. Most of them are secondary choices. But to let them govern most of our waking hours is to miss the point of life. There are also ultimate choices that are of ultimate concern, which we can recognise because they are self-fulfilling — the opposite feeling to emptiness. More than that, we come to recognise that the only adequate response to ultimate concern is passion, even infinite passion! It is the 'I can do no other' syndrome. Martha's way is not contemptible. Indeed it is the way which keeps the world running. There are innumerable concerns in our lives that demand attention; even devotion, but they do not demand infinite attention and infinite passion. Profits are a concern of business but they are not the ultimate reason for existing. The end and object of the nation's existence is not its standard of living.

Ethicist Peter Singer (1993) has written a book on *How Are We to Live?* The first three chapters are devoted to stories of business people who failed to make the ultimate choice until it was too late. Their lives remained unfulfilled despite huge worldly success. They remained Marthas all their lives.

Is there any central ethical principle that could serve as a guide to ethical conduct? One proposal is the so-called 'utilitarian ethic' of Jeremy Bentham. (The word 'utility' in this context means to judge actions by their consequences or uses.) Bentham eventually formulated his doctrine as aiming at 'the greatest happiness for the greatest number'. That is what he saw governments and the legal systems for. This ethic would involve some sort of arithmetic adding the goods and subtracting the bads — the famous 'hedonic calculus' of maximising pleasures and minimising pains — which is easier said than done. Bentham built his laissez-faire economics on the basis of utilitarian hedonism. He saw economic value as measured by pleasure.

Peter Singer (2001, p 16) adopts a somewhat different yet utilitarian ethic: to choose a course of action that has the best consequences for all affected. 'Best consequences' is understood as meaning what, on balance, furthers the interests of those affected rather than merely what increases pleasure and reduces pain.

This utilitarian principle would include the Golden Rule: to give the same weight to the interests of others as one gives one's own interest. One formulation of the Golden Rule is that we do to others as we would have them do to us. The Golden Rule was well known to the Jews and Greeks, although mostly in a negative form. Rabbi Hillel, an older contemporary of Jesus, had summed up the teachings of Judaism on the Golden Role: 'Do not do unto others as you would not have done unto you' (Armstrong 2001, p 141). Jesus tells us in a positive form: 'Whatever you wish that men would do to you, do so to them' (Matthew 7: 12). As far as it goes the Golden Rule is good in principle, but how can we tell what is good for all others? Furthermore, does this principle of consequential ethics go far enough? We think not.

The Golden Rule is transcended in further words of Jesus which speak, not of reciprocity as the ultimate standard of ethics, but of love. The Christian ethic insists that the needs of neighbour shall be met, yet without a careful computation of relative needs. The Golden Rule must be transcended for it does not tell us what we should wish that men would do to us. And our wishes express not only our right but also our wrong and indeed even our foolishness. This is why Paul Tillich (1955, p 32) says this sets the limit of the Golden Rule, and it is why he calls it 'calculated justice' as opposed to 'creative justice'. Only for him who knows for what he *should* wish and who actually wishes it, is the Golden Rule ultimately valid.

The 'Christian realism' of Reinhold Niebuhr agrees with Paul Tillich on this judgement. He says that without the concern for others which originates in love, the determination of moral obligations quickly deteriorates into 'mere calculation of advantage' (Niebuhr 1949, p 193). Without love, the reciprocity, which was supposed to lead us beyond individual interests, may prove in the end to be just another instrument for advancing them. Only love can transform calculating justice into creative justice. Love makes the Golden Rule a valid ethic. This is the highest way of all. There is no greater statement of it than this:

> If I were to speak with the combined eloquence of man and angels I should stir men like a fanfare of trumpets or the clashing of cymbals, but unless I had love I should do nothing more. If I had the gift of foretelling the future and had in my mind not only all human knowledge but the secrets of God, and if in addition I had that absolute faith which can move mountains, but had not love I tell you I should amount to nothing at all. If I were to sell all my possessions to feed the hungry and, for my convictions, allowed my body to be burned, and yet had no love, I should achieve precisely nothing. Love is slow to lose patience. It looks for a way of being constructive. It is not possessive: It is neither anxious to impress nor does it cherish inflated ideas of its own importance ... Love knows no limit to its endurance, no end to its trust, no fading of its hope: it can outlast anything. It is the one thing that still stands when all else has fallen (1 Corinthians 13: J B Phillips' translation).

This sort of love has nothing to do with romanticism. Love's work is hard work. It works against conventions and opportunism, is alert to need in season and out of season, working its transformations without ceasing. Love, by whatever names you might wish to call it, is central to the activities of creative organisations from the manager and his or her team to the CEO. Its emphasis is not utilitarian. Its emphasis is on values that are fulfilling for human life and society at large.

QUALITY OF LIFE AND THE MODERN SOCIETY

In this section we pursue quality of life in organisations in the context of the wider aspect of the community in which the organisation is set, that is to say both socially and politically. A humane society is one that encourages fulfilment of human life and enrichment of the quality of life through the practice of the principles of love — even in business! Some of the ways of promoting this in the workplace are discussed in Chapters 4 and 7 about hours of work and stress.

We are often asked: Where are the values of modern young people to come from? At one time churches provided an answer for most people. That is no longer the case.

Our quality of life depends also on the wider society in which we live. A society whose policies make the rich richer and the poor poorer is a bad society. The focus of attention in a society guided primarily by economic goals, especially a society guided by economic rationalism, is not one that enhances quality of life, for it puts the emphasis on material goods. Man does not live by bread alone.

John Maynard Keynes (1930) was appalled at the demoralising influences of economic affluence and its exaltation of what he called some of the most distasteful human qualities. Yet in his essay on the 'Economic possibilities for our grandchildren' he looked forward to a time of abundance which would assure a decent standard of living for everyone. He predicted the day when economic problems would take a back seat where they belong, and the head and the heart would be occupied by the real problems such as human relationships. He was alluding to, but did not use the phrase, quality of life. Keynes' forecast was wrong. He incorrectly thought people would prefer more time for 'real' issues of life than to spend more and more time accumulating wealth. He did not anticipate the choices made by the Baby Boomers' generation.

In Australia, as well as in other developed countries, we define progress mainly in material terms. The Prime Minister of Australia, John Howard, time and time again set the rate of economic growth or the gross national product (GNP) as the prime criterion by which to judge his government. Increase the production of goods and all else will fall into line. It doesn't. GNP becomes a golden calf. To so worship is to pay dearly (see Chapter 3).

Where then is the younger generation to look for its ethical ideals? In an address to businessmen in New York, Larry Rasmussen, professor of Ethics at Union Theological Seminary in New York, discussed how the quality of life of a society requires healthy communities with face to face participation: families, neighbourhoods, the workplace, churches and other faith communities, and schools. He said these are the anchor communities, which are most directly responsible for the formation of human character and the values of that society. He argued that no amount of market and business efficiency and no level of technical expertise can substitute for the social glue provided by these sectors of society working together. The quality of life floats on a sea provided by what some now call the 'civil society'. So it matters tremendously the particular values that a civil society tends to promote (Rasmussen 1996).

A sense of community, so desperately lacking in many human groups, is dependent to a large extent upon the civil society having social arrangements that help people to discover a sense of meaning and a commitment to life. Whereas at one time this role was played by churches, today it has to come from a wider community of the civil society. The networks and institutions that bind society together are its 'social capital'. This includes its political systems. Right action is learned in these contexts. The good person learns to act in ways that develop the capacities human beings have. The good person does not settle for less than human possibilities allow. To settle for less means that human nature has been sold short.

A major factor in raising or lowering the character of people is the political structure of the society in which they live. Politics is the art of so adapting that structure as to raise the sense of duty in each to all. All politics can be ultimately tested by that criterion. It is the test that democracy first passed, with some blemishes, in ancient Greece. Here was a society based on the assumption that all its members are called upon to contribute to its people's well-being in the whole of their faculties. 'Idiot' was the name Aristotle gave to a person who refused to participate in public affairs.

According to Curtis (1938, ch 11), it is no accident that Athens could give to the world poets like Sophocles and Euripides, artists like Pheidias, a statesman like Pericles, a teacher like Socrates, and a thinker like Plato. This amazing originating power was, as her own historians felt, released by a system which laid the tasks of government on more of its citizens than other states, despite its practice of slavery. No doubt other causes were also operative. William James (1917) made the point that, sporadically, great people come from everywhere, but from a community to get vibrating through and through with an intensively active life, many geniuses come together in rapid succession. This is what happened in the sudden bloom in Greece, later in early Rome, and again in the Renaissance. 'Blow must follow blow so fast that no cooling can occur in the intervals. Then the mass of the nation grows incandescent, and may continue to glow by pure inertia' (James 1917, p 188). We long in hope for such a society.

The suggestion is that in these great flowerings of society many people became involved in the issues of the day and were guided by a succession of great and inspiring leaders. Is it possible then, for the managerial hierarchy in organisations to harness the creative power of their employees, so that the tasks of managing and organising could be laid on the largest possible number of employees while at the same time being influenced by leadership from above? The organisation itself becomes part of the civil society.

THE ORGANISATION AS PART OF CIVIL SOCIETY

Ricardo Semler, CEO of Semco has managed to do what the ancient Greeks had done, to lay the challenges that he saw facing Semco at the doorstep of all his employees. He has done this so successfully that executives from companies such as IBM, General Motors, Ford, Kodak, Nestlé, Goodyear, Bayer, Chase Manhattan, Siemens, Dow Chemical and Mercedes-Benz have made regular pilgrimages to his non-descript industrial complex on the outskirts of the huge Brazilian city of Sao Paulo (Semler 1994; 2003). He has done this moreover in a South American society, which is still discovering the nature of democracy after decades of authoritarian rule. What he has done is good for business and also for society in its struggles to find democratic values.

In his groundbreaking book *Maverick*, Semler (1994) outlines the grave situation that Semco was facing at the time. The hallmarks of the organisation were poor performance, diminishing profits, low morale, employee burn-out and lack of initiative and creativity. Semco was facing a crisis on a number of different levels. Having heard the regurgitated wisdom of consulting companies and managerial gurus, Semler decided to try something radical.

Semler says, 'before I could reorganise Semco I had to reorganise myself. Long hours were the first issue I tackled. They were one of the biggest symptoms of time sickness, a disease that afflicts far too many executives ... So many executives find that the daily quota of 24 hours is too few to get to everything and still have any left over' (Semler 1994, p 59). As a result of these long work hours, Semler resolved not to take work home, not to work on weekends, and most importantly to leave the workplace at a reasonable hour each day. In order to achieve these goals he had to shift other underlying beliefs first.

His own belief system and philosophy had to change. When asked the reason for their success, entrepreneurs are fond of saying 'A lot of hard work'. But hard work by itself is not enough, Semler argues. To say it is possible to

establish a successful business just by arriving early and staying late is like saying that every mailman can be a Bill Gates. 'There is a prevailing conviction
that sweat is obligatory, and with each new drop an executive moves a little
closer to financial heaven. I had to rid myself of this notion. It isn't healthy. It
isn't even true' (Semler 1994, p 60).

There is a silent understanding that the quantity of work is more important than the quality of work. Executives today feel the pressure from their
bosses to out-work colleagues and present an image of hard work and sacrifice. By this reasoning, having a heart attack because of work leads to true
glory (Semler 1994). A person who manages their time is often suspect of
being slack or not having enough to do. An executive who judges their contribution in hours will mutter things like 'Well, as we all know how unfair it
was they didn't promote me. Everyone here knows that I'm here at seven in
the morning until nine in the evening.'

The last aspect that Semler (1994) had to change was rationalising the
late hours by saying that things are a little uncertain at the office right now.
I'll just work a little longer until they straighten out. It is generally difficult
to argue with someone who says 'my organisation is going through a
restructure, changes at the top, my boss just quit, merger preparation or post
merger crises, lack of sufficient staff to complete this project, unexpected
change in deadlines.' One may rationalise that these are reasons for working long hours. Semler argues that 'to allow such events to shape one's
working day is to become like a cork that bobs up and down on the sea'
(Semler 1994, p 61).

Semler seized the opportunity to change Semco when it was down and
out. He factored the quality of life (as an uncompromising variable) into a
business world dominated largely by profit margins and shareholder wealth.
He brought about radical changes in management practice by changing his
own philosophy and beliefs first, which had a tremendous effect on all those
working for Semco for they too participated in deciding what had to be
changed. As a result of such changes, it is little wonder that some of the
world's leading companies send their executives to study such changes.
Semler focused on the quality of life of his employees.

It has been argued that what Semler achieved could not be replicated in
a very large company. If that is the case why do large companies, such as those
mentioned above, bother to come to his doorstep? They must be learning
something. Brazil is becoming a centre of corporate social responsibility
because of entrepreneurs like Ricardo Semler. Another one is Oded Grajew,
founder of the Ethos Institute of Social and Business Responsibility with its

headquarters in Sao Paulo. It has over 300 companies as members (Holliday, Schmidheiny and Watts 2002).

Another corporation where management is concerned about the quality of life of its employees, which has a flow on to the community, is Flight Centre. According to Blake (2001), it is the world's fastest growing travel company and a billion-dollar success. This company places its employees first on a list of priorities, and ensures that their goals and needs are in alignment with the overall vision, values and philosophy of the company. Flight Centre is a place where systems and processes are 'created for our people, by our people, in an environment that stimulates change. Bureaucracy, red tape and sacred cows are outlawed' (Blake 2001, p 27). The management constantly monitors and deals with unseen and difficult to measure factors such as morale, team spirit, team leadership, each individual's self-esteem and the way team members relate to each other. These factors ultimately have an impact on customers, market share and profit margins, which in turn, affect share price and shareholder value.

Blake says that Flight Centre recognised the need for people to identify with something larger than themselves and therefore strove to provide a meaningful workplace, a supportive team environment and the opportunity to make a difference. In a world gone crazy, Flight Centre provides a place to 'come to each day that respects your very humanity, where you are treated fairly, where there are a set of sensible rules of the game, rather than a boss's unpredictable whims and generates ownership of results' (2001, p 61). So people are not rewarded because they can get 'stuff' done, but rather, they are promoted to higher positions because they have demonstrated that they have highly evolved communication and people skills. Managing the people side is the key to this company's success. This involves the management focusing on and constantly improving the quality of life of its employees. But at the same time it says something about the sort of society the company wants to see around it.

In his book *The Living Company*, De Geus (1997), a former Shell executive, compares the difference between an 'economic company' and a 'living company'. The economic company exists to make profits and lives for its shareholders. It is a mechanistic model, like a puddle forming on the ground when it rains and where raindrops (meaning people) collect and stay. De Geus develops the metaphor by explaining that puddles have relatively short life spans and are vulnerable to stagnation and changes in the environment such as heat and drought.

The living company is more like a river that is continually replenished by each drop of rain. Unlike the puddle the river contributes to the life on its banks (the greater community). By means of these metaphors De Geus emphasises the importance of quality of life in companies. Employees feel that they are contributing to something worthwhile, rather than simply working to exist. And quality of life contributes to the growth, development and prof-its of the company and as well to the greater good of the community in which the company lives. It is a beacon both to its employees and to society at large.

In this chapter we have given some examples of the meaning and importance of the quality of life. But how is quality of life measured? The next chapter furthers this discussion by focusing on measuring quality of life as an index.

3

THE WEALTH OF NATIONS

In Australia and other developed nations, we have
defined progress in mainly material terms and measured
it in terms of a rising per capita GDP (Gross Domestic
Product). The equation of more with better — of standard of living with quality of life — is coming under critical scrutiny in the research literature, but remains largely
unquestioned in mainstream public and political debate.

Richard Eckersley, 'Redefining progress', 1998, p 3.

MEASURING THE QUALITY OF LIFE OF THE NATION

The material wealth of a nation may be regarded as a measure
of its standard of living. The material standard of living is measured by the
GDP. But this is not an adequate measure of the quality of life. Attempts have
recently been made to devise a credible measure of quality of life. The United
Nations developed its Human Development Index (HDI) for this purpose. It
urged that more attention should be paid to the quality rather than the quantity of growth. It recognised five damaging kinds of growth:

- that which does not translate into jobs

- that which is not matched by the spread of democracy

- that which destroys cultural identity

- that which despoils the environment and wastes resources needed for
  future generations

- that where most of the benefits are claimed by the rich.

It calls these, respectively, 'jobless', 'voiceless', 'rootless', 'futureless' and 'ruthless
growth' (UNDP 1996).

At the present stage of its development the HDI combines only two indicators together with GDP: life expectancy and educational attainment. When this is done Canada comes out on top of HDI rankings, although it is ninth in GDP per capita. Sierra Leone ranks dead last on the HDI. Of the 'emerging economies', tracked each week by *The Economist's* own ranking, Israel has the highest ranking followed by Singapore. India has the lowest score (Anon 2000a).

The World Health Organisation is in process of developing an index of quality of life that attempts to be cross-cultural. It is based on individuals' subjective assessment in six areas: physical, psychological, level of independence, social relationships, environment, and spiritual (WHOQOL Group 1995).

INDEX OF SUSTAINABLE ECONOMIC WELFARE

The Index of Sustainable Economic Welfare (ISEW), which includes 20 indicators, is more widely developed at this stage (Cobb et al 1995). It takes into account consumption, distribution of wealth, environmental health, the cost of unemployment and many other indicators. Whereas in the United States the GDP per capita rose steadily between 1950 and 1995, the ISEW showed a rise in quality of life of some 2 per cent between 1950 and 1976. But thereafter, despite a rising GNP, it fell by over 15 per cent by 1995. Britain, Denmark, the Netherlands, Germany and Australia all show a similar trend over the past 50 years, with ISEW increasing with GNP up to the 1970s, then levelling off or falling away while GNP continued to climb. Likewise, whereas per capita consumption in the United States in the last 20 years rose 45 per cent, there was a decrease of 51 per cent in the quality of life as measured by another index of social health (Handy 1998).

The ISEW has been enlarged by the Australia Institute to use some 25 indicators. This index is called the Genuine Progress Indicator (Hamilton and Saddler 1997). The indicators include items such as income distribution, costs of commuting, costs of noise pollution, costs of water pollution, and costs of crime (see below).

HUMAN WELL-BEING INDEX

A bold new index called the Human Well-being Index (HWI) has been developed by Prescott-Allen (2001) with the co-operation of six international organisations. It is bold because it has been applied to 180 countries for which some data could be obtained for at least half of the nine indicators used. These indicators are: health, population (eg life expectancy), household wealth, national wealth, education and communication, freedom and governance, peace and order, household equity, and gender equity. The

180 countries were then put into five categories: 'good', 'fair', 'medium', 'poor' and 'bad'.

Only three countries came out on top as good: Norway, Denmark and Finland. They were closely followed by Sweden. The top three countries performed well in all indicators. Ten other countries have a standard of living as high as the top three, but their wealth is not as evenly distributed.

Two thirds of the people of the world live in countries classified as poor or bad. Fifty-one countries, with 54 per cent of the world's population, were classified as having a poor HWI. They include China, most of Asia and the Middle East, and Northern Africa.

Forty countries, with 12.5 per cent of the world's population, were classified as bad. They include most of the rest of Africa and some parts of Asia.

In between the good and the bad are the fair and medium countries. Thirty-four countries with 16 per cent of the world's population had a fair HWI. They include North America, most of Europe, Australia and New Zealand.

Fifty-two countries, the largest group with 17 per cent of the world's population, had a medium HWI. They include most of South and Central America, South Africa, and Northern Europe, including Russia.

Looking at the world as a whole, of 180 countries studied in terms of their quality of life:

- 37 countries are fair or good
- 52 countries are medium
- 51 countries are poor
- 40 counties are bad.

The country with the lowest HWI is Somalia, closely followed by Sierra Leone, Burundi, Congo DR, Angola, Liberia and Afghanistan. Countries with a bad total score all have a poor or bad score for health and life expectancy, wealth and education. They are trapped in a vicious cycle of underdevelopment as illness and illiteracy cripple lives, debt stifles the economy, and governments fail to lead. Nigeria, for example, has emerged from 16 years of military dictatorship with a life expectancy of a mere 50 years, a fertility rate of five children per woman, with 43 per cent of children stunted, half the households without safe water, GDP per person under US$800 and with its institutions in ruins.

In summary: a fortunate few countries have a good life, but the gap between them and the rest of he world is enormous. This is the big picture, which necessarily will change as better data becomes available and as well-being changes with time. But, for whatever its deficiencies, the HWI studies should spur us on to the task of creating a better world for humans to live in. We need to have targets such as the World Health Organisation's plans for ridding the world of its three main diseases (malaria, AIDS and tuberculosis) and the UN objective of raising the life expectancy of all countries to more than 75 years by the year 2015.

ECONOMIC GROWTH AND THE QUALITY OF LIFE INDEX

In Australia between 1950 and 1966 GDP per capita increased almost three-fold (a rise of 200 per cent). This suggests that Australians had become much better off. Not so. The General Progress Indicator (GPI) reveals a different picture. From 1950 to 1966 the GPI rose by only 80 per cent. However, GPI showed no increase at all from 1970 to 1996, whereas GDP increased over this period by 90 per cent (Hamilton and Saddler 1997). These figures are in line with the perceptions of Australians about their quality of life.

In an extensive survey of 1200 Australians, Eckersley (1999) found that over a third (36 per cent) believed that life was getting worse, with slightly more (38 per cent) saying it was staying about the same. Only 24 per cent thought that life was getting better. The survey found that 75 per cent of Australians rated being able to spend more time with family and friends as very important for their quality of life. Some 66 per cent said that having less stress and pressure in their lives was very important. Only 38 per cent rated as very important having more money to buy things.

Mackay (1997) says his investigations reveal there is a growing community concern in Australia about the gap that exists between people's values and the way they live. They would like to be less materialistic but tend to acquire more and more. They seem unable to go where they want to go (see 'Generational change' in Chapter 4).

Yencken and Porter (2001), in their 'A just and sustainable Australia', have further analysed the present situation of economic growth in Australia and its failings as a measure of progress. Their 16 recommendations include:

- generating more jobs and spreading them more equitably
- improving support for individuals and communities through better community services
- more equable health services
- overcoming the disadvantages of minorities
- strengthening human rights with a bill of rights.

(A number of these recommendations are taken up in later chapters of this book.)

The moral of the story of this chapter is that GDP and economic growth in developed countries are no longer measures of quality of life. Because of the inadequacy of statistical data, the new indices of quality of life for developing countries tell the story with somewhat less confidence.

The supposed rationale that economic growth is an indicator of quality of life is flawed in four important aspects. Eckersley (1998b) identifies these as:

- It overestimates the extent to which past improvements in quality of life are attributable to economic growth. 'Economic growth' may include environmental damage from pollution as growth several times over: when it is produced, when it incurs health-care costs, when legal costs are incurred, and when it is cleaned up.

- It reflects too narrow a view of quality of life, and fails to explain why, after fifty years of growth, so many people appear to believe life is getting worse. The belief that material progress equates with a better life is so ingrained in our culture that we are overlooking the importance of other factors — in particular the personal, social and spiritual relationships that give life a sense of meaning, and people a sense of self-worth and purpose.

- It underestimates the gulf between the magnitude of the environmental challenges we face and the scale of our responses to them.

- It neglects the social costs of growing inequality.

An *Atlantic Monthly* article asked in its title 'If the economy is up, why is America down?' Pusey (1998) asked the same question of Australia. His answer is that ordinary people are not the winners in the growing economy. Indicators of a growing economy tell nothing about the inequality of the distribution of the growing wealth. It is very unequal. There are more losers than winners. In Australia in the 15 years from 1983, there was a substantial redistribution of income from the bottom 70 per cent to the top 10 per cent. At the same time there was a shift of 15 per cent of GDP away from wages, mostly to corporations. An increasing number of polls in the 1990s in Australia indicated that people did not feel good about their society. More than half the respondents in a CSIRO poll in 1997 said that their quality of life had deteriorated. An increasing proportion of people believe that Australia is becoming less equal and less like their ideal (Cox 1998).

Instead of the evening news each day on radio and television giving inordinate reports of the daily movements of the Dow Jones, Hang Seng, All Ordinaries and GDP, we would be better off to know the movements of a qualify of life index, as it would present a viable picture of people's lives in the context of their social and economic environments. Our hope is that as nations come to recognise the inadequacies of economic growth as a measure of quality of life, so too will business organisations and the media.

There is as yet no one system of measuring a business organisation's extent of participation in the triple bottom line of profits, society and environment. Knowles (2000, p 54) uses a 'five star' system for screening social responsibility and concern for the environment: no star represents indifference to the issues; five stars represents a high level of attention to the issues. The system is devised as a guide to ethical investment. A good example of environmental responsibility is the high rating given to Westpac Investment Management (WIM). In 1999 WIM entered an agreement with the Monash Centre for Environmental Management to screen companies on the basis of their corporate environmental performance. An initial list of 150 companies listed on the Australian Stock Exchange, including WIM, have been given environmental ratings.

But rating environmental issues is more readily done that rating for social responsibility. As yet there is no standard system for measuring the ethical stance and social responsibility of organisations. This is a much-needed project for the future. (Some indicators are given in subsequent chapters, and the Good Reputation Index is an example given in Chapter 1.)

Part 2

QUALITY OF WORKING LIFE

Progress in quality of working life includes concerns with hours of work, intensity of work, flexibility of working time, real income, productivity, efficiency, safety, freedom from stress, a proper balance between work and home life, and equality for women. For every step forward we make in one of these concerns there seems to be a step backwards in another.

There is a grave failure to recognise a professional obligation to face up to the negative factors in the workplace. The short-term answer to a corporation's concern about the bottom line of profits, such as downsizing, has been disastrous for the work force as well as failing as a long-term solution for the corporation. A major cost of downsizing and longer hours for those who remain in the work force has been a phenomenal increase in stress. The Baby Boomers' generation is the first generation of Australians to have identified stress as a debilitating consequence of everyday life, despite that generation's much higher standard of living compared with previous generations. The quality of working life is threatened while stress remains so widespread in the working world. By identifying the causes of stress we are in a better position to reduce its toll.

4

HOURS OF WORK, INTENSITY OF WORK AND REMUNERATION

The satanic mills were heedless of all human needs but one; relentlessly they began to grind society into its atoms ... the inner temple of human life was despoiled and violated.

Michael Polyani, *The Great Transformation*, 1957, p x.

Progress in the workplace is judged by a number of criteria. Sue Richardson (1998) lists four:

- hours worked

- the real income of workers

- the productivity of workers

- the quality of working life (job security, job satisfaction and relative power of workers).

AUSTRALIA AS A TRAIL-BLAZER

One image of Australia is that it is 'the lucky country'. Just over a hundred years ago the English novelist Anthony Trollope said, on a long visit to Australia, that it was becoming 'a worker's paradise'. His reason for saying this was that in 1885 in Sydney, stonemasons won an eight-hour day and a 40-hour week. And in 1886 a mass meeting of workers and employers of stonemasons in Melbourne resolved that an eight-hour day be introduced. They too won. Later that same year in Melbourne, 700 members of the mechanical trades discussed the expediency and practicability of the eight-hour day. They too won.

Dr Thomas Embling, who wanted people to be kinder to one another, gave them the slogan 'Eight hours labour, eight hours recreation, eight hours rest'. The victory of these workers was celebrated by an annual holiday in which workers march through the streets of the big cities holding banners extolling the virtues of eight hours work, eight hours recreation and eight hours rest (Clark 1995; Blainey 1994).

A later trail-blazer for the shorter working week was the Australian Commonwealth Public Service, which was awarded a 36.75 hour week in 1902 (Verrender 1997). Thus it was that Australia pioneered the eight-hour-day movement and for the first time in the world divided the 24 hours into eight for work, eight for sleep, eight for relaxation.

That day is rapidly fading. With less than two workers in five now working an eight-hour day, and workers nationally working an average of 43 working hours per week, Australians have earned the dubious reputation of being one of the hardest-working peoples in the developed world (Buchanan and Bearfield 1997). In the United States the average working week is just slightly longer at 43.8 hours (Catalano 1993). Those most affected by long hours, much longer than the average, are lawyers, architects, managers, accountants, executives and office workers. The Japanese probably work the hardest of all, possibly some five and a half weeks total per year more than American workers, and they take less than eight days annual holidays (Beder 2000). However, because of the difficulty of comparing countries, due to ways hours are assessed, some think Japan is about the same as Australia (Bachelard 2001).

CHOOSING TO WORK LONG HOURS

There are some in the community who work very long hours because they like it. Many research scientists come into this category. Research is their hobby. Some, of their own choice, work more than ten hours a day, six or seven days a week. They don't belong to any union nor do they need to. Some research scientists work long hours because they work in highly competitive fields such as molecular biology. Their telephones maintain constant touch with the advances their colleagues are making. There is an element of a big game being played on the frontiers of knowledge. Moreover, the person who is ahead gets the largest of the research grants. Having started on that road there is the 'Matthew effect' — 'To him who has, more shall be given' (Matthew 25:29).

One of us recalls a visit to a leading biological laboratory at the Massachusetts Institute of Technology, and being surprised at the white boards lining a long corridor. In case you got a bright idea in the corridor you immediately put it down on a white board and discussed it with the next passer by. No idea was to be lost.

David Shenk recalls:

> When I worked in the lab as a full-time scientist, I'd wake up in the morning thinking about a single research idea, then I'd go to work and think and read and talk only about that idea. I'd often go back to the lab at night to keep working on it. And this could go on for days and weeks. It was the most exhilarating, creative time of my life. But today I find that my time is fragmented by more and more demands: faxes, voice mail, e-mail and letters; the insistent pull of television, newspapers and radio; not to mention my family and friends (Suzuki and Dressel 1999, p 81).

For other scientists today, particularly in biotechnology, the exhilarating long hours in the laboratory become taken over by industrial and administrative problems as their discoveries become industrial (see Chapter 7).

Others create their own hours of work, notably those in the law who charge per minute of their time with a client to satisfy the greed of the wealthy. That is a choice made by the bosses whose underlings have to follow suit or be fired. A somewhat similar situation applies to medical practitioners in some medical centres who are reimbursed according to the number of patients they can squeeze into a brief timeslot.

FAIR RATES OF PAY

Besides reasonable hours of work individuals might expect to have reasonable and fair rates of pay. The two have not always gone together, though they were not far apart in their early history in Australia. A landmark decision in this respect was the ruling in Australia in 1907 of the new Court of Conciliation and Arbitration to establish a basic wage for unskilled workmen and a fair and reasonable wage for others. Fair and reasonable was a wage 'sufficient to ensure a workman and his family food, shelter, clothing, frugal comfort, provision for evil days, etc, as well as reward for special skills of an artisan if he is one' (Clark 1995, p 478). This was the beginning of a rising umbrella of social security. In the first 25 years of the twentieth century the United States eventually overtook Australia in its standard of living for wage earners. As to the present, Australia still has the protection of a basic wage, but the United States, as we indicate below, has a substantial number of 'working poor'.

Over the past 20 years in Australia average real wages have grown by 10 per cent. This increase has been unevenly distributed. Men in the top

20 per cent of the pay distribution gained about 12 per cent, whereas men in the bottom 30 per cent had lower real wages in 1995 than they had in 1975.

WORKING HOURS IN AUSTRALIA IN RECENT TIMES

In this section we discuss work primarily in terms of working hours per day and per week. Annual holidays and various leave entitlements help to determine the total hours of work in a year. These are considered only briefly. The story as told below is quite a complex one with its various twists and turns. Those who prefer a summary should turn to the one at the end of this section.

Between the early 1960s and the early 1990s only a third of employees in Australia had a 38-hour week. The average hours worked by full-time employees was 41 hours. In the late 1990s the average hours worked was 43 hours. Some 55 per cent worked 40 or more hours. One in three full-time employees worked for 49 hours a week (Dusevic 1997; Buchanan and Bearfield 1997; 1998; Gittins 1997). This is a cruel regression, in stark contrast with the ideals of one hundred years ago.

The severe downsizing and restructuring strategies, pursued by many corporations in Australia in the early 1990s, left more than half a million job-less per year in the early 1990s. This included 30 000 banking jobs and 50 000 manufacturing jobs downsized out of existence in the first half of the 1990s. And downsizing continues in Australia and elsewhere (Lecky 1998). Companies learned to use fewer workers to produce more. With so many unemployed, management had the whip. Many people stayed on, less for love of their job than for fear of losing it (Paul 2000). This period has been bad news for the worker (see 'Downsizing and stress' in Chapter 7).

In these years one in three white-collar employees worked overtime, and two-thirds of these did it for free. Besides the burgeoning problem of over-work there is a serious problem of underemployment of part-time and casu-al workers. In Australia there are more than 15 million people over the age of 15. Of these, 6.7 million are employed full-time and 2.3 million employed part-time. Of those employed part-time, over 430 000 would prefer to work additional hours while many of the full-time workers would prefer to work fewer hours. Over 200 000 people work less than 10 hours a week but all of them are seeking additional hours. The number of underemployed workers has grown steadily since the late 1980s (Denniss 2001).

Blue-collar workers were better off. Only one in five worked overtime for free. However, if the overtime had been harnessed into new jobs, some 200 000 new full-time positions might have been created. This did not happen for reasons we discuss later. Some 30 years ago there were as many as

15 workers for every manager. In the late 1990s there were only eight work-ers for each manager, all working much harder (Dusevic 1997). This too is a serious regression.

The situation is even worse. Oddly enough, long working hours has also meant greater intensity of work in Australia. In 1995, a questionnaire survey involving 37 000 employees made an attempt to quantify intensity of work. Employees were asked how their intensity of work had changed during the last 12 months and to reply on a score of low, medium or high. Table 4.1 shows three components of intensity were recognised: the effort put into the job, stress in the workplace, and pace of work.

TABLE 4.1 Increase in intensity of work in Australia: 1994–95

Components of intensity	Percentage
Increased effort put into the job	> 59
Increase in stress	50
Increase in the pace of work	46

SOURCE Morehead et al, *Changes at Work*, 1997.

Over 59 per cent of employees said that effort had increased; 50 per cent said that stress had increased; and 46 per cent said there had been an increase in pace of work. Managers experienced the greatest increase in the three components: 39 per cent had a high score on the index. Overall 28 per cent of all employees had a high score. Increased effort was more likely to be reported by employees in finance and insurance (69 per cent). Some 61 per cent of these employees reported increase in stress, and 52 per cent reported increase in pace of work (Morehead et al 1997). Buchanan and Bearfield (1998) found that not only did managers work the longest hours, they were also the group of workers which had the largest percentage of people who wished to work fewer hours.

Responses in 1997 of more than 200 employees indicated that 76 per cent of managers in the advertising, marketing and communication sectors were working up to ten hours longer a week than they had been five years earlier. There were fewer managers around and those who had survived the downsizing worked harder. Further, 68 per cent of those in non-managerial positions clocked up more hours than five years earlier (Hornery 1997).

In the 1920s and 1930s the fight for reduced working hours was an important strategy of the Australian union movement for a more equitable sharing of wealth. This culminated in 1947 in the adoption of the 40-hour week by the Commonwealth Court of Conciliation and Arbitration. It involves an eight-hour working day over a five-day week during 11 months of the year over a 45-year working life. The union programme for further reduction in working hours resulted in a campaign for a 35-hour week. It had limited success. Employers in the metal industries conceded to a 38-hour week, which spread to some other sectors. Some other industries such as coal, mining, oil and stevedoring achieved the 35-hour target (Verrender 1997).

The average working week in Australia became longer from the early 1980s (Verrender 1997). Since the mid-1980s the proportion of full-time workers working beyond 40 hours has grown to 40 per cent. Now, it is not unusual for white-collar workers to arrive at the office at 7:30 am and not leave until 9:00 pm. A study in 2001 reveals that one in five Australians now work more than 50 hours a week. The study covered workers in 12 industries including engineering, medicine, teaching, the public service, horse racing and mining. Whilst some expressed a love of their work, overwhelmingly most were concerned with the negative effects of long hours which were damaging to family, friendships and community life. Wives felt like single parents or 1950s housewives. Many were lonely. The main cause of long hours amongst this group was fewer people doing more (Horin and Wilson 2001).

Another Australian study revealed that between 1982 and 2000, full-time male employees worked an extra 4.3 hours a week. Full-time female employees worked an extra three hours a week. Between 1998 and 2000 an extra 48 minutes were added to the average working week of full-time employees. This is an extraordinary finding given that declining full-time working hours are more common in other OECD countries. In comparison with all other OECD countries, Australia appears to have had by far the largest increase in average working hours for full-time employees since the 1980s. No longer is Australia regarded as the land of the long weekend (Robinson 2001).

Nor do the working hours cease on arriving home. There is a proliferation of communication via e-mail, voice mail, SMS (short message system, or text messaging), mobile, internet technology and interactive television. Together with clients operating from different time zones, this all adds to the day's work. So the 60-hour working week is the norm for many (Verrender 1997). Now just over one third of the labour work force work standard hours per week. Of the remainder just under one third work overtime and just under one fifth work part-time. Around 80 per cent of blue-collar workers are paid for overtime, but only one third of white-collar workers are paid for overtime. In 1997, a survey asked 700 employees if they would prefer to work fewer hours? The results are shown in Table 4.2.

TABLE 4.2 Australian workers wanting to work fewer hours

Type of worker	Percentage
Professional/managerial	35
White-collar	23
Blue-collar	22

SOURCE Buchanan and Bearfield, 'Reforming work time', 1997.

The single most popular topic in work reform in Australia in recent years is flexibility in working time arrangements. These include changes in rostered days off, flexibility in starting and stopping times, flexibility of breaks, and limits to the amount of overtime in an one year. Despite fears to the contrary, increased flexibility in working time for employees and employers can be achieved simultaneously with security of employment (Buchanan and Bearfield 1997).

To summarise this complex story: Australia pioneered the shorter working week in the end of the nineteenth century. It gave the world the slogan 'eight hours labour, eight hours recreation and eight hours rest'. In the 1920s and 1930s the fight for reduced working hours was a strategy of the Australian union movement for a more equitable sharing of wealth. It culminated in 1947 in the awarding of the 40-hour week by the Commonwealth Court of Conciliation and Arbitration. The union programme for a further reduction to a 35-hour week met with only limited success. The average working week became longer from the early 1980s onwards. At the beginning of the twenty-first century less than two in five workers have an eight-hour day. In the central business districts, the 60-hour week has become the norm. Much downsizing in the 1990s has resulted in fewer workers. Longer working hours has brought with it a greater intensity of work for these fewer workers, especially for managers. Australians are now amongst the hardest working people in the world, being probably exceeded only by workers in the United States and Japan.

WORKING HOURS ELSEWHERE IN THE WORLD

What has happened in Australia has parallels in other English-speaking communities. In the United States, unemployment is at a 25-year low. It has been reduced by limiting welfare and enabling employers to offer ever lower wages to unskilled workers. But having a job these days does not mean having a living wage. It could mean earning US$6 an hour on a night shift from midnight to 8:00 am. Virtually everyone in the United States, not incarcerated, can get a job. But many workers are exhausted.

Some 30 per cent of Americans consider that many workers earn pover-ty-level wages, hence the phrase 'working poor' for the large under-class of the menial and low paid (Horin 1997). It is not a happy prospect. Of the 127 million people working in the United States in 1996, 38 million worked part-time. Another 35 million, though working, weren't paid enough to support a family. Some 19 million of those who were counted as employed worked in retail business and earned less than US$10 000 per year, usually without any type of health or retirement benefits (Hawken, Lovins and Lovins 1999, p 53).

Between 1979 and 1992 the *Fortune* 'Top 500' companies in the United States decreased their work force by downsizing over 4 million workers. The 100 biggest US companies reduced their work force by 22 per cent between the years 1978 and 1996. During the 1990s a million workers were laid off in the United States each year. Downsizing continues. Jobs are far more insecure than they used to be. The average US firm loses half its employees every four years (Beder 2000, pp 132–33). This is a sorry state of work in America today.

There has been much opposition in the United States to shortening working hours to a five-day week of eight hours a day. Workers in the cloth-ing industry won this in the 1920s. But American steelworkers continued with 12-hour shifts. Legislation in the United States during the Great Depression set the standard working week at 40 hours over five days. But long hours continued through the use of overtime. This continued until the 1970s when hours of work started to increase again. In the early 1990s, the average American full-time worker was working 140 to 163 more hours each year than in the 1970s. One in four Americans work 49 or more hours a week on the job and for more weeks per year (Beder 2000, pp 230, 245).

In the United States between 1995 and 1999 the number of workers call-ing in sick because of stress in the job has more than tripled. Half of all Americans report some kind of stress, and 63 per cent say they would rather have more time off than more money. Their problem is to get a proper bal-ance between work and life. A recent survey has found that a majority of American workers are willing to relinquish income to gain more family and personal time. About two thirds of those surveyed would give up an average of 13 per cent of their salary. Less than one quarter were unwilling to give up any salary at all (Jamieson House Employment Group 1996). American work-ers have legally mandated 16 vacation days per year, the lowest in any Western country. By contrast Australia has four to six weeks for vacation each year, and Swedes have 32 days a year (Robinson 2000).

The Japanese work five and half weeks a year more than Americans, and 10 weeks a year more than Europeans. They take less that an average of eight days annual holiday, although they are entitled to more. On top of a 60- to 70-hour week they are expected to spend time entertaining customers and clients (Beder 2000). In Japan, workaholism is a social problem. A 1999 survey found that Japanese workers are more likely to go without breakfast, spend long hours commuting, hardly talk to their wives and get less than five hours sleep at night than was the case with workers 25 years ago. About 10 000 Japanese people aged between 34 and 61 die each year from overwork, which is as many as die in motor car accidents (Beder 2000).

The Japanese Government became a promoter of fewer hours spent on work, and efforts were made to get workers to take a vacation. One company even created a competition for the Dream Vacation (Kriakov 2000). It's about time. Too many workers in Japan fall prey to *karoshi* or 'death by overwork'. These victims labour for weeks without adequate rest, then collapse and die without warning. About 40 claims for compensation are filed each year in Japan, mostly by widows of victims. Recent work has shown that there is a strong correlation between and excessive overtime in the three months prior to death. People who worked more than 100 hours overtime in the final month and more than 80 hours per month in the previous five months were far more likely to die. Other factors that lead to are irregular working hours, the number and length of business trips, and high temperature and noise in the workplace (Hadfield 2001).

It has been estimated that Canadian businesses lose C$12 billion every year due to stress related disorders. More Canadians are now recognising that long hours of work contribute to stress, depression, burnout and loss of productivity (Lehmkuhl 1999). A major enquiry commissioned by the Canadian Government carried out a modelling of the impact of a large-scale reduction in working time on the economy and job creation. As a result, Canada introduced the Work Well Network to co-ordinate the promotion of a four-day week with controls on overtime (Jamieson House Employment Group 1996).

In 1993 the European Union produced its Working Time Directive, which was intended to have the effect of reducing the maximum hours worked by its employees (European Union 1993). The 48-hour maximum week (including overtime) was presented as a health and safety initiative. It stipulated rest breaks where the working day is longer than six hours, a minimum rest period of one day a week, and an annual paid holiday of four weeks. (Certain workers are currently excluded from the directive, including those in the transport sector, doctors in training, and offshore workers.)

The Working Time Directive became law in Britain on 23 November 1998. Sectors excluded from the law included workers involved in transport, chief executives and those with autonomous decision-making powers (Kodz et al 1998). Despite the law, the Quality of Working Life Report for Britain a year later (Anon 2000b) reported that in that year:

- 82 per cent of executives work over 40 hours a week

- 32 per cent of executives work over 50 hours a week

- 10 per cent of employees work over 60 hours a week

- 76 per cent of employees work more than their contract hours a week.

Most of these workers said that their long hours were necessary to meet deadlines. Some 86 per cent said that it left no time for other interests, and 79 per cent said it adversely affected the relationship with their partner. Only 15 per cent of mangers felt their organisation helped to balance work and home commitments.

Compliance with the Working Time Directive is mandatory for member nations of the European Union. However, its introduction has been fraught with controversy. French trade unions welcomed the proposal, but the business community condemned the legislation as costly, complex and restrictive. Furthermore, the French Government urged employers not to cut pay commensurate with working shorter hours. The Mitterand Government introduced a phased reduction in the working week to 39 hours, and increase in annual leave to five weeks (Buchanan and Bearfield 1997, p 3). An agreement has been reached between the major employer group Paronat and four large unions to cut the five-day 39-hour week to a four-day 33-hour week (Jamieson House Employment Group 1996).

In the private sector as a whole the 35-hour week has, since 2000, established itself firmly as a part of French culture. Many observers say it has fulfilled the government's stated objective of creating new jobs. A government survey found that 59 per cent of those affected say it has improved their lives. Applying the law to civil servants in France, of which there are nearly 5 million, has proven more problematic. The dispute centres on the government's refusal to create new positions to compensate for the working time lost (Goodman 2001). Truck drivers, doctors and tax collectors have complained about injustices arising from the enforced hours. There are problems, but the instigators hope these will be ironed out.

Germany has reduced the working week in some industries to four days at 28.5 hours (Buchanan and Bearfield 1997, p 3). Italy has not complied with the directive. Spain formally did, but not without huge overtime hours (Brack 1998). Germany and France have chosen to share work more equitably and have successfully created more jobs. They have cut hours, extended vacations, shortened the working week, and given more holidays and sabbaticals for study and retraining.

Other steps to 'humanise' work include a Swedish scheme for a gradual transition from work to retirement for those over 55. There is some evidence that older workers employed part-time are more productive and their health is better. Under the Orlov law in Denmark, the state funds a career break for up to one year's leave for professional training, parental leave or a sabbatical (Buchanan and Bearfield 1997).

SHORTENING THE WORKING WEEK

We have already discussed some successful attempts to shorten the working week, particularly in Australia and parts of Europe. It can be done.

One attractive argument is that if hours of work were shorter, workers would enjoy a better quality of life, and more people could be employed, thus lessening the ranks of the unemployed. In the view of Buchanan and Bearfield (1977) work-sharing has limited potential to create a significant number of jobs. One reason they give is that most of the hours in the long-hour day in Australia, as in other countries, are not renumerated. So to employ more people is likely to cost more. What is called for is a much more radical redistribution of work. France has legislated for a 35-hour week. If a 15-hour week at current rates of pay meant that the unemployed could all be employed, why not aim for that? Such a long-term objective might be attained by degrees after 50 years, so suggests Hamilton (2003, p 218) who also reminds us that such a proposal was seriously put by Maynard Keynes in 1930.

Those who are against shorter hours of work argue that dividends will be less, that people do not necessarily want to spend more time at home, and that leisure would become a burden rather than a gain because people will not know what to do with it. Those against shorter hours also argue that the work will not be done in the time allocated because of downsizing having reduced the number of workers and those left having to work harder.

This may be logical enough but is it fair and ethical? We think not. It may, though not immediately, increase profits, but it will be at the expense of quality of life. It is very difficult for workers to argue for a shorter working week in the environment of downsizing. One primary reason is the fear of being regarded as a slacker, or worse, the fear of being sacked. 'If you don't like our work ethic go somewhere else' is the corporate catch-cry. It is therefore very important that change involves change in the mind-set of senior management (which is what happened with Daniel Petrie in Microsoft, as discussed in

Chapter 5). It involves a shift of emphasis from greater profits to better quality of life.

This shift has another side to it: a shift from materialistic consumerism to other values such as sharing and service in the community. The writer and social critic John Ruskin said, at a time when England was a very competitive and materialistic community, 'There is no wealth but life'. He was not against a work ethic, but he was against making work a be-all and end-all of life. There are higher goals in life to aspire to. Work is meant for people, not people for work. People matter. To believe that requires a robust faith in the human. As social ethicist Ronald Preston has written: 'Everything works at bottom with a "faith", in the sense of some fundamental propositions about humans and their place in the universe on which they build, and behind which they cannot go' (Preston 2000a, p 256).

The US labour movement's first great campaign for shorter working hours was the 'Kellogg six-hour day'. 'Eight hours for work, eight hours for sleep, eight hours for what we will' chanted the late nineteenth-century unionists. They argued that technological progress and mounting abundance of goods should make possible a steady decrease in time spent on the job. WK Kellogg agreed. In 1930 the cornflakes capitalist announced that nearly all the workers in the huge plant in Battle Creek, Michigan would henceforth enjoy a six-hour day. The company anticipated greater efficiency from contented employees who would now have time for their families and hopefully for some voluntary labour at the local church or school. For nearly two decades it worked. Employees welcomed the hiring of additional workers during the Depression years. And most seemed not to resent the drop in pay that accompanied the shorter hours.

The idyll did not last. After World War II, Kellogg promoted an ethic which tied higher wages to boosts in productivity. Most male workers eager to take part in the consumer bonanza opted for an eight-hour working day. The ethic of higher wages for longer work won out. In 1985 the giant cereal company eliminated the last six-hour job (Kazin 1996). The eight-hour or more job is fine for those who enjoy their work, but what about those whose job is dreary, repetitive and uninspiring? There are still plenty of those around as witness, for example, the female Kellogg employee at Battle Creek:

> Sure everybody wants a Prince Charming job. But the jobs I know about, and that the people I know are likely to get, are mostly a pain in the butt. Everybody but a complete idiot or a college professor who has never hit a lick of work in their lives looks forward to quitting time, and the sooner it comes the better (Hunnicutt 1996, p 4).

Kellogg's original dream was the American dream that technology would result in shorter working hours. Except for this experiment, and maybe a few others, it hasn't happened.

The general picture in the developed world, with few exceptions, is that people are working longer and with greater intensity and less security than ever before. Attempts to rectify this state of affairs are being made with much difficulty, but a happier future in the workplace depends upon the zealous pursuit of reform and large-scale reform.

Barbara Pocock (2002) suggests the following as possible steps forward in Australia:

- enterprise bargaining to contain hours and overtime. However, only 37 per cent of Australians are covered by such arrangements and only the most powerful are likely to be able to win reduced hours.

- legislative caps and limits as adopted in some European countries. There are mechanisms by which state and Federal governments could use the corporations powers to this end.

- future pay rises traded for reductions in working hours. In the six years to 2000 productivity rose by 10 per cent. If we took that productivity rise in the form of reduced hours we could have reduced a 40-hour working week to 36 hours. Instead we have seen that productivity feed shareholder value and executive salaries as the hours have grown.

- the long service system in Australia provides a good base on which to build general 'leave banks' for employees. These banks could be built up by means of employee and employer contributions as well as in other ways.

These proposals are creative approaches to the growing work-time squeeze that impoverishes so many households.

5

STRIKING A BALANCE

Our basic conviction is that persons are internally related to one another (ie their relationships define their identities as persons) so that any view of people that treats them as self-contained individuals falsifies the real situation.

Herman Daly and John Cobb Jnr, *For the Common Good,* 1989, p 169.

IMPACT OF WORK ON FAMILY AND RELATIONSHIPS

How happy are Australians with their work? When 37 000 employees were asked in 1995 if they were satisfied with their job, some 63 per cent said they were satisfied. Of specific categories, 73 per cent of managers were satisfied, but only 63 per cent of professionals were satisfied. Paraprofessionals and clerks were least satisfied (Morehead et al 1997). In an attempt to focus on the large picture, Australian Prime Minister John Howard nominated four priorities for his government. One of the top four was 'quality of life expressed as a balance between work and family' (Walker 2002). That was a step forward just to recognise the concept of quality of life. We await real action.

Dissatisfaction with work increases when employees find their job is having a negative impact on home life. Their work became less productive. Some 4000 men and 800 of their partners in the mining industry in Australia were interviewed about the effect of work on home life. The interviews extended from managers to miners and drivers. Middle managers were least satisfied with their work, especially those with offspring aged 9-21 years. Employer support for family life was found to improve commitment and performance (Pratt 1998).

A study in Britain showed that fathers who were involved with their children, such as helping younger children with their homework and older children with social issues, were more successful in their careers. Conversely the least involved fathers or workaholics who gave everything to their work were often struggling to cope and found difficulties in their career. Family-friendly policies of employers are not only good for the family but also for the business (Golan 1997b).

A study in Australia of 111 organisations including white-collar, blue-collar and public sector employees agreed that concern for the family was improving. Senior management was responding. But barriers such as increased demand of work, lack of education of middle management and lack of flexibility remain (Moodie 1997). There is still tension between what companies want, namely productivity, and what the employee needs to do to be a good partner and parent. There is not enough analysis in the workplace that looks to the needs of men as parents and the need for children to have contact with their fathers. Workplaces still make the assumption that fathers are not involved, as are mothers, in parenting (Adamson 2002).

Initiatives that are helpful in creating a better balance between work and family include emergency leave, study leave, career breaks, permanent part-time work, working from home, paid maternity leave, counselling, reward bonuses, and a more flexible work plan. Yet employees do not take advantage of basic entitlements, such as leaving on time, overtime and rostered days off (Loane 1997). The finance sector in Australia is considered to be a leader in family-friendly policies, according to a study of the banking and insurance industry. Employers have been slow to catch on to the benefits of paid maternity leave. Only 38 per cent of female workers have access to it. Those who are eligible receive something in the range six weeks (IBM) to 12 weeks (Australia Post), which falls short of the 14-week international benchmark. In Sweden, paid maternity leave is 15 months and comes from social security (HC 2002b).

Unhappy homes are a work hazard! A study in California indicated that excessive hours of work, whether chosen or imposed, makes workers less well rounded and less creative. A direct effect is the neglect of family. In some cases increased emotional stress was bought on by troubled children who seemed to be a direct effect of lack of time given to them. Productivity and performance at work were affected. The well-being of children was a leading casualty of lack of balance between work and home.

Conversely, a good parent makes a good worker (Golan 1997a). A study by the Chicago think-tank 'Families and Work' asked 1000 children what they would most like to change about their parents working lives. To the surprise of the parents, the answer wasn't the work itself but the stress they brought home from work. It was not that the parents worked, but how they worked (Doogue 2002).

BALANCING LIFE BETWEEN WORK AND HOME

In many developed countries, including Australia, the balance has tipped too far in favour of working life and has left insufficient room for home life. McCallum (2000) recognises two aspects of this intrusion. First, many workers are employed to perform set tasks, rather than for set working hours, so that work intrudes into evenings and weekends. More than half the employment in Australia is of this nature. Second, notions of professionalism are curtailing freedom of action even outside working hours. The use of lengthy written contracts which often incorporate codes of conduct coupled with a corporate image have led to tightening of employer controls. McCallum (2000) presents many legal cases in which freedom of speech and other activities out of working hours have been penalised by employers on the grounds that these behaviours have reflected negatively on the company. The private life of the employee out of hours seems to become part of the working life, and so is an intrusion on home life. Thankfully, in many cases judges rule against such intrusions.

McKenna (1997, p 98) points out that some of us have a great personal life and a so-so career. Others have a tremendous career and a compromised personal life. Still others have a little of both some of the time and a little of neither some of the time. Are there any who have all of it all of the time? The critical point comes when someone asks of themselves: Is this all there is? Is this what I want for my life? Such questions can lead one to seeking change in the present job or look for another one.

There are a variety of possibilities in seeking to find a balance between life and work. A study by the Families and Work Institute in the United States showed that in 1991 twice the number of men under 40 said they would forgo raises in salary and advancement for a better home life than had been willing to do so five years earlier (McKenna 1997, p 264).

A study by the Australia Institute reveals that in the past 10 years, 23 per cent of Australians aged 30-59 have forgone income for the sake of a more balanced lifestyle. They have switched to a less demanding, less stressful and less well paid job, reducing hours or dropping out of the work force altogether. Some have taken on work with NGOs or part-time work. Some have moved from city to country. It is about putting quality of life before income.

They are making for themselves a new culture called 'downshifters'. They are a challenge to those employers who are blind to the needs of their employees (Hamilton and Mail 2003).

There is now available a variety of options for flexible work solutions to help keep life and work in balance. Biggs and Horgan (1999) have explored these options in considerable detail. They include: working at home part-time, working at home full-time, flexible working hours, shorter working hours, part-time work, job sharing, and family-friendly practices such as paid parental leave. Some of these options are considered below. Biggs and Horgan (1999) argue that all of them have benefits to the organisation, despite arguments organisations may put up against such practices.

Organisations worldwide are increasingly offering flexible work arrangements. In the United States, 66 per cent of employers were offered flexible work arrangements in 1994. In Australia 77 per cent of workplace agreements included a range of flexible working conditions, and in 1997 over 2.5 million employees had variable starting and finishing times and could work extra hours to take time off (Biggs and Horgan 1999, p 9).

One solution to the problem of balancing work and home is to work at home. In the United States between 1991 and 1997, paid work at home became increasingly attractive. The number of workers at home rose from 7.2 million in 1991 to 9.5 million in 1997. In 1991 some 39.2 per cent of self-employed and 43.5 per cent of salaried home-workers were executives, managers or professionals. By 1997 the proportions had increased to 44.4 per cent among the self-employed, and 51.2 per cent among the salaried workers. The most common reason people give for working at home is that it gives more autonomy and it is easier to co-ordinate work and family needs. Women were more likely than men to work at home because they found that such an arrangement was family-friendly (Stainback and Donato 1998).

Working part of the time at home is an option for some workers. In the United States, some 20 per cent of the work force at IBM spend at least eight hours of each working week working at home. Typically, those working at home are surrounded by telephones and a computer but may sit at a window where they can see their children at play. People who do this find they are more likely to be working 55 hours a week and not 40. However they are judged by their results, not by hours of work (Hewett 1997).

In Australia in 1995, 26 per cent of employees worked some hours a home. Four per cent worked more hours a home than elsewhere. This was a rise of 11.5 per cent since 1992 (Biggs and Horgan 1999, p 150). By the year 2000 almost one million Australians worked from home. About half of those are women. But it seems unlikely that the large proportion working at home is due to the workplace becoming more family-friendly or more flexible. The most common reason for Australians working at home is to set up and operate a family business. Some 38 per cent of those working at home were parents of children under 15. Almost 400 000 of those whose jobs were based elsewhere worked from home as well as a form of unofficial unpaid overtime (Burke 2001).

A study was made of 87 professionals and managers in the United States and Canada who had chosen to work less than full-time to try and balance better work, home life and lifestyle. Seventy per cent of the senior managers were highly supportive of the programme; 90 per cent reported positive effects on the family; and 91 per cent were happier and more satisfied with the balance between work and home. But what effect did their partial absence have on those left to work full-time? About half of their co-workers were highly supportive of the arrangements of their colleagues. The others were not so enthusiastic, for various reasons, including the claim that some of the work of people with reduced loads ended up with them (Lee and MacDermid 1998).

Daniel Petrie was a senior executive in Microsoft in Seattle who later headed Microsoft Australia. He became appalled at the number of people who worked 50, 60 and even 70 hours a week. This obsession he came to see as an addiction. He questioned whether people should trade in their lives for a company. Initially he found that people who questioned a company's work ethic were seen as no longer committed. There were many reasons for questioning the dominating work ethic, a main one being the neglect it involved of the family and other relationships.

Petrie adopted another ethic. He argued that if the job could not be done in a focused nine or ten hours a day, then the employees were either incompetent or were trying to do too much with too few resources. Petrie learned how to maximise the time he was at work. Fewer and more efficient meetings became part of his schedule. Petrie reduced his work time to 30 hours a week. He allowed more time to participate in family activities, engage in study and pursue writing interests. He recommended that no meetings be scheduled before 8:30 am and none after 5:00 pm. He reckoned that people who were one hundred per cent committed to the company made very bad managers. They did not really know how to manage people. Youthful obsession he reckoned was fine for a while but eventually you had to take responsibility for your life and the lives of those close to you. The principles he laid out for himself he regarded as those that were to be practised for the rest of his company (Petrie 1998a; 1998b).

In Australia the search for a better quality of life and more satisfaction with work is leading more and more chief executive officers to resign and seek less demanding positions with greater satisfaction for their lives (Macken 1997). It is little wonder, since surveys show that executives are working harder than ever. Seventy-five per cent of those earning more than A$100 000 were found to be working more than 50 hours, and a similar proportion of those aged 55 and over were working more than 40 hours (Lawson 1996).

Some of the best people leave a company because their goals no longer coincide with those of the company. An international consulting firm was worried when some of their brightest and best left the company after two or three years. They were not leaving for larger salaries or more seniority. Some went into teaching, others to probationary work or even just backpacking around the world. It appears that their own priorities were no longer in line with the goals of the organisation, which left no room for further self-expression and creativity. The organisation lacked 'soul' for them (Handy 1998, p 159).

There are long-standing arguments for shorter hours of work. More time is available to lead a balanced life between work and living, especially for participation in family life. There is more likelihood that stress and related illnesses would become less prevalent. There is evidence that productivity and efficiency is greater when fewer hours are worked. Even though the take-home pay may be less, the upside is that quality of life is better.

In 1944 several hundred senior executives from Fortune 500 companies in the United States were asked for a show of hands based on the following questions:

- Do you want to work harder five years from now than you are today?

- Do you know anyone who wants to work harder than they are now?

- Do you know anyone who is, or are you yourself, spending too much time with your children?

No-one raised a hand. Presumably they wanted to live, not just to work. American employees find that they are working 100 to 200 hours more per year than people did 20 years ago, and they don't particularly like it (Hawken, Lovins and Lovins 1999, pp 55-56). According to the third annual *Quality of Working Life Report* in Britain, organisations are failing to curb the long-hours culture and help employees achieve any balance in their lives (Anon 2000b; Worrall and Cooper 1999).

'Improving quality of life improves quality of work', says a 1998 report of the Radcliffe Public Policy Institute of New England in the United States. It states that the struggle to meet business goals and to achieve high quality in work and family life are not mutually exclusive. On the contrary it says that attention to issues of quality of life can be beneficial to a company. It represents a win–win scenario for both business and employees (Anon 1998), while increased productivity increases dividends to shareholders.

Striking a balance doesn't just mean taking time off here to put it there. It can mean doing more in less time by increasing the efficiency of work. In Greek there are two words for time. *Chronos* is chronological time. No second is worth any more than any other second. The clock dictates the rhythm of our lives. But the second Greek word for time is *kairos*. It means 'quality time' or 'appropriate time'. It is how time is experienced, how much value you get out of time rather than how much *chronos* you put into it. We recognise *kairos* when we ask: Did you have a good time? We are not asking the amount of time spend in a particular way, but about value, the quality of that time. With *kairos* goes the idea also of appropriate time. It is inappropriate to work on something when you are dead tired, inefficient and possibly accident-prone. Hence the concept of the fullness of time. The book of Ecclesiastes devotes much of one chapter to this meaning of time, beginning with the familiar words:

> To every thing there is a season, and a time to every purpose under the heaven: a time to be born and a time to die, a time to plant, and a time to pluck that which is planted ... a time to mourn and a time to dance ... a time to embrace and a time to refrain from embracing (Ecclesiastes 3).

Life is a balance of how we spend our time to give maximum quality time. We need more *kairos*.

Women who have a family have special difficulty in balancing life between work and home. It is very easy for them to get overburdened lives. It could even be said that women are in crisis over their work and family commitments. They are doing an accounting of their lives and finding that the ends don't meet. There are an increasing number of women with families who also have a paid job. In Australia between 1981 and 1997, two-income families increased from 41 per cent of all families to 56 per cent. The single male breadwinner family, which represented 53 per cent of all families in 1981, was barely more than a third of all families in 1997. Fewer 'stay-at-home-mothers' means more needs for child-care, fewer volunteers, suburbs that are largely empty during the day, domestic tasks outsourced to cleaners, and community being found in the workplace rather than with neighbours.

Barbara Pocock (2001) and her team interviewed 150 women in

Adelaide for her book *Having a Life*. Most of these women were happy in their work, around which much of their lives was centred. But there is a price to pay. Most of them had great problems balancing work and home. They worried that their children are unhappy or unsafe. Their domestic tasks became very taxing, leading to serious anxiety, exhaustion to the point of illness, feelings of guilt, lack of in intimacy with their partners, and impoverished relationships. It seemed to be difficult for them to get their partners involved in domestic tasks to relieve the burden. They were caught between their own ambitions, the family's need for more money, and the notions of what constitutes good motherhood. There were great difficulties when a child became sick and needed a lot of attention. The sorts of jobs they had seemed to make little allowance for the flexibility needed to allow for such situations or for other emergencies.

Casual work provides greater flexibility and many choose this path. But casual employment is insecure and has no sick leave. An important reform to rectify the present inadequacies is for governments to fund maternity leave for at least three months, to provide subsidies for child-care, and legislate to remedy the disadvantages of casual work. Men also need to change and share more in the demands of the home. Sweden could provide a model: for couples to qualify for 12 months' maternity leave, fathers must be willing to spend six weeks at home.

Following submissions from the Australian Council for Trade Unions to the Australian Industrial Commission, it found that a steady increase in working hours with consequent adverse effects on health and safety justified enshrining in the award system the worker's right to refuse 'unreasonable' overtime work (Gough and Price 2002). This is an important win for balancing work and outside commitments such as home responsibilities. It means that a worker, or a union on behalf of many workers, may legitimately refuse to take on overtime work that is prejudicial to the employees' quality of life.

This section has shown that there are many ways in which a better balance between work and life can be achieved but there is still a powerful resistance to complete any reform. We know what should be done. The next move is to do it.

A GENERATIONAL CHANGE IN ATTITUDES TO LIFE AND WORK

Attitudes to balancing life and work have changed over the generations. For example, during the first two-thirds of the twentieth century, Americans took a more and more active role in the social and political life of their communities — in union halls, in bowling alleys, and around committee tables and dinner tables. Year by year they became engaged more in community projects, trusted each other more and gave more generously to charity. People discovered it was possible to be involved in the community outside work as well as to work. Then in the last third of the century they began to do all of these things less often (Putnam 2001). The people involved included the Baby Boomers, born between 1946 and 1964, who were the best educated generation in American history. They were affluent and enjoyed community vitality in their youth. But as adults they endured harder times, though much less so than their parents did during the Great Depression.

Putnam (2001) has analysed in detail the possible causes of the decline in civic engagement in the United States. One factor is pressure of time and money, including the pressures of two-career families. But this, he thinks, accounted for no more than 10 per cent of the total decline. Other changes were going on at the same time. Suburbanisation and electronic entertainment may have accounted for 35 per cent of the change. Putnam attributes the remaining 55 per cent of the change to what he calls 'generational effects'. By this he means that society changes although the individuals don't. Such a societal change could be the dominance of the computer compared with the age without computers. The cohort born before the Baby Boomers lived in a different society compared to the Baby Boomers who were born just after World War II. All sorts of influences could have contributed to this generational change. For example, the changing character of work from manufacturing to services and the movement of women into the paid work force were amongst far-reaching upheavals in American society during the latter part of the twentieth century.

For the work force in Australia during recent decades, which includes the Baby Boomers and their offspring, the nature of work and employment relations have changed, as has the attitude to work (Callus and Landsbury 2002). As we have already documented, these Australians are working longer and harder. Many have less secure jobs than the previous generation. There has been a growth in part-time and casual jobs. Fewer people have a life-time career in the same job with the same employer.

Hancock (2002) shows that from the late 1980s, issues to do with management and flexibility of the labour force became more prominent, but the quality of working life diminished. Quality of working life includes job-security, regularity of employment, intensity of effort, and a satisfactory relationship between work and life.

Oppenheimer (2002) reports on the work of Duncan Ironmonger, which shows quite another trend — that volunteer work was the largest growth area of work in Australia during the 1990s. Remarkable indeed was the huge team of 60 000 volunteers who played such a prominent part at the Sydney 2000 Olympic Games. This change in Australia seems to be contrary to the trend in the United States referred to above.

There has also been a marked shift in employment from manufacturing to services from the 1970s through the 1990s (Wooden 2002). According to Dunphy and Stace (2002) the basis of organisational success has changed in the later 1990s, moving from an emphasis on cost reduction to value added through innovation.

Mackay (1997) has investigated generational changes in attitude of Australians over the three generations which he calls the 'Lucky Generation' born in the 1920s; the Baby Boomers born in the years 1946-1964; and the 'Options Generation' born in the 1970s. His studies reinforce the conclusions reached by Callus and Landsbury referred to above. What follows is abstracted from Mackay (1997) with particular reference to the changing attitude to work and quality of life over these three generations.

The Lucky Generation were the children of the Great Depression and the young adults of World War II. They regarded their transition from a tough childhood to mid-life prosperity as the result of a very favourable hand of fate. Now in their late adulthood, they have become critical of the state of the world, especially its materialism. They see too many working mothers neglecting their children, and look back to their own working days which gave them great security and purpose.

The Baby Boomers, also known as the 'Me Generation', lived in a construction boom, a manufacturing boom and a mining boom. They experienced material comfort as a birthright. They were materialistic, hedonistic and big spenders. In an attempt to maintain a high standard of living, they created the two-income household, and therefore the working mother. Mackay (1997) considers this is the first generation to have identified stress as a debilitating consequence of everyday life. Their idea of stress is inextricably connected in their minds to the idea of busy-ness. They would like much more time, and some of them have been forced to rethink the role of work in their lives. They have watched as Australia split into the haves and the have-nots.

A study by the Australia Institute (Hamilton 2002) points out that the Baby Boomers today are three times better off than their parents of the same age, and five times better off than their grandparents. Yet the broad mass of middle-class Australians believes their incomes are insufficient to provide for what they consider are their needs. There is a big difference between their real needs and their wants. The problem is not inadequate incomes but inflated wants. The growth in long hours of work has been driven by increasingly ambitious lifestyle goals. Yet these same people are coming to realise that they place too much emphasis on money and material goods to the neglect of what really matters — their quality of life. The real have-nots are not these people, but the 10 per cent Australians who are really struggling to make ends meet. Yet a fifth of the poorest households say they do not have difficulties affording everything they really need, suggesting that they have some money left over for 'luxuries'. On the other hand the middle-class Australians feel they don't satisfy their needs. Feelings of deprivation are conditioned by expectations leading to what has been dubbed 'affluenza'.

Luxury Fever, by Frank (1999), identifies the same problem in middle-America. Middle-class Americans are feeling compelled to spend more in order to keep up. But the added luxury does little to boost their quality of life. The proportion of 'suffering rich' in Australia is even higher than in the United States.

The Options Generation was born in the 1970s. Despite their conformity in dress, their recurring theme is individuality. Their options are open, and work is merely one of them. The reality of unemployment is stark for this generation. Some 750 000 Australians under the age of 24 live in households where no-one is currently earning wages. Almost one million dependent children live with only one parent. This is also the generation that has given us 'street kids' in disturbingly large numbers. This generation is growing up with the idea of job insecurity firmly in their minds. Even when they get a job they are aware that they could lose it and have to move to something else. Mackay (1997, p 178) makes this critical comment: 'It is of great importance that our young people who are unable to obtain employment are not seen by others or by themselves as having somehow failed. The plain fact is that it is our society, which has failed them.' That is terribly true.

Youth unemployment is an overwhelming social problem. Work is becoming associated with risk, mean spiritedness, uncertainty and anxiety. It is increasingly seen in the context of corporations that, when forced to choose, favour short-term returns to shareholders over provision of secure employment for their employees (Mackay 1999, p 112). Some members of the Options Generation have relegated work to a less important role than was played by work in the lives of their parents and grandparents. They want a greater flexibility in their work than is offered to them. They ask: In what way will work enhance our lives? We have tried to respond to their question in this book.

Mackay's (1997) study demonstrates a changing relation to work from the security of the Lucky Generation to an over-worked Boomers Generation to an insecure Options Generation. It is tremendously important that the forces in society bring back a balance and sense of quality of life in the face of an uncertain future.

INEQUALITY FOR WOMEN IN WESTERN COUNTRIES

In striking a balance between life and work, the status of women in the work force is dependent upon an equality with men that they do not yet experience. Equality for women should include equality of pay, equality for advancement, freedom from sexual harassment, and participation in the public world, including work in the professions and in business. (The concerns specifically to do with United Nations conventions are discussed in Chapter 8.)

A major change in the labour force in recent times has been the increased participation of women, especially of married women. In a typical family in Australia in the new millennium, the man works for more than 40 hours per week, and the woman undertakes part-time or full-time employment. Men have insufficiently changed their domestic habits, so that women still also do most of the household chores and more than their fair share of rearing children. Many women work part-time, but this for many is a second best. Appropriate full-time jobs are not available, with government cutting back on child-care, which has become less affordable and less available (McCallum 2000).

A second major aspect of existing inequality for women is their chance of promotion and equality of pay. Although the percentage of women in the workplace over a wide range of sectors in Australia was 46 per cent in 1995 (Morehead et al 1997), only 3 per cent of senior managers were women. Furthermore, women were paid only 79 per cent of what men earned, they represented only 4 per cent of all board members, and only 1 per cent of the executive directors (McKenna 1997). Between 1994 and 1996 the number of women entering senior management positions increased at a glacial pace by only 0.15 per cent per year (Larriera 1996). By 2002 the percentage of women who held board positions was 8.2 per cent, while 54 per cent of companies had no women at all in executive management roles. Only two companies had women chief executives, putting Australia well behind Canada and the United States (Harris 2002).

Justice Mary Gaudron of the High Court of Australia (the only woman member since her appointment 13 years ago) criticises the very small percentage of women judges as a whole. She considers the major contributing factor is prejudice against women (Jacobsen 2000). In the United States there are only three women chief executive officers amongst the Fortune 500 organisations, and only 63 women among the top 2500 executives in all walks of life from Wall Street to academia (Hulbert 2000).

Australia has one of the highest rates of women–owned businesses, but one of the worst records for promoting women to the top of companies. In most Western countries, 1–5 per cent of executive directors in corporations were women. Australia's performance at the lower end has not improved over several years. In New Zealand about 37 per cent of management positions are held by women, compared with 27 per cent in Australia. New Zealand in this respect ranks equal first in the world with Russia (Horin 2001). Australia ranks ninth in the world in 'gender empowerment', an index that includes legislative and practical equality of pay and access to jobs. Norway ranks at the top followed by Sweden, Denmark and Canada (Harvey 2001).

Women hold 13 per cent of seats in national parliaments, and 7 per cent of ministerial posts worldwide. In Papua New Guinea only 2 per cent of parliamentary seats are held by women contrasted with 43 per cent in Sweden (Nierenberg 2002). Almost all senior military and police commands are held by men, and practically all of the world's largest corporations have male leaders. Men also dominate positions of intellectual and religious authority (Connell 2000).

In industrial countries as a whole today the income of women is on the average only 59 per cent that of men. In the manufacturing sector women's wages as a percentage of men's wages has a low of 55 per cent in the Republic of Korea and a high of 97 per cent in Turkey. For Australia the figure is 79 per cent.

In the early 1970s all industrial countries outlawed discrimination in pay based on gender. However, only a few countries such as Australia and Sweden made much progress. In Britain the *Sex Discrimination Act* of 1975 made it unlawful to treat women less favourably than men in education, training, employment, or in the provision of goods, facilities or services. An indication of progress toward greater equality of opportunity in employment in Britain came with the growth of Opportunity 2000. This business–led campaign was launched in 1991 with support from the Conservative Government 'to increase the quality and quantity of women's participation in the work force by the year 2000'. The organisation claims to count among its founding members a quarter of *The Times* top one hundred companies. By 1996 its members included over a quarter of British work force. Almost one third of the member companies offer flexible work arrangements, and half provide child–care or career–break option (Wajcman 1999).

Western societies have made some progress toward gender equity, yet men continue to monopolise the elite levels of corporate power. Despite widespread legislative changes aimed at reducing inequality of women, the policies have not been greatly successful in achieving the changes they were supposed to achieve.

Judy Wajcman (1999) has investigated the reasons for this in considerable detail. Her central argument is that management incorporates a male standard that positions women as out of place. Whether it is argued that women's sub-ordination can best be overcome by a focus on equality as sameness with men, or by recognition of the gender difference, women in both cases are positioned as the problem with men's life regarded as the norm. The outcome is that in order to succeed, women are expected to become like men. The culture of organisations is dominantly male.

Women work under a no-win paradox. They need to work to be fully realised as women, but in order to do the work they have to silence a good deal of themselves. A Doonesbury cartoon has Michael asking a hard-working woman at her desk 'How do manage to keep all the balls up in the air at the same time? How do you balance a demanding career, a family and a social life without losing your mind?' 'Simple', she responds, 'I have insomnia, I have no friends, kids I barely know, and a husband who's about to file for separation' (in Morrison et al 1992, p 1).

The term 'glass ceiling' refers to a set of invisible barriers obstructing women's opportunities for advancement. Wajcman (1999), in her study of managers in Britain, identified the following five barriers: prejudice of colleagues, clubiness of senior management, sexual discrimination/harassment, the lack of career guidance, and family commitments. There is a great divergence between espoused company policy and reality. While it is relatively easy for women to gain employment at the lower levels in organisations, it is much more difficult for them to reach middle and senior executive positions. The ethos of the managerial job as male is especially strong at the most senior levels. Wacjman (1999) found, in her study of British companies that the few women who succeeded have similar backgrounds and attitudes to the men. For example they work the same long hours.

What of the future? 'Affirmative action' of the 1980s was not the success some had hoped. 'Diversity management' of the 1990s may shape up better. The intention is to value and manage diversity. This is to focus on the value of differences between people and how to get the best out of them. The issues involved have been much discussed but leave much still to be worked over (Wajcman 1999). Maybe more than a generation will be needed for real change while men and women still struggle to accommodate each other's shifting roles and expectations.

INEQUALITY FOR WOMEN IN ISLAMIC COUNTRIES

The exclusion of women from public life is a dominant feature in most of the Muslim world. Muslim societies are substantially less productive by denying opportunities to women. A study by Landes and Landes (2001) investigates this in the light of history. Hundreds of years ago Islamic civilisation was at a pinnacle of global achievement, politically and intellectually. Muslim empires ruled from the Middle East west to Spain and Portugal and east to India and the borderlands of China. Then something went wrong. In the thirteenth and fourteenth centuries Islamic theologians shut down liberal theological schools. As a result of banishing so-called heresy from an increasingly dog-matic Islam, the high culture lost its grasp of a wider world and its adaptabil-ity. Reactionary features hardened. The exclusion of women from public life, slavery and a huge gap between the rich and the impoverished were part of the price to be paid. The Industrial Revolution made things worse. By the second half of the twentieth century the difference between standards of liv-ing of the West and in the Muslim world were enormous.

The treatment of women in the Muslim world today differs in different parts of that world. Pakistan, Bangladesh, Turkey and Indonesia have all been ruled by women in recent years. But nevertheless, compared with the West, the lives of women in most of the Muslim world are very circumscribed. This fundamental inequality, says Landes and Landes (2001), makes Muslim soci-eties substantially less productive and is part of the reason why they have fall-en behind the West. It may also help to explain why they find the West so culturally threatening.

PROFESSIONAL OBLIGATION

This chapter and Chapter 4 have covered a wide area of facts about the mod-ern workplace. One item stands out from all these facts: the present failure to recognise a professional obligation to face up to the negative facts of the workplace. There comes a time when we must take a position that may be neither safe not popular — but because it is right. There are some notable attempts, particularly in Europe, to address some tyrannous aspects of the workplace, but still too little is done to improve the situation. More and more organisations are paying lip service to the triple bottom line. But how many of them follow words with action? Very few!

This chapter is replete with data that demonstrates there is a limit to the number of hours anyone can work and still be efficient and productive. And yet organisation after organisation believes that long hours mean more productivity. It doesn't. Why are organisations so behind in their thinking about work? So many of them are stuck in an antiquated mode where more is always supposed to be better. It isn't.

It seems to us immoral, and in the end unprofessional, to sack a thousand workers and expect the staff that are left behind to double their efforts. Yet this is right now the professional ethos of many organisations. It indicates a failure of professional obligation in its ethics. It is high time that we see things for what they really are. Not everything that is faced can be changed but nothing can be changed until it is faced. We would hope that more organisations would be willing to face up to the evident facts of the workplace, and to revolutionise their way of thinking and acting. The world would then be a happier place. Profits would still be made, but not at the expense of everything else. (This issue is further pursued in Chapters 7 and 8.)

6

HAZARDS

Reducing the risk of accidents at work is one of the
principal factors in improving the quality of working life.
Mona Salin, Swedish Minister for Industry, press release, 2001, p 1.

Investment in health care means a more productive
work force in the future.
John Kenneth Galbraith, *The Good Society*, 1996, p 54.

When asbestos worker Clarence Borel walked into the
offices of a legal firm in a small Texan town [in 1969] to
ask for help, he unwittingly tripped over the first in a
long line of financial dominoes that would eventually
rock the world's best-known insurance market to its
foundations. Indeed, this single act triggered one of the
most spectacular avalanches of industrial litigation
[concerning asbestos] the world has yet seen.
John Elkington, *The Chrysalis Economy*, 2001, p 187.

Occupations differ in the extent to which health and safety
become critical concerns because of the nature of the work. People working
in the mining industry put safety at the top of their agenda, as would those
working in demolition involving asbestos. There is always a trade-off between
the level of risk, the levels of safety and health desired, and the costs that
determine how high on the agenda risk is put. Consider the cases of driving
safety, airline security, and cigarettes.

In the late 1960s General Motors was confronted with a list of demands
from a small number of stockholders organised by Ralph Nader. They
demanded that General Motors design a car to be crash-testable at 60 miles

per hour, devote as much money to pollution control as to advertising, and provide 50 000 mile, five-year warranties on all cars. General Motors' management said that the demands would price the company out of the market. Consumers would be unwilling to accept the larger price tags that social responsibility brought (Donaldson 1982). Prior to mandatory seat belts, few manufacturers paid even the small amounts necessary to install them as options. General Motors argued that it was giving the people what they wanted and what they were prepared to pay for. The technology to make cars safer was developed for many years prior to being introduced, the main reason being the fear that customers would be unwilling to pay the extra cost of a safer car.

After the bombing of Pan American flight 103 en route to New York, US officials knew that the additional measures that were then taken to strengthen aviation security were hardly foolproof. The airlines had prevailed in the subsequent debate in arguing that more effective security would be too costly for them and too unpopular.

Cigarettes are the leading underlying cause of death from fire. In the United States alone, 1000 people each year are killed in smoking-related fires. In Australia cigarette butts thrown from cars are thought to be a major cause of bushfires. Why then are cigarettes not made 'fire-safe', designed to go out shortly after being left unpuffed. They can be made. But they are not on the market to any extent. The cigarette companies claim that smokers would find them unacceptable. Evidence now suggests otherwise. It looks as though the real reason is product liability. This means that admission that earlier versions were unsafe could expose the cigarette companies to lawsuits from people injured in fires caused by standard cigarettes. So cigarette manufacturers continue marketing an unsafe product when a safer product is possible (Randerson 2002).

THE ANNUAL TOLL

Work is a dangerous place. Occupational injury, illness and death are epidemic worldwide. There are 200 000 fatalities, 120 million injuries and 68-157 million new cases of work-related disease each year. In Australia there are 2900 deaths each year as a result of work-related injury and illness, and 200 000 injured and ill each year. The cost to Australia is about 5 per cent of GDP or at least A$20 billion per year (Mayhew and Peterson 1999). Many thousands of people are employed in dealing with occupational health and safety in Australia.

Accidents and work-related illness cost the British economy £6-12 billion per year. This is between 5 per cent and 10 per cent of all British industrial companies' trading profits, and averages £200-400 pounds per worker. The total cost is equivalent to 2-3 per cent of GDP (Health and Safety website 2001). Every year in the United States, over 6000 Americans die from workplace injuries. An estimated 6 million people suffer non-fatal workplace injuries which alone cost the economy more than US$110 billion a year. These are astonishingly high figures for a country that has high standards for the working environment. The mission statement of the US Occupational Safety and Health Administration is to assure, so far as possible, every working man and woman in the nation safe and healthful working conditions (Gates 2001).

ILLNESS, INJURY AND DEATHS

There are many types of illness and injury associated with the workplace. Table 6.1, based on a sample of 3316 employees at Australian workplaces with 20 or more employees in 1995, shows that the disabilities range from stress to a variety of wounds.

TABLE 6.1 Workers' susceptibility to injury or illness, Australia 1995 (%)

Employee characteristics	Fracture	Dislocation/strain/sprain	Open wound	Bruising/crushing	Burns/scalds	Eye injury	Stress	Other
All employees	5	43	17	20	8	7	26	17
Male	6	44	22	20	9	9	23	16
Female	3	42	10	20	8	3	32	18
Occupation								
Managers	5	34	11	12	4	0	49	9
Professionals	3	33	8	16	1	2	41	22
Para-professionals	4	45	10	22	1	5	34	18
Trades persons and apprentices	5	43	28	17	19	13	13	14
Clerks	3	37	8	13	2	4	42	17
Sales and personal service workers	4	51	16	24	10	3	23	16
Plant and machine operators and drivers	6	46	23	23	10	10	19	14
Labourers and related workers	6	45	21	23	10	8	18	19

NOTE Percentages from 3316 employees with at least one work-related injury or illness.
SOURCE Morehead et al, *Changes at Work*, 1997, p 125.

The most frequently reported injuries were dislocations, strains and sprains (43 per cent) followed by stress (26 per cent). The type of injury or illness was related to occupation. Sales and personal service workers were more likely than others to report dislocations, strains and sprains while tradespersons were more likely to report open wounds or burns and scalds. Stress was highest among managers, professionals and clerks.

Another workplace injury, back pain, has reached epidemic proportions in Australia. It is not just a problem of the elderly. Millions of people suffer chronic pain in their bones and joints, much of it due to poor working conditions. Peter Brooks, the co-ordinator of the International Bone and Joint Decade, says that more and more people of working age were sufferers of aches and pains including back pain (Brooks 2001).

The breakdown of injuries and diseases by industry in Australia are shown in Table 6.2. Agriculture, forestry and hunting top the list of injuries. Mining comes next, with manufacturing and transport not far behind. Mining has the highest incidence of diseases by far, as well as the combined rates for injury and disease. The figures for 1999-2000 rates of injury per thousand workers find sheep shearers on top with 144, and railway workers next with 143, with others much behind these figures. The actual number of claims for sickness or injury was greatest for truck drivers and lowest for teachers (though teachers had a high rate of stress-related illnesses). There is a pattern of the number of claims being greater for lower skilled workers than those in more complex and more dangerous jobs — telephonists claimed more than police officers. The incidence of back injury is high in nurses (Vincent 2002).

The incidence of deaths in various industries in Australia is shown in Table 6.3. The incidence of fatal work-related injury was on average 8.1 deaths per 100 000 employees per year, but varied from 0.4 for clerical workers to 396 for loggers. Some 95 per cent of deaths were males.

A surprisingly large number of deaths are due to occupational exposure to hazardous substances. In the three years 1989-92, there were 2290 deaths per year due to exposure to hazardous substances. About 60 per cent of these deaths resulted from cancer, and 60 per cent of these were due to lung cancer. Of the remaining deaths, 35 per cent were due to heart disease and the rest to various diseases. Some 70 per cent of deaths were males. The vast majority of deaths from malignant mesothelioma are due to exposure to asbestos fibres. Australia has the highest rate of this disease in the world, a legacy of the high use of asbestos in building in the past. The push to remove asbestos-containing material from buildings exposes a new generation of workers to this hazard. Due to the long latency between exposure and development of symptoms (about 38 years) the peak incidence is not expected until about 2010.

TABLE 6.2 The incidence of injuries and diseases according to industry, Australia 1995 (per 1000)

Industry	Injuries	Diseases	Total
Agriculture, forestry, fishing and hunting	40.6	5.5	46.2
Mining	44.1	19.3	63.4
Manufacturing	34.5	12.4	47.0
Electricity, gas and water	20.3	9.9	30.5
Construction	34.3	10.3	44.7
Wholesale trade	17.0	3.2	20.2
Retail trade	13.4	1.9	15.4
Accommodation, cafes and restaurants	19.3	2.6	21.9
Transport and storage	36.4	11.1	47.5
Communication services	21.4	2.0	23.5
Finance and insurance	3.2	1.9	5.1
Property and business services	11.1	2.9	14.0
Government, administration and defence	21.6	10.4	32.0
Education	9.2	4.3	13.6
Health and community services	22.3	4.6	26.9
Cultural and recreational services	14.7	2.5	17.2
Personal and other services	20.4	6.3	26.7

SOURCE Mayhew and Peterson, *Occupational Health and Safety in Australia*, 1999, p 31.

TABLE 6.3 Work-related deaths by industry, Australia 1982–84

Industry	Deaths per 100 000 each year
Logging	396
Commercial fishing	143
Mining	70
Transport and communication	38
Agriculture	19
Clerical workers	0.4
All occupations	8.1
Male	12.1
Female	1.3

SOURCE Mayhew and Peterson, *Occupational Health and Safety in Australia*, 1999, p 33.

LOW-FREQUENCY/HIGH-SEVERITY ACCIDENTS

Explosions and fires are likely to have severe consequences in the workplace, but they are relatively rare events. Likewise the assault or murder of a taxi driver comes into the same category. They are low-frequency/high-severity accidents. (On the other hand, trips, falls, cuts and bangs are relatively common events in most industrial settings. They are high-frequency/low-severity accidents.)

The Piper Alpha oil platform in the North Sea went up in flames in 1988 with the loss of 167 lives. There had been lack of co-ordination between shifts to do with maintenance work, which resulted in a gas leak and fire. The fire extinguishing system had fallen into partial disrepair. The fire spread with catastrophic results. Nine months later in 1989 a similar series of events occurred on an ESSO platform in Bass Strait in Australia. By great good luck that fire was controlled, and although some workers suffered burns, no-one died. Repeated disasters such as this suggest that industry is slow to learn from its mistakes and tends to lack corporate memory (Hopkins 1999). Is the only way we can win by losing? No, if we put our minds to it, we can create learning organisations (see Chapter 11).

Here follows a case history of a tragic coalmine disaster, and what can be learned from it. Eleven men died in an underground coalmine at Moura in Central Queensland in 1994. They died following an explosion which, with hindsight, was quite predictable. The circumstances should never have been allowed to occur, and the owner, BHP, acknowledged it should be held accountable. Moura is just one in a long line of explosions in Australian coalmines. Since 1987 in New South Wales and Queensland there have been nine explosions in which ten or more men were killed. In addition smaller numbers of men are killed every year in underground accidents.

The sequence of events leading to a coalmine explosion are well understood. Coal has a tendency to slowly heat up in a process known as spontaneous combustion. If the process is allowed to continue unchecked the temperature of the coal will eventually reach the ignition point of the gas methane. If there is a sufficient concentration of methane in the area it may explode. This is what happened at Moura in 1994. A similar set of circumstances resulted in an explosion that killed 13 men in a mine in 1975, just a few kilometres away from Moura, and another 12 died in an explosion at Moura in 1986. This gives a total of 36 men killed in explosions around Moura in 19 years bringing great grief to the small town of 3000 people. Each time the town vowed that this would not happen again — but it did.

The inquiry into the 1994 disaster indicated a great failure of communication. Signs of spontaneous combustion were detected by miners in the weeks preceding the explosion. They were even recorded by supervisors of work crews. But these records were unnoticed by management, which failed to respond. The problem is: How does the unwelcome news get to the top? There was other evidence that all was not well in the mine, but it was ignored and miners were sent down the mine on night shift when this should never have been allowed. The inquiry led to the conclusion that unless companies make strenuous efforts to carry out rigorous and searching audits of their safety systems, even the best systems cannot guarantee safety.

What is the relation between profits and safety? Moura was under pressure to produce as fast as possible. The area being mined at the time of the explosion had achieved the highest production rate ever seen in the mine. To have to stop production to deal with spontaneous combustion would have disrupted this achievement. Thus there is an economic incentive in the short term to ignore the problem of safety as long as possible. In the long run this is disastrous. There is need for a deeper learning process about safety in the top echelons as well as by the miners themselves. The necessary technology to avoid high-severity disasters is well established, but its implementation evidently is not. Disasters are preventable and should not happen (Hopkins 1999).

OCCUPATIONAL VIOLENCE

Occupational violence is special case of low-frequency/high-severity injury that has become an increasing concern. It is known to occur to very young workers in video stores, public transport, service stations, corner stores, community services, and taxis. Two per cent of all work-related traumatic deaths in Australia are from occupational violence. One industry that has been studied from this point of view is the taxi industry. Throughout the world taxi drivers tend to work long hours for relatively low remuneration. This has its stresses for the taxi driver. But taxi driving is also a high-risk occupation (Mayhew 1999).

The preferred robbery targets in Australia have shifted from banks to all-night chemists, service stations, and taxis. Workers there are alone, vulnerable, unprotected and relatively easy prey for theft, fare evasion, vandalism and even murder. Taxi drivers encounter stick-ups, belligerent drunks, women in labour, psychopaths and fare-evaders. The commonest forms of aggression are shouting, swearing and threatening. Assaults and murders may be for kicks or for the small amount of money taxi-drivers carry with them. Key risk factors are night work on Fridays and Saturdays, intoxicated passengers, lack of knowledge of the roads, extended waiting times, and inability to speak English fluently.

In Sydney there are about ten robberies of taxis per night. Some 60 per cent of robberies resulted in little or no injury; some 30 per cent resulted in minor injuries; and 8 per cent resulted in serious injuries. Physical protection of drivers is difficult. Many Australian taxis have no division between the front and back seats. Although alarm systems are of some use, attempts to overcome this problem have had limited success.

Interviews with taxi-drivers in Australia have revealed eight major risk factors:

- most assailants are male

- most assailants are young

- most assaults occur between 6:00 pm and 5:00 am

- alcohol is factor in many assaults

- customers who booked their taxi were of lower risk than those hailed from the street or from a taxi rank

- requested destinations of assailants were typically of lower socio-economic status

- customers from disadvantaged socio-economic groups who were desperate for money are a high risk

- fare evaders tend to run away, and only when pursued is the risk of assault high.

These risk factors have four underlying elements:

- the economic urgency of taxi-drivers to accept work in hazardous situations

- inappropriate design of taxis

- widespread social acceptance of inappropriate behaviour

- inadequate responses of governments to the level of occupational violence.

Reduction of vulnerability depends upon recognition of the risk factors and the development of protective arrangements of work and of protective devices. Again, it is case of we know what to do but we don't do it (Mayhew 1999).

IMPROVING OCCUPATIONAL HEALTH AND SAFETY

A major source of information and advice is provided by national occupational health and safety commissions. For example, the national commission for Australia provides regular reports to governments and industry encouraging all to learn more about the real situation. Some annual reports of companies, for instance those of Australia Post and BHP, include what they are doing to reduce hazards. The Mineral Council of Australia conducted a national survey to identify safety culture and to recommend action (NOHSC 2000). Even so industry as a whole has a long way to go to improve health and safety, and to promote awareness through learning programmes. Much is still to be done where the workplace is still a hazard for many.

It can be argued that ethical responsibility concerning health and safety is good, because it is good for business. But this should not be the main motive for being ethical. 'We should be ethical', says Simon Longstaff (1997, p 261), 'even if there is no profit to be made ... even if there is a cost'. He goes on to say that what is needed is practical wisdom built on the foundation of virtues such as moral courage, justice, benevolence, temperance, fortitude and charity. The choice we make depends upon what we think life is for. Is it primarily for material gain, no matter the cost; or is it for a quality of life that is fulfilling and inclusive? We pursue one of the costs, namely stress, in the next chapter.

7

STRESS

In the face of strong winds, let me be a blade of grass.
In the face of strong walls, let me be a gale of wind.

Robert Sapolsky, *Why Zebras Don't Get Ulcers*, 1994, p 280.

God give us grace to accept with serenity the things
that cannot be changed, courage to change the things
that should be changed and the wisdom to distinguish
the one from the other.

Reinhold Niebuhr, quoted in Ursula Niebuhr, *Justice and Mercy*,
1974, p vi.

A WORLD PICTURE

Usually we deny the reality of things we cannot change, and too often acquiesce in things we ought to change. In this chapter, as in the previous chapter, we challenge customs and traditions in the workplace that ought to be changed. According to Gro Harlem Brundtland (2000), the director of the World Health Organisation, work-related illnesses and injuries including stress are responsible for the death of more than 1 million people in the world every year; 250 million accidents, and 160 million new cases of work-related illness occur every year. The cost to economies has been estimated at 4 per cent of the world's total GNP. There is a clear inverse relationship between work-related illness and productivity. This chapter is primarily about stress in the workplace and the need for flexibility, resiliency, picking one's battles and one's weapons as suggested in the quotations heading this chapter.

The International Labour Organisation made a study of mental health in the workplace in Germany, Finland, Poland, Britain and the United Sates (Gabriel and Liimatainen 2000). Their report indicated that as many as one in ten workers suffer depression, anxiety and burnout. Some 3-4 per cent of GNP is spent on mental health problems in the European Union.

In the United States the national spending associated with depression is US$30-44 billion each year. In many countries early retirement due to mental health has increased to the point where this is becoming the most common reason for allocating disability pensions. The costs for employers are low productivity, reduced profits, high rates of staff turnover, and increased costs of recruiting and training replacement staff. For governments the costs include health-care costs and insurance payments, as well as loss of income at the national level.

In the United States, clinical depression has become one of the most common illnesses affecting one in ten working-age adults and resulting in a loss of about 200 million working days each year. It has been estimated that 54 per cent of absences from work in the United States are due to stress. In Finland over 50 per cent of the work force experience some kind of stress-related symptoms such as depression, anxiety and exhaustion. In Germany, depressive disorders account for 7 per cent of premature retirements. In Britain one in 20 mature-age workers experience major depression, and nearly three in ten employees have some sort of mental health problem. A 1996 British Trade Union Congress survey of 7000 workplace health and safety representatives found that 68 per cent reported stress as the most serious occupational health and safety issue in their workplace. In Australia one in four people take time off due to stress at work, making it the most reported work-related illness in the Australian workplace (ACTU 1998).

The causes of these mental health problems are various: high unemployment, job insecurity, overwork, tight deadlines, new technology, and demands in both quantity and quality of production. Constant change, restructuring and downsizing have been a major cause of stress. To maintain their position or to seek further seniority many workers have willingly or unwillingly become addicted to work. The good news is that more and more individuals are coming to question if this way of life is being successful, and organisations are coming to recognise the seriousness of mental health problems of employees. For example, in the United States, programmes have been implemented to support work/family/life-issues. In Germany stress-reduction programmes have been underway for many years. They include relaxation procedures, role-playing, and training in self-confidence and interpersonal skills.

Stress relates to lifestyle. A lifestyle study of executives in Asia in 1998 found that the least stressed executives were in Indonesia, yet even there 58 per cent of executives felt 'stressed out'. Asia's most stressed executives were in Hong Kong, where 80 per cent felt stressed. Australian executives were the second-least stressed (62 per cent) in the region, after Indonesia, Filipinos, Singaporeans and South Vietnamese. Thai executives experienced stress close to that of Hong Kong (Harris 1998). That's a lot of executive stress!

A great deal is known about what can be called the physiological correlates of stress. A stressful situation leads to changes in the levels of particular hormones, which in turn affect the normal functioning of the body. Knowledge of these details has led to advances in the medical treatment of stress. It is not our purpose to deal with this here. Instead we suggest to those interested in following up this area two splendid reviews of the whole subject: John Merson's *Stress: The Causes, the Costs and the Cures* (2001); and Robert Sapolsky's *Why Zebras Don't Get Ulcers: A Guide to Stress, Stress Related Diseases, and Coping* (1994).

What then can be done to reduce the toll of stress in the workplace? Amanda Sinclair (2002) reminds us that there are two sides to stress that have to be dealt with. One is toxic workplaces. The other is 'the devil within who allows ourselves to be defined by what we do, how much we earn and the hours we put in. Shifting these habits is not easy' (p 66). Unless we do shift them we easily drift into disconnection, depression, feelings of failure, humiliation and despair, that can lead to serious medical ailments.

We seem to be surrounded on all sides of the workplace with pressures that can be disarming. On the other hand, there are certain human rights that we should be aware of and take steps to defend. This is the subject of Chapter 8.

Stress relates significantly to particular professions. Jobs traditionally associated with high levels of stress are air-traffic controllers, airline pilots, police, medical doctors (especially in their first year of hospital residency), and nurses (Freeman 1998). Here follows some example of stress in different professions.

POLICE

In the United States, police and emergency services suffer higher than average levels of depression, alcoholism, anxiety disorders and post-traumatic stress. The incidence of suicide in the New York City Police Department reached six and a half times the civilian average. Stress in this case leads to emotional exhaustion and a reduction in feelings of sympathy or respect for citizens who are apprehended. Police are subject to levels of stress most of us are able to avoid (Merson 2001).

A 1998 report estimated that the number of police in Australia on stress leave had risen from 21 in 1995 to 455 in 1998. The New South Wales State Ombudsman was highly critical of the inadequate response of the police service to dealing with stress in the police force. The service needed to introduce ways of identifying officers who are not coping with their struggles in highly stressful situations. Such an officer is more likely to make errors of judgement that could cause serious harm (Merson 2001). Reforms have been introduced following the Ombudsman's report.

GOVERNMENT OFFICE EMPLOYEES

A study of stress in 17 000 male government employees in London was begun in 1978. Rather surprisingly, the single most important factor determining whether someone died early of a heart attack was their position in the organisational hierarchy. People at the bottom of the organisation had three times the risk of heart disease as those at the top. The risk increased stepwise from the top down. The risk was correlated with the level of certain components in the blood, suggesting that stress was the primary cause of the problems of being in the lower levels of the hierarchy. The causes of this stress seemed to be the extent to which a worker lacked control over what he or she did. Modern evidence is now suggesting that new structures in the bureaucracy are moving the stress up the corporate structure. The more enlightened organisations and government institutions seek to identify causes of stress and take appropriate action (Merson 2001).

AUTO-WORKERS

Stress-related illnesses rise amongst automobile workers as the speed of the production line is increased. It began with the so-called 'scientific management' of Frederick Taylor, first applied to the assembly line of Ford automobiles. It found its zenith in the Japanese production line known as *kaizin*, which puts pressure on each section of the line. As workers are pushed to the limit of their capability, their stress-related illnesses rose. Japan's Institute of Public Health refers to this syndrome as *karoshi*:

> a condition in which psychologically unsound work practices are allowed to continue in such a way that it disrupts the worker's normal work and life-rhythms, leading to a build up of fatigue in the body and a chronic condition of overwork accompanied by a worsening of pre-existing high blood pressure and finally resulting in a fatal breakdown (Merson 2001, p 134).

In the 1970s, the Swedish aero-space and automobile company SAAB turned on its head the conventional wisdom of Ford and Taylor. They abandoned the production line control system and in its place set up a series of teams each of eight workers. Instead of carrying out one monotonous function the teams were given the responsibility of producing and testing a complete component. They were able to rotate different jobs and learn different skills. The effects were greater enjoyment of work, reduction in stress, lower cost in control systems and fewer losses due to poor quality. The success of SAAB led to Volvo taking a similar approach in which each team assembled a complete vehicle (Merson 2001).

SCHOOL TEACHERS

There is increasing evidence that teachers in the Western world in the 1900s have been experiencing increasing levels of stress. In the Western world teachers form the most numerous professional or para-professional group in the community. In Australia, for example, teachers outnumber all doctors, lawyers, nurses and dentists combined; one in 30 members of the work force is a teacher. In the 1900s there has been increasing pressure on teachers in many countries partly due to a worldwide educational reform movement. Educational systems have changed in areas of teaching practice, curricula and an emphasis on accountability and self-management (Dinham 1997). In Western Australia, for example, a study of 576 secondary school teachers revealed that 45 per cent have medium or high scores of stress. This is twice that of the general population (Tuettemann and Punch 1992).

A study of 1000 Dutch school teachers, compared them with members of other social professions for the prevalence of 'burn-out'. (Burn-out refers to a serious form of stress with symptoms of emotional exhaustion, depersonalisation and reduced personal accomplishment.) Teachers were found to be especially vulnerable to burn-out, more than workers in any other social profession (De Heus and Diekstra 1999).

In Britain, primary school teachers are working 53 hours a week, which is four hours a week more than six years ago. The average working week in secondary schools now exceeds 51 hours, up by 3.4 hours. A study of the working week of 3400 teachers and heads in England and Wales found that staff worked overtime of up to 15 hours a week in the evenings and at weekends. Half the 300 heads and deputies in Warwickshire working in 250 schools responded to a study in May 2000. It found that one in four reported serious health problems, including depression and chronic insomnia, which they attributed to overwork and stress. More than half said their family life was suffering as a result of stress in the job. Some reported break-up of their marriages due to stress. Others complained that they saw little of their families. Some were working 70 hours a week, often until 11.30 pm. Twenty per cent admitted drinking too much, with 15 per cent considering themselves to be alcoholics (Anon 2000c).

Five potentially stressful factors or stressors are recognised in teachers:

- inadequate access to facilities such as photocopying machines and class preparation areas

- student misbehaviour

- the intrusion of school work into out-of-hours time

- total hours of work

- society's expectation of teachers seen as excessive.

The degree of stress rises steeply with the number of stressors to which teachers are exposed (Tuettemann and Punch 1992; 1996).

Other studies have found that hours of work have become very stressful. Dinham and Scott (1996) found in their study of teachers in New South Wales that only 33 per cent of their respondents were satisfied with their workload. Their work had become more time-consuming, with more and more tasks being added to their teaching resulting in less and less time available for innovative preparation. Further, increased workloads had a negative effect on the teachers' personal lives. Only 27 per cent of respondents were satisfied with the effects of their work on their personal and family life.

Tuettemann and Punch (1992; 1996), in their study of teachers in Western Australia, found that the absence of stress is positively correlated with four factors:

- influence/autonomy — the teacher's perception of the extent of their influence and independence

- efficiency/achievement — the teacher's sense of competence and achievement

- support of colleagues

- praise/recognition — the acknowledgment and praise the teacher receives.

This points the way to a school environment that is less likely to provoke stress. So teachers and principals are encouraged to develop supportive environments in the school that promote a sense of kinship and support. These findings are not specific to Western Australia, but have been demonstrated in other Australian states (Tuettemann and Punch 1992, 1996). For example, a survey of secondary school teachers in Victoria found that over 20 per cent reported some degree of stress from their work (Sorros and Sorros 1992).

A study of teachers in New South Wales found that those in middle management positions, that is to say heads of departments, are the most stressed. Principals and their deputies and other teachers are less stressed. A teaching load combined with diverse duties and responsibilities is making the positions of departmental heads quite difficult (Dinham 2001).

STAFF IN UNIVERSITIES

Although universities have traditionally been regarded as working environments of low stress, during the 1990s there has been increased pressure on staff. This has been associated with reduced government funding, particularly in Australia, New Zealand and Britain.

A comprehensive study of 9000 respondents in 17 of the 38 public universities in Australia has been made by Tony Winefield (2001). It began with a pilot study in 1994 in the University of Adelaide and was completed in the year 2001. Measures were made of degrees of satisfaction in work and stress. Job satisfaction was substantially lower, and stress substantially higher than was documented in 1994. The overall levels of psychological stress were disturbingly high, with nearly half the respondents being classified as possible 'cases', and nearly a third as possible 'severe cases'.

This survey shows that, compared with a sample of the Australian population, the university population had double the percentage of possible 'cases' and triple the percentage of possible 'severe cases'. Academic staff in newer universities were worse off than those in older universities. Four aspects of the job with which there was overall dissatisfaction were:

• chance of promotion

• rates of pay

• industrial relations between management and staff

• 'the way the university is managed'.

The main causes of dissatisfaction with the job had to do with:

• hours of work (mainly working long hours)

• industrial relations

• autonomy

• variety

• responsibility.

Stress was higher in academic than in general staff. Organisational changes in recent years have meant that decision-making in universities has become less collegial and more managerial and autocratic. Control has tended to move from academics to senior managers. At the same time, decreased funding and increased demands for accountability have put greater pressures on staff. Present results suggest that stress is highest in the Arts (which includes the humanities). The study reveals serious problems in Australian universities associated with reduced funding, commercialisation, managerial culture, and restructuring.

Commercialisation is becoming an increasing problem for universities, particularly in biotechnology. There is little doubt that commercialisation of scientific research has in many cases led to a diminution in the free flow of ideas and serious conflict of interest, leading some scientists to feel that the quality of life in their laboratories has suffered (Moynihan 2002).

Bill Haseltime was a professor at Harvard University. His discoveries led to the making of drugs from proteins. He founded Human Genome Sciences. In just over a year the company went from nowhere to a market value of US$9.3 billion to make headlines in the *Financial Times* and *Fortune*. Life's values and demands inevitably changed (Pagan Westphal 2002). Professor Richard Lewontin (1991) of Harvard University says that no prominent molecular biologist of his acquaintance is without a financial stake in the biotechnology business. He goes on to discuss the inevitable conflict of interests, including restrictions in scientific interchanges which go against the freedom of communication which has been so characteristic of science until now.

CLERGY

Another profession that has become stressful, somewhat surprisingly, is that of the clergy. The following evidence of stress in the clergy in Australia and the United States is taken from Paul and Libby Wetham's (2000) book *Hard to be Holy*. The Australian data is based on two surveys of ministers, priests and pastors — one of 60 male clergy, and the other of 4500 clergy.

In the United States clergy are ranked third highest of all professions to seek divorce. American clerics were found to experience more loneliness, burn-out and diminished marital adjustment than church laity. They experience a 'diminished quality of life'.

In Australia also, marriages of clergy are under extreme strain. There are very low levels of intimacy in their closest relationships, regardless of denomination. In addition to marital problems, the other two main sources of stress are overwork with inability to resists demands, and a crisis of faith. A survey of 142 clergy in the Anglican Church of Australia revealed that 45 per cent were close to burn out; 5 per cent were so stressed that immediate remedial attention was considered necessary. The most comprehensive study in Australia indicated that burn-out is a major factor in the lives of nearly a quarter of all clergy.

Australian clergy work the longest hours of any profession and are amongst the lowest paid. Half of them have difficulty in finding time for recreation and do not take holidays when they should, and one in three has major concerns about their financial situation.

Contributing also is that clergy have the second-highest mobility rate of all professions (next to the army). They are also expected to be all things to all people: counsellor, evangelist, preacher, educator, visitor, priest, scholar, social reformer and organiser. Some 43 per cent of Australian clergy feel that they waste time on tasks not central to their role, and that their congregations often disagree about their leadership role (if the minister would only visit more people, if the minister would only preach better sermons, if the minister would only do this). Clergy are expected to be paragons of virtue and are put on a pedestal, which is often alienating. This leads to great loneliness. When asked to list ten people they turned to for help, members of their congregation were nominated the least. Clergy have few close friends inside or outside the church. All this would seem to be in great contrast with the affirmation of Jesus repeated 16 times in the New Testament: 'Love one another. In the same way that I loved you, you are to love one another' (John 15:12).

At the extreme end of the spectrum of behaviour of clergy is sexual misconduct, which has been associated with the impoverished nature of relationships of clergy. Most data on this has been gathered in the United States. One US survey of 300 clergy across denominations reported that 23 per cent admitted having done something that they felt was sexually inappropriate with someone other than their spouse. A further 12 per cent admitted having sexual intercourse with someone other than their spouse, sometimes a parishioner. There are also cases of sexual abuse, which are given much publicity when revealed.

A problem for the churches is how to change things so that the quality of life of the clergy meets the ideals of the profession. There are clergy whose quality of life is truly exemplary, and these are the ones who have the least problem of stress and burn-out. Paul and Libby Wetham (2000) give many suggestions as to how quality of life of clergy can be improved, most of which revolve around making the church a more supportive community for clergy and congregation alike.

Barbara Taylor (2001), who is an Episcopalian priest, suggests that it is no solution to follow the trend of many large churches in the United States. They resemble corporations, complete with departments, ranked staff members and organisational charts. This picture tends to look like a pyramid with straight lines of power that run from top to bottom. The trouble is that the work of a local church is to be with people and serve their needs when these needs arise. Life in this situation, as in many others, is what happens to you when you are making other plans. Taylor tells that she would pull out her compass in the morning, plot a straight course to her goal for the day and find that she was six miles off the path by noon: 'It was all those people who fouled things up' (p 30). There is another way to conceive of life together, but it requires a different world view — not a clockwork universe in which individuals function as springs and gears, but one that looks more like a network in which the whole is far more than the parts.

A scientific research laboratory is not a church, but maybe it has some similar features. Ultimately the work done there is for human good, yet it tends to be organised like a workshop. One of sciences great exponents, Robert Sapolsky (1997) of Stanford University confessed 'Sometimes, it would be nice to simply see the face of someone we helped' (p 74). This stands in contrast to jobs in social services where the complaint is more about the number of faces one sees in any day. The number can become so overwhelming as to lead to burn-out.

JOURNALISTS

Gardner and colleagues (2001) conducted intensive interviews of 60 journalists in the United States to find out the well-being or otherwise of their profession. Most of those interviewed were conscious of a crisis in their profession. Many find that it is difficult to honour the precepts of their profession. They work in a state of tension, with stakeholders threatening their core values. They feel the need to take time to investigate a complex story, but instead the public wants gossip and scandal, while management seeks greater profits in a hurry. In 1999, the *New York Times* reported that relatively few people paid attention when Bill Clinton's impeachment vote was televised, but the Monica Lewinsky interview drew an incredible audience of 70 million (Gardner et al 2001, p 134). Journalists are conscious of a decline in values and ethics in their field. Good work is difficult to do with market incentives driving performance. This is particularly true of television, where the primary mission is to get ratings. That means a shooting here, a homicide here, a child abuse case — that's business. But this gets boring for the good journalist.

This has not always been the case. Many of the influential newspapers in the United States that flourished in the first half of the twentieth century were owned and controlled by wealthy families who felt close ties with their communities and who believed that journalistic integrity was good for their business. The same tended to be true in the early phases of radio and television. In the last few decades the business climate has changed rapidly. There has been a waning of family control. Katherine Graham believed that her own newspaper, the *Washington Post*, and the *New York Times* and the *Wall Street Journal* — still family influenced — could not have made some of the decisions they made, especially the great risks over the Pentagon Papers, if they had been corporate papers. Their decision to publish was 'a terribly big risk' in her view (Gardner 2001, p 137).

Adolph Ochs Sulzberger, the owner of the *New York Times*, instituted a rule that would set his paper apart from the scandal sheets of the day: 'All the news that's fit to print' heads the front page of every issue. It promised everything important, and relief from seamy gossip that was saturating competing papers. This strategy was a winner. From the 1800s through the early 1900s many American papers followed the path of the *New York Times*. So good practice can mean good business, and good business created the conditions that freed journalists to pursue their craft with skill and honour. Practices that might have helped the bottom line, but damaged the company's reputation in the long run, were ruled out. But the proprietors of this period have been superseded by quite a new brand of CEOs who are more rapacious. The exceptions are still papers such as the *New York Times*, the *Washington Post*, *The Economist* and the *Wall Street Journal* and their counterparts, especially in Europe.

The modern discontent led to high-level commissions in the United States, with titles such as Committee of Concerned Journalists. In 1947, one such commission was headed by the famous young chancellor of the University of Chicago, Robert Maynard Hutchins. Its report, *A Free and Responsible Press*, set out the essential standards and purposes of the tradition of journalism, and the definition and the meaning of good work for journalists in a free press. The Hutchins report was ahead of its time — and it was dropped like a lead balloon. More recently, defenders of journalism's noble traditions in an environment of the greater crisis, anticipated by Hutchins, have heeded the recommendations of his commission. Codes of conduct and proper standards have been recommended and widely disseminated. The good news is that efforts at affirming journalism's core mission have arisen from within the body of concerned journalists.

SYMPTOMS OF STRESS

Not everyone is equally susceptible to stressful situations. Challenge can be stimulating and good when it motivates action and interest. The word 'stress' applies to situations that are debilitating. Those who succumb most to stress tend to have a dependent lifestyle, low self-reliance and low initiative. Typical symptoms of stress are irritability, emotional swings, fatigue, lack of concentration, headaches, sleeplessness, indigestion and susceptibility to infection.

According to the Melbourne-based Centre for Professional Development, indicators of an unhealthy workstyle are lack of clarity and focus, a tendency for after-hours conversation to evolve around work, a lack of fulfilling relationships, and a failure to contemplate the more spiritual aspects of life (Cooper 1997). There are basically two ways of dealing with a stressful situation: change the situation, or change how you go about facing it. Some make the lifestyle switch when children arrive in the family. They spend more time at home. Others choose self-employment (Hughes 1988). Still others may opt out of their present work for something entirely different (if they have the resources to make such a major change).

St Vincent's Clinic in Sydney found that 13 000 executives it surveyed were drinking to excess and working long hours that left little time for family. Sixty-six per cent were not exercising enough, and had no idea that a more balanced life was necessary if they were to reduce their soaring rates of stress. They had to face up to their false sense of male invulnerability and to more direct contact with their emotions so that they recognise when they are tired and irritable and perhaps even close to suicide. It is not surprising that more women than men initiate divorce. Men are often surprised at their wife's decision to separate. A newspaper death notice of a bereaved wife said it all: 'Taken time off at last' (Edgar 1998).

The International Labour Organisation emphasises that work should leave time for rest and leisure, for service to society and for self-fulfilment and personal development. It adds that these goals are unattainable if workers' lives are dominated by occupational stress (ACTU 1998).

DOWNSIZING AND STRESS

In capitalist countries, the 1990s was a time of exceptional economic growth, yet also of downsizing (see also Chapter 4). The loss of a job, and the attempts of those declared redundant to find alternative work, has had a profound effect on human lives. The American sociologist Richard Sennett (1998) considers that the working conditions of modern capitalism are eating away at loyalty, commitment and the kind of long-term thinking that used to make even the most routine work a central ingredient in orderly life. He paints a bleak picture of what happened to downsized executives and their colleagues in IBM. Yet he is not without hope. While he sees the modern American denied the satisfaction of order and security in the workplace, some are nevertheless beginning to learn to rebuild their lives from scratch.

So an unintended consequence of modern capitalism is that it has strengthened the value of place, aroused a longing for community and for some a new valuation to attachment and depth, perhaps most of all in family relationships. However, in the climate of downsizing there are many casualties and only a minority get back on their feet. A study of more than three hundred large companies in the United States reported that in 40 per cent of the companies downsizing resulted in undesirable consequences for the organisation as shown in Table 7.1. Pfeffer (1998, p 176) comments: 'Even as they talk about people as key strategic assets, firms jettison these assets with abandon'.

TABLE 7.1 The undesirable consequences of downsizing

Consequence	Percentage of firms reporting
Lower morale amongst remaining work force	61
More need for retraining of remaining staff	41
More use of temporary staff	36
More overtime	35
Increased retiree health-care costs	30
Entire functions contracted out	26
Wrong people lost	20
Severance costs greater than anticipated	16
Too many people lost	6

SOURCE Pfeffer, *The Human Equation*, 1998, p 176.

Retrenchment at age 45 or 50 is a major blow. But it does not have to be the end of the world. It depends on how one deals with personal disaster. It can be the end, or it can be an opportunity to rethink one's life. It does not have to be destructive. People have to change and they do (Margo 1998). As to the surviving staff, the best managers relate to them in an honest and fair way. They must assume the surviving staff will readjust to new aims and ensure that the process is fair, ethical and compassionate. Sadly however, this is not always the case (Clanchy 1997).

One cause of stress following downsizing and longer hours is intimidating behaviour of bosses. In Australian studies — by Doherty (2000), and Sheehan and colleagues (2002) — of 5000 employees 18 per cent said that their bosses made unrealistic requests, demanding longer working hours. More than 30 per cent said their bosses were more belligerent than they were ten years ago. The bosses themselves were under pressure from boards and shareholders, and many were finding difficulty in coping with the additional stress. The worst offenders were in the legal profession and in government departments.

The economic cost of workplace bullying has been estimated at between A$6–13 billion as a result of mental illness, headaches, sleeping problems, and a rise in drug and alcohol use. Some consequences of bullying in the workplace are absenteeism, staff turnover, costs of legal advice and support in court and tribunal actions, compensation pay-outs, and lost productivity. To make help more accessible, the ACTU has established a helpline for workers to report on workplace bullying.

Bullying in the workplace is also common in the business world elsewhere. Surveys in the United States, Britain and Scandinavian countries reveal that up to 98 per cent of employees experienced bullying in their working lives, while 38 per cent had experienced bullying over the previous six to 12 months. Sometimes a 'healing manager' steps in to keep the gears moving. They are called 'toxic handlers' and are unsung heroes who save the day but often pay a high price (Frost and Robinson 1999).

An attempt to quantify the effect of British bosses on workers' stress has been made by Feldman (2002). He tested the blood pressure of 25 health-care assistants who had two supervisors on alternate days of the week. He also gave them a questionnaire to find out how they felt about their bosses. Assistants who had one boss they liked and one they didn't had higher blood pressure than the control group who had two supervisors they rated equally pleasant. On the days they worked for a boss they dreaded, their average blood pressure jumped from 113/75 to 126/81. That is high enough to cause a significant health risk over time.

LONG WORKING HOURS AND STRESS

Long working hours in the workplace is often cited as a major cause of stress. In the year prior to 1995, a study of all full-time workers in Australia found 26 per cent reported stress as the most recent form of illness they had. The highest levels of stress were reported among managers (49 per cent) and clerks (42 per cent: Morehead et al 1997).

In a survey of 10 000 workers in 1997, the ACTU found that one in four Australian workers takes time off each year for stress-related illness. Stress was the most reported illness, with sprains and strains coming second. Respondents to an extensive questionnaire indicated which of 16 listed workplace conditions affected their state of well-being (ACTU 1998). The results are shown in Table 7.2.

TABLE 7.2 Adverse workplace conditions

Workplace conditions	Percentage
Increased workload	70.3
Organisational change/restructuring	68.2
Poor career opportunities	46.2
Uncomfortable temperatures	45.9
Job insecurity	42.9
Insufficient training	42.6
Communication difficulties	42.4
Long hours	38.7
Poor work organisation	35.1
Conflict with management	33.1
Excessive performance monitoring	26.8
Unresolved health and safety issues	24.5
Not enough rest periods	23.4
Difficult relations with clients	22.6
Excessive noise	19.9
Child-care difficulties	11.8

SOURCE ACTU, 'Report of the OH&S Unit', 1998.

By far the most cited of these listed conditions was increased workload (70 per cent). Next came organisational change and restructuring (68 per cent). Twelve of the 16 workplace conditions were reported by a quarter or more of the respondents. The five most frequently listed workplace conditions — increased workload, organisational change and restructuring, poor career opportunities, uncomfortable temperatures and job insecurity — were reported each time an interim survey report was produced.

There were differences between occupational groups. Some 82 per cent of managers and administrators found organisational change and restructuring a source of stress; whereas 52 per cent of labourers were so affected. Long hours affected 59 per cent of professionals, managers and administrators, but only 33 per cent of labourers. Uncomfortable temperatures and noise affected mainly plant and machine operators. There were no occupational differences for increased workload. When asked what were the three main causes of stress, poor management was listed by more than 40 per cent of respondents. The study showed that many judged management to be authoritarian, uncaring and incompetent.

Respondents were asked what they thought were solutions to stress. The main response was better management or more communication and consultation (53 per cent), then came more staff and resources (30 per cent), followed by lighter workload and less monitoring (16 per cent), and better organisation of work (14 per cent). The majority were of the view that the answer to stress at work is in the workplace. Only 2.2 per cent of respondents nominated stress management programmes or courses as the answer to stress. It is the causes rather than the symptoms that have to be addressed. A philo- sophical psychiatrist remarked to the theologian Paul Tillich: 'What is the use of my work with my patients, even if most successful, when I have to send them back into this society?' (Tillich 1968, p 128).

The ACTU report (1998) concluded that something urgently has to be done about the deleterious effects of the increasing hours of work and lack of breaks which are the result of staff reductions and burgeoning workloads. To fail to act amounts to a 'breach of duty of care' of employers and man- agers. So concerned is the ACTU that it has issued a draft booklet for dis- cussion by employers and employees: *Stop Stress at Work: A Guide for Workers*. The ACTU hopes that this will stimulate some joint action to remedy the serious situation in the Australian workplace.

THE FINANCIAL COST OF STRESS

Stress is very costly, not only in terms of suffering but also in its financial cost to industry and to the nation. In the United States, stress claims have tripled since 1980 and account for 15 per cent of all occupational sickness. In Britain, more than 40 million working days a year are lost to stress, which is estimat- ed to cost 3.5 per cent of GDP (Donaghy 1995).

It is the same story in Australia. The estimated cost of stress in public ser- vice claims in New South Wales in 1994 was A$35 million, having been A$5.6 million in 1990 (Sharp 1995). In 1993-94, claims for stress made against the Federal Government's workplace health insurance for its half a million staff members amounted to 25 per cent of the total cost. In 1994-95, the Australian Commonwealth's liability for stress claims was estimated at A$50 million (Comcare Australia 1995). In 1998-99, stress still accounted for 18 per cent of the total cost of claims (Comcare Australia 1999), and the total num- ber of accepted stress claims rises at an annual rate of about 20 per cent. Of special interest is the breakdown of the causes, as shown in Table 7.3.

TABLE 7.3 Causes of stress among Commonwealth public servants: 1994–95 (%)

Interpersonal conflict	24
Pressure of work	24
Anxiety caused by change	22
Physical and verbal abuse	17
Performance counselling and other management procedures	7
Forced relocation and organisational restructuring	6

SOURCE Comcare Australia, *Annual Report 1994–95*, 1995.

Part 3

LEARNING TO ENHANCE THE QUALITY OF WORKING LIFE ACROSS NATIONS

If the modern organisation is to make progress in the quality of working life, it needs to become a learning organisation. This may require a major restructuring, involving the active participation of all levels of the work force, to renew its culture. A foundation for this approach is a deeper understanding of human nature and the basic human rights that flow from this (Chapters 8 and 9). The renewed culture must be adaptable to changing circumstance or the organisational change may fail, as it often does. There can be either progress or regress. The key words are 'learning' and 'change', 'understanding' and 'compassion', 'values' and 'pride' (Chapter 10). The final chapter of this section leads us to identifying ten core principles for increasing the quality of working life in the brave new world that lies ahead.

8

RIGHTS

Man is born free but everywhere he is in organizations.
From T Donaldson, *Corporations and Morality*, 1982, p 109.

Whereas it would once have been a case of out of sight,
out of mind, in today's world human rights — civil,
political, economic, social and cultural — are moving to
center stage.
John Elkington, *The Chrysalis Economy*, 2001, p 20.

Whoever altered Rousseau's famous slogan, as above, must have been thinking of life in a large modern corporation. As organisations become larger, they become more bureaucratic and centralised, with the tendency to lose sight of the human beings who make it all possible. Hence the importance of a focus on human rights in the workplace.

Rights were originally conceived to protect individuals from excessive control by the majority or political power. For example, the words of the American 'Declaration of Independence' declare that the state does not have the right to take away, without due process, the lives of the citizens, their liberty or their right to pursue their own happiness. Human rights are now relevant to a wider concern that includes the relation between employer and employee. This is the subject of this chapter.

(Many of the ideas and examples in this chapter are taken from *Human Rights, Corporate Responsibilities*, a splendid dialogue edited by Rees and Wright (2000). Particular chapters in this valuable book are identified here by reference to the respective authors.)

CORPORATIONS AND HUMAN RIGHTS

There are those who argue that corporations have no special obligations beyond their duties to shareholders. However, society and shareholders today have grown to expect corporations to give something back to the communities that support them, and are prepared to make decisions based on the social and environmental credentials of companies. Business has social responsibilities.

In the United States, corporations in the state of Delaware assume an identity under the law as citizens of that state. They are assigned the same rights and citizen status as individual people. They are expected to fulfil their legal responsibilities in this context. Some are prepared to operate with a broader mandate, which they make for themselves, and extend their concern to human rights. As another example, in New York, Social Accountability attempts to standardise human rights and labour practices across industry. Companies that meet its requirements are awarded certification and can legitimately seek market advantages over less acceptable competitors (Birch and Glazebrook 2000).

By contrast the vast majority of Australian firms have no formal recognition of their human rights responsibilities. Of the top 100 Australian firms in the Good Reputation Index, only five have a publicly stated commitment to the Universal Declaration of Human Rights (Wade 2001).

What could help is a 'social contract' between corporations and society. The social contract is two sided. One side faces the consumer and the society at large, while the other faces the employee in the workplace and requires the enhancement of his or her interests. (Usually corporations are better equipped to register input from consumers than from employees, as the former relate directly to sales.)

The term 'social contract' was introduced by the Enlightenment philosophers Hobbes, Locke and Rousseau, for the relation between society and state. It became a basis of discussion of human rights in the West (as we indicate later). A social contract for a corporation would provide a justification for the existence of the corporation much like a mission statement.

Donaldson (1982) analyses the possibilities, advantages and difficulties of creating social contracts for corporations — not just, as in the past, for governments. He quotes John Maynard Keynes:

> I think that capitalism, wisely managed, can probably be made more efficient for attaining economic ends than any alternative system yet in sight, but that in itself is in many ways extremely objectionable. Our problem is to work out a social organization which shall be as efficient as possible without offending our notions of a satisfactory life (Donaldson 1982, p 78).

The problem is how to put this last paragraph into practice and make it positive.

THE UNIVERSAL DECLARATION OF HUMAN RIGHTS

The United Nations Universal Declaration of Human Rights (1948) affirmed the fundamental worth of each individual, and called for everyone to have the opportunity to fulfil his or her potential. It says that the potential could be realised only when civil and political rights, freedom of speech and belief, freedom from fear and want, and other economic and social rights were recognised and met.

Rights proclaim responsibilities. They proclaim a universal standard to protect against the tyranny of the state and more recently against exploitation by the corporate world, in particular multinational companies. The latter have become important because, from a list of the world's hundred largest economies, 50 are corporations. Only 50 are countries. General Motors' sales revenues equal the combined GDP of Tanzania, Ethiopia, Nepal, Bangladesh, Zaire, Nigeria, Kenya and Pakistan. Forbes' top 400 richest people had a net worth in 1993 equal to the combined GDP of India, Bangladesh, Nepal and Sri Lanka (Handy 1998). The annual income of Motorola is equal to the annual income of Nigeria's 118 million people (Corporations and Human Rights 2002, p 2).

Such corporations are semi-states, and their leaders have enormous powers for good or evil. When corporations are bigger than nation states, you have to apply the same rules of human rights, freedom and responsibility to them. But, as yet, corporate power and its systems of checks and balances are not well understood. Corporate power at its current level was not foreseen by early law-makers and constitutional scholars. It seems now to be a field of much discussion and dispute amongst those in favour of and those against globalisation of trade.

The UN Secretary General threw the multinational companies a challenge in July 2001. He invited them to be partners in a Global Compact in a quest to promote responsible corporate citizens, especially to promote labour rights. A number of companies — including Shell, BP, Amaco and Texaco — have responded to the invitation (Inter Press Service 2001). Ford's CEO has made a commitment consistent with the Global Compact by stating that company's three priorities in the triple bottom line: environmental (climate change), social (human rights) and economic (Wall Street) (Elkington 2001, p 120). We watch hopefully.

Since this challenge, the World Watch Institute has issued the following three priorities for business (French 2002, p 198):

- participate in the UN's Global Compact and other corporate codes of conduct, and accept independent monitoring and verification of compliance with them

- respect the goals and provisions of international environmental, human rights, and labour treaties and standards

- forge partnerships with NGOs, governments and international institutions.

The Declaration of Human Rights can be thought to embody two categories of rights: individual civil liberties ranging from free speech to freedom from torture, and communal rights such as health, food, shelter and work. Although the declaration itself is not a binding legal document, in later years both sets of rights did enter into force as binding international laws in the Covenant on Civil and Political Rights, and the broader Covenant on Economic, Social and Cultural Rights. The Universal Declaration of Human Rights (UDHR 1948) was awarded a Guinness record for the most translated and disseminated document in the world, together with the International Covenant on Economic, Social and Cultural Rights (ratified 1966) and the International Covenant on Civil and Political Rights (ratified 1966) which gave a legal framework to the declaration.

The declaration is based on the presupposition that all human beings have basic needs and therefore similar rights. It is a statement of what it means to be human. These are the rights one has simply because one is a human being. As Rees and Wright (2000) have emphasised, human rights exist to encourage humanness in every transaction and policy decision. Yet the persistence of poverty, the exploitation of children and the oppression of indigenous peoples indicates the persistence of inhumane practices.

A culture that cannot believe in, discuss and develop the best human qualities is one that inevitably suffers from dreadful injustices. We need constantly to ask: How good a human nature does our society permit and how good a society does our human nature permit? We need to be constantly reminded of such questions. This was done most eloquently by Barry Jones, former minister in a Federal Labor Government in Australia, when making his farewell speech to the Australian Labor Party:

> My main preoccupation, even obsession, in public life has been the promotion of the 'abundant life': the conviction that the overwhelming majority of people are capable of responding to a far greater richness of experience than is commonly recognised. The central question for all radical reformist parties ought to be, apart

from the economic agenda, what are human beings
capable of? Do we aim at the highest common factor
or the lowest common denominator? (quoted in Horne
2001, p 141).

Human rights extend equal concern and respect for all peoples. The 'all'
is crucial, even though some nations don't want to be bracketed with the West
in its call for human rights. We don't have, nor do we need, a list of human
rights for each country in the world. This is because there is not a multiplicity of human natures. There is one human nature (Chapter 9). There is indeed
a multiplicity of human cultures, but they exist within the one human nature.
When we say human rights are universal we mean that they apply to all
human beings.

The basic human rights of a Malaysian or a Singaporean are the same as
those of a New Yorker or Australian. When non-Westerners proclaim that
Western human rights are not applicable to them what they usually mean is
that their societies have different cultural practices. They hardly argue that
human nature in Asia is different from human nature in the West. The influence of a Confucian ethic in some Asian countries, for example, lays great
emphasis on relations with one's family and intimates and there may be less
concern for the equality of women with men. But the basic rights of women
are the same, whatever their country of origin, wherever they are and whatever anyone may say to the contrary. If, in practice, women are not given
equal rights with men this is a serious cultural deficiency that can be cor-
rected as understanding grows.

The Universal Declaration of Human Rights sets out minimum conditions for a dignified life, a life worthy of a human being. It is a widely accepted consensus. The founders of Australia's first university, the University of
Sydney, 150 years ago recognised that human values were universal when they
gave the nascent university its motto *Sidere mens eadum mutao* — which translated is 'though the stars may change, men's minds remain the same'. Human
nature didn't change then when people moved 20 000 kilometres from one
side of the Earth to the other.

The tradition that stems from all the great religions of the intrinsic worth
of the individual remains the most solid bulwark of human rights (see
Chapter 9). Each generation has to interpret its understanding of intrinsic
value into the language of human rights. The roots of the Western approach
to human rights can be traced back to the seventeenth century, particularly
in England. John Locke's view of human nature, and his view of human rights
that followed from that, became incorporated in the mainstream of political

debate in that century. It became the basis of what he called the civil society. Locke was regarded as having done for human nature what Newton had done for the physical world. Society and the state are devices to guarantee the more secure enjoyment of human rights, and a government is legitimate to the extent to which it protects human rights through its laws and practices.

Locke's ideas were embodied in Thomas Jefferson's 'American Declaration of Independence', and much of the American Bill of Rights is a direct paraphrase of Locke. Indeed its concept of human nature ('All men are equal by nature' said Locke) has been called that of 'Lockeian man'. Both documents were based on the Lockeian ideal of self-evident human rights. These were defined by Locke as life, liberty and property. Thomas Jefferson changed them to 'life, liberty and the pursuit of happiness'. Jefferson began the declaration by describing these fundamental principles as 'sacred and undeniable'. It was Benjamin Franklin who deleted this phrase and put in its place the words that now stand in the declaration — 'self-evident'. The language was simpler and less elevated. These documents appealed to Enlightenment thinking with its ideals of independence, autonomy and equality.

HUMAN RIGHTS AND CULTURAL PRACTICES

Some cultural practices are antithetical to the Universal Declaration of Human Rights, and are slowly disappearing. Chattel slavery, once common, is now almost universally condemned. So is the caste system in India. It involves the separation of people into four groups or castes kept separate by extraordinarily powerful and detailed rules of ritual purity. Placement in this social hierarchy is by birth. There is a radical incompatibility between caste and human rights, since caste denies the equality of all human beings. All Indian governments since independence have rejected the caste system — yet it still exists, particularly in the countryside. Indian governments have pressed hard for human rights as against caste and have eroded caste significantly (Donnelly 1989).

Are there human rights in Islam? Many Islamic scholars maintain that the basic concepts of human rights are embodied in Islamic law, and some argue that these rights can be traced back to texts in the Koran. The Koran has indeed many noble utterances about humans. Donnelly (1989) argues that these 'rights' of Islam are not really rights but duties required of a good Muslim. Muslims are regularly enjoined to treat their fellow humans with respect and dignity. The bases of these injunctions are more like divine commands establishing duties rather than rights. Islam teaches that it is the duty of the state to enhance human dignity and alleviate conditions that hinder individuals in their efforts to achieve happiness. There is plenty in the tradition of Islam to encourage decent and helpful relations between one another. That there are contrary practices, such as bodily mutilation and the killing of 'infidels' in some Islamic communities, is no different in principle from the existence of contrary practices in Western states that proclaim human rights.

In Africa the high degree of aversion to international monitoring of human rights led to the African Charter on Human Rights and Peoples' Rights in 1981. It put an emphasis on collective or peoples' rights, such as the rights to peace and development. As yet it has hardly established itself as an effective monitoring body despite the many abuses of human rights in the region (Donnelly 1989).

The universality of human rights must be realised through particular action of corporations and nations. We should keep on asking: Why do some societies widely respect human rights while others systematically violate them? Some political regimes are inimical to the practice of human rights. This is true of totalitarian states. Nazism had a view of human nature that divided people into desirable citizens and outcasts. The latter included Jews, homosexuals, gypsies, communists and political opponents. These had no rights, not even the right to life. One can argue that only in liberal democratic regimes can civil and political rights be protected (Donnelly 1989).

WORKERS' RIGHTS

The Universal Declaration of Human Rights recognises workers' rights as universal human rights. Labour standards are elaborated and protected by the International Labour Organisation (ILO) with its 'Declaration on Fundamental Principles and Rights at Work'. Its principles have to do with freedom of association, the right to organise and bargain collectively, discrimination in employment, equality of remuneration, forced labour, migrant workers, workers' representatives, and standards of social policy. It has an effective monitoring system with a tripartite structure in which workers' and employers' delegates from each member state, along with government representatives, are voting members of the organisation . With the 'victims' represented by national trade union delegates, it is difficult for states to cover up failure to discharge their obligations.

In recognition of the increasing role of multinational corporations, the ILO adopted the Tripartite Declaration on Principles Concerning Multinational Enterprises and Social Policy. It emphasises the part multinational corporations can play in promoting labour rights throughout the world. Multinationals tend to seek out the lowest labour costs, relocating their place of production as wage levels change. This has led to a downward spiral of wages, as one country competes with another. This is a problem. There are exceptions. Body Shop, for example, seeks to establish an environment of fair wages wherever it operates. Such exceptions are all too rare however.

Nike, one of the offenders, has been criticised for the low wages it pays its workers, and its often unsafe working conditions in Asian countries. The corporation shifted its shoe and apparel production from Oregon to Korea, Indonesia and Vietnam, and then to China and Bangladesh to take advantage of low wages in these countries. Following criticism, it has adopted a code of practice, which is fine in theory but may yet have to be tested fully. Nike is an example of the difficulties of developing fair labour standards when production occurs in a number of countries with different jurisdictions. Enforcement of standards may in the end depend upon the ILO's attempts to enforce its standards (Duffield 2000).

Some corporations have included UN workers' human rights in their stated business principles. The retailer Reebok found that by incorporating human rights into its business practices it achieved better morale amongst workers, a better working environment, and higher-quality products. Other textile manufacturers such as Gap have found that actively engaging with NGOs to develop fair labour initiatives has helped to protect their reputation (Holliday, Schmidheiny and Watts 2002).

The Shell Petroleum Development Company was targeted by the Ogoni people in southern Nigeria for its long involvement in oil production in Ogoniland, and its alleged complicity in human rights and environmental abuses. The plight of the Ogoni was dramatic enough to spur major collaborative effort among international human rights and environmental organisations. Much of the publicity came in response to the eloquent appeals of Ken Saro-Wiwa, the president for the Movement for the Survival of Ogoni people (MOSOP). MOSOP was founded in 1992 specifically to campaign against what it referred to as Shell's reign of 'environmental terrorism'. The once lush agricultural land of the Niger Delta had become covered with an oil slick stretching for kilometres, vegetation had died, and some rivers ran black. Gas flares near villages were said to poison the air, causing acid rain. Unlined toxic waste pits allowed pollutants to seep into drinking water supplies.

The Nigerian Government introduced violent tactics against the complaining activists, committing gross violations of human rights. In 1995 Ken Saro-Wiwa and eight other MOSOP leaders were executed in retaliation for their activities. Shell, in the meantime, accepted no responsibility for what initiated the government's violent tactics. Eventually, in response to intense international pressure, Shell launched a review of its international business practices. As a result it outlined new core values to guide its business ethics, including responsibilities to the environment and to social concerns. It is a tragedy that this was not done before its destructive activities became entrenched. The sacrificing of small communities like those in Ogoniland is unfortunately a common phenomenon around the globe (Sachs 1995).

Human rights and environmental issues are often inextricably bound together. A tragic example involved the murder of Chico Mendes in 1988. He waged a battle against deforestation in the Amazon rainforests of Brazil. His principal aim was to protect the rights of fellow rubber trappers in the forest. But he had enemies — land hungry cattle ranchers, one of whom masterminded his assassination. An Amnesty International report revealed that there were more than 1000 land-related murders in rural Brazil in the 1980s, and fewer than ten convictions. Environmentalists working in the Amazon region learned from Mendes that one of the best ways of preventing deforestation is the human rights approach — to reform the law and empower people to mount protests to defend their health and livelihood. The Mendes Reserve, a tract of nearly one million hectares of protected rainforest that stands as a tribute to his memory, is an example of the results of such legislation (Sachs 1995).

The rights of workers is an issue raised by the existence of sweatshops, which still seem particularly prevalent in the garment industry. Describing the typical garment workplace, the general secretary of the International Textile, Garment and Leather Worker's Federation in the United States, Neil Kearney, said:

> The reality today is that most of the 30 million jobs in the fashion industry around the world are low-paid, often based in export processing zones where worker rights are usually suppressed. Wages are frequently below the subsistence level and falling in real terms ... Management by terror is the norm in many countries ... Attempts to unionise are met with utmost brutality, sometimes with murder (Pincus 1998, p 767).

Low wages are a prime magnet for multinational firms coming to Third World countries. In 1990 a glossy full-coloured advertisement appeared in a major American apparel trade magazine showing a woman at a sewing machine and proclaiming that she can be hired in El Salvador for 57 cents an hour. Next year her salary was reduced to 33 cents an hour. This was not uncommon in that country at that time (Pincus 1998).

It is not necessary to go to Third World countries to find sweatshop conditions. According to Pincus (1998) America's garment industry grosses US$45 billion per year and employs more than one million workers. There was an uproar in 1995 when Secretary of Labor Robert Reich announced the names of several large retailers who may have been involved in sweatshop operations in California. In one plant, Thai workers were paid less than one US dollar an hour. A spot check of garment operations in California in 1994 revealed that 93 per cent had health and safety violations. Robert Reich claimed that he had discovered in the US sweatshops conditions as bad as the worst in Third World countries. Since his revelations various measures have been adapted to try and rectify he situation both in the United States and abroad.

On occasions women migrants in Australia have worked at home for manufacturing industries for low wages and poor conditions. When discovered, attempts have been made to rectify the situation. The Centre for Working Women Co-operative reported on conditions of 'outworkers' in Victoria in the 1980s (Anon 1986). The term is used for those people who do the work in their own homes. Such work is obtained from a factory or shop, and is usually paid at piece rates. Outworkers are usually women migrants from non-English-speaking backgrounds. Many of them work for the garment industry and use their own sewing machines. The sweating of women outworkers in Australia is not new. The latter half of the nineteenth century saw a period of rapid expansion of manufacturing and a rise in the numbers of women outworkers in the garment industry in Australia. Their conditions were poor and wages were low. There followed a massive campaign by the anti-sweating league. An outcome was the *Shops and Factories Act* of 1873 to protect the workers. The ACTU took steps to oppose anti-union employment practices so common with employers of outworkers. Many migrants find it difficult to find a job in a factory so become outworkers. The legal status of outwork is problematic because of the variety of Acts and their possible applications. Middlemen between the factory and the outworker can be intimidating and even threatening. Most outworkers receive no worker's compensation for injury. Women outworkers usually do monotonous and repetitive work at high speed. Repetitive strain injuries are common. Stress is also a common condition. Because of their economic condition they continue working even though they should take time off to recover. One cannot but feel that some employers have taken advantage of women migrants who speak little English and are desperate for work.

There are various advantages for employers employing outworkers. They mostly stem from being able to use workers outside of award conditions.

Outworkers are often paid under-award rates, and few receive sick pay or holiday pay, and employers have fewer overheads.

The report of the Centre for Working Women Co-operative (1986) makes a number of recommendations, including the employers granting of regular award rates of pay to outworkers, providing workers' compensation, keeping adequate records, and the workers having appropriate status with unions. Yet one is left with the sense that much more needs to be done to get rid of the sweatshop conditions that outworking can lead to.

The problem of workers' rights is also a major concern of the ILO. It estimated that in 1997 some 800 million workers around the world were unemployed, and that at least 1.2 billion were living in poverty. Such estimates, along with such events as the Asian economic crisis, have brought the issue of international labour standards to the fore in international forums including the WTO and OECD. The problems are diverse and numerous, particularly the enforcement of such agreements as are made. The OECD identified a set of 'core' labour standards, based on a range of ILO human rights conventions, in 1996. (Core standards are distinguished from non-core standards such as minimum wage conventions.) The ILO's core standards are:

- the right to collective bargaining and freedom of association, allowing workers to establish and join organisations, and protecting against anti-union discrimination

- freedom from exploitative child labour, which attempts to prevent children from entering full-time work before a certain age or completion of a basic education

- freedom from forced or compulsory labour, including freedom from forced prison labour

- equal opportunity standards, which are designed to ensure freedom from discrimination in the workplace.

The above employee rights include free speech and due process and to them could be added privacy and participation.

The moral case for core labour standards is strong, and the economics are advantageous. An OECD study concluded that failure to observe core labour standards can hamper economic efficiency of a country and the growth of its exports. Compliance can be achieved in some cases through trading bloc arrangements. For example, the Maastrich Treaty has a 'social chapter' on working hours, parental leave and works councils designed to harmonise law and social conditions throughout the European Union. Some companies under pressure from their unions and customers have withdrawn investment from particular countries. For example, Levi–Strauss withdrew from China, at least for a period (Green 2000).

At a more personal level than the core labour standards of the ILO, an Employee Bill of Rights has been drawn up by Sonnenberg (1993, pp 23-26). In this bill of rights employees have the right to:

- decide how best to achieve their goals
- be treated as part of an organism rather than as interchangeable parts of a machine
- be viewed as unique individuals
- be challenged
- be treated with dignity and respect
- try and fail
- know their employers have confidence in them and their abilities
- be treated in a fair and honest fashion
- have their professional standing recognised
- have freedom of expression
- be informed
- be able to approach management
- know their efforts are appreciated.

To set forth such rights is to send a message that the corporation believes that its employees are its most important asset and that they will be treated with dignity and respect.

Jack Welch Jnr, the celebrated chairman and CEO of General Electric wrote in its 1989 annual report:

> We want GE to become a company where people come to work every day in a rush to try something they woke up thinking about the night before. We want them to go home from work wanting to talk about what they did that day, rather than trying to forget about it. We want factories where the whistle blows and everyone wonders where the time went, and someone suddenly wonders aloud why we need a whistle. We want a company where people find a better way, every day of doing things; and where by shaping their own working experience, they make their lives better and your company best. Farfetched? Fuzzy? Soft? Naive? Not a bit. This is the type of liberated,

involved, excited, boundary-less culture that is present
in successful start-up enterprises. It is unheard of in an
institution our size; but we want it, and we are determined to have it (Sonnenberg 1993, p 33).

This had been Welch's vision all his life. With every step he claimed that
he tried to live up to this vision and, by his own account, did so all the way
to the top, as revealed in his account of his life with the huge firm of General
Electric. He expected himself and his staff to have 'the four Es' of leadership:

• high levels of energy

• the ability to energise others

• the edge to make tough yes–and–no decisions

• the ability to execute on promises.

Associated with ratings of his staff on the four Es is a reward system of salary
increases, stock options and promotions. Those lowly rated and not showing
improvement might be asked to look for another job. Employees were regularly invited to complete a questionnaire which included questions such as
'Has your career with GE had a favourable impact on you and your family?'
Union leaders were regularly asked for their views. 'Treat people with dignity and give them voice' was Welch's motto (Welch 2001, pp 158-168).

RACISM AND HUMAN RIGHTS IN THE WORKPLACE

All people, whatever their skin colour, belong to the one species *Homo sapiens*. We share one humanity. The more we know about human 'races', we find
that variation within race in any particular characteristic is greater than variation between so-called races. The more we know the less possible is it to separate races except in the most superficial characteristics such as skin colour.
There is no biological basis for making a distinction between races. The only
way some people have managed to divide *Homo sapiens* into races is to select
one or a few characteristics such as skin colour on which to base their clas-
sification. The next step is to brand some races as inferior to others. Ignorance
about race has led to the most pernicious effects in society, such as slavery and
the Nazi holocaust. The idea that large groups of people who are differentiated from other groups by superficial characteristics, and adding to that differences in supposed mental qualities such as intelligence, is a myth (Birch
1999; Ehrlich 2000).

A serious responsibility of corporations is the elimination of racial discrimination in the workplace. In multicultural societies such as Australia's,

employees from many different nationalities work alongside one another. Corporations benefit from promoting diversity and freedom from discrimination. The race discrimination commissioner of the Australian Federal Government issued a training package Race for Business in 1998 to assist employers in identifying and dealing with race discrimination in business. It was recognised at the time that many employers particularly in aviation, banking and retail industries were leading the way in good practices.

One such leader was the fruit company Berri, a large corporation with employees from 40 different ethnic backgrounds. In 1998 it conducted an anti-racism advertising campaign on television which highlighted the deleterious effects of racial intolerance and the advantages of diversity. The programme led to much valuable public discussion and greater tolerance of diversity in that community.

A focus on the individual and the special talents that individuals bring to an organisation is at the core of valuing diversity. People have different talents, and they thrive under different circumstances. Workplaces need to change to incorporate the variety of employees who constitute the modern work force. In multicultural countries such as the United States and Australia, the work force no longer consists of only white males, but includes females, immigrants and minorities. 'Scientific management', developed by Frederick Taylor, and Fordism of the conveyor belt era are the epitome of the homogenous work force; the man as machine where one size fits all. Post-Taylorism and post-Fordism moved away from the machine metaphor of work, to work with more complexity and less rigidity. It needs now to move further in the direction of the culture of the organisation fitting the diverse talents of employees.

A number of corporations in Australia have taken steps to address issues affecting Australia's indigenous peoples. One of these is the Yandicoogina Land Use Agreement between Hamersley Iron and the Gumala Aboriginal Corporation, signed in 1997. It concerned Hamersley's Yandicoogina iron ore mine, and covered 26 000 square kilometres in the Central Pilbara in Western Australia. The agreement is regarded as a benchmark in relations between mining and Aboriginal land rights.

As another example, Kakadu National Park in the Northern Territory is co-managed by the government's park service and the Aborigines who have inhabited the region for more than 50 000 years. Co-management has fostered effective nature conservation, a tourist industry that provides Aborigines with a steady income, and the preservation of traditional communities. Further examples of these and other issues discussed in this section are given by Robinson and Sidoti (2000). Indigenous people also have rights to do with their heritage both cultural and intellectual. Some possible solutions in attempting to resolve such problems are considered by Janke (2000) for Australian indigenous peoples.

RIGHTS OF WOMEN AND CHILDREN IN THE WORKPLACE

The UN Convention on the Elimination of all Forms of Discrimination against Women was ratified in 1979. The UN Convention on the Rights of the Child was ratified in 1979. Inequalities of women at work as compared with men concern inequality in pay, inequality in promotion, extent of participation in full-time employment, freedom from sexual harassment and the right to organise. These concerns are discussed in Chapter 5. Here we deal with some issues related to the declaration of rights for women and children.

The Levi-Strauss company set guidelines for is contractors on the rights of women and children, and as a result left its operations in Burma and is phasing out contracting labour in China. By contrast, Nike is reported to have continued employing Asians despite widespread criticism of its poor record on rights there. The UN Commission on the Status of Women has drafted a variety of treaties such as the Political Rights of Women and the Convention on the Elimination of Discrimination against Women. The latter has been ratified by more than 90 states.

The tension between economic interests, cultural tradition and the rights of children comes to the fore in issues to do with child labour. The ILO estimates that the number of workers aged under 15 in the world exceeds 250 million, 61 per cent of whom are in Asia and another 32 per cent in Africa. Their work is characterised by low pay, long hours and unsafe working conditions. The ILO maintains that child labour is in breach of international conventions on the rights of children. It should be outlawed and replaced by investment in public education (Rees and Wright 2000b).

HUMAN RIGHTS OF PARTICULAR MINORITIES

In addition to the rights of women and children there are other groups of people whose rights are often ignored or misunderstood. People with disabilities are such a group, and issues such as building access and public transport show much progress. The same cannot be said of other areas of concern. The working rights of people with mental illness are a major concern, particularly in those countries which have greatly reduced the population in mental hospitals. Savings resulting from this are not being redirected sufficiently to mental health services in the community.

The UN Declaration of the Rights of Disabled Persons was ratified in

1971 and the UN Resolution of the Rights of the Disabled Persons was rat-ified in 1991. We are slow to change. The Sydney Opera House, which was opened in 1973, is a physically unfriendly place for the aged and physically handicapped. Only now are changes being made to rectify this deficiency.

Gay men and lesbians are another group of workers who experience dis-crimination. This discrimination may be more than just a preference for het-erosexual applicants for vacancies. It is an act of discrimination when an employee is expected to not bring his or her same-sex partner to a business social gathering. It is an act of discrimination when an employee may, perhaps in response to some award or retirement, be expected to not express gratitude in public for the role of his or her partner of the same sex. Legal steps have been taken in all states and territories of Australia to combat discrimination on grounds of sexual orientation. In the United States, seven states and the District of Columbia have enacted laws that prohibit discrimination by pri-vate employees on the basis of sexual orientation. Some 130 cities and coun-ties have done the same (Woods 1993). Yet discrimination and prejudice continue in employment as well as in the community at large.

There is much to be done in education of the community about gays and lesbians. There is, for example, a widespread misunderstanding that supposes that sexual orientation is a choice. It is not, any more than being left-handed is a choice. Medical and scientific evidence confirms that sexual orientation is something one is born with. There is no moral case against being gay or lesbian any more than there is a moral case against being left-handed or hav-ing black skin.

If people really understood this they would understand that gays and lesbians should be given exactly the identical rights of heterosexuals, including considering homosexual bonding equivalent to heterosexual bonding. This stance is quite widely appreciated in academic communities such as universities where discrimination is a minimum. It is an attitude that should be as widespread in the business community. Some moves are taking place especially in the United States, as the following examples from Woods (1993) indicate.

Microsoft, Digital, Apple Computer, Oracle and many smaller software firms were trend-setters by having explicit non-discrimination policies. They have been followed by AT&T, Xerox, DuPont and others. Microsoft, with its 14 000 employees, has a special staff to implement its diversity and non-dis-crimination programme. It includes blacks, Hispanics, Jews, women, deaf, native Americans, East Indians, gay, lesbian and bisexual workers. Gay, lesbian and bisexual employees are Microsoft's largest diversity group.

In 1991, Lotus Development extended its company health benefits to partners and eligible dependents of lesbian and gay employees. It was followed by Levi-Strauss in 1992, and several other industry rivals including Microsoft since. Yet despite these healthy indicators, there is still in the world of business a deep need for diversity, acceptance, inclusiveness and tolerance.

So-called diversity policy in employment, which once meant recruiting more women or people from different ethnic backgrounds, is now recognised by more institutions to encompass a much greater variety of subcultures in the workplace (Turner 2002). For example Telstra's diversity council promotes the advancement of women, cultural diversity, people with disabilities and work/life balance. IBM's head of global diversity has formed taskforces to look at work from the perspective of African Americans, Asians, disabled people, gays, Hispanics, native Americans, white males and women.

Age is the next big item that needs much greater attention. In an ageing population, such as ours, more older people are looking for jobs yet finding that they are discriminated against. On the other hand, there are problems in having older workers supervised by much younger managers that need to be faced with fairness.

AM I MY BROTHER'S KEEPER?

The doctrine of human rights implies that I am to be my brother's keeper. Yet the extent to which we are called to be responsible to one another is controversial.

Adam Smith, in *The Wealth of Nations* (1776), argued that individuals and business should seek to maximise their own self-interest and in doing so the 'invisible hand' of the free markets would maximise the well-being of society. Private vices become public virtues. The University of Chicago economist Milton Friedman regards Smith's thesis as the foundation of modern economics. It is the proposition that leads to the concept of *Homo economicus*. Hence Whitehead (1938) argued that the study of political economy in its first period after the death of Adam Smith in 1790 did more harm than good. On the one hand it destroyed many economic fallacies, and taught how to think about the economic revolution then in progress. But on the other hand it riveted attention on 'a certain set of abstractions which were disastrous … in dehumanising industry' (p 232).

To the question asked of Cain — 'Where is Abel thy brother?' — Cain answered 'Am I my brother's keeper?' People who give the same answer incur Cain's guilt. Smith's theory that the promotion of self-interest led to goods and services for all left little room for the renaissance of the 'whole man'.

Hence the judgment that Smith's society left little room for Renaissance man. Opulence could indeed exist in such a society, but it would not be rich in many-sided men (Brownoski and Mazlish 1960, p 349).

Fortunately there has been a paradigm shift amongst some economists who now argue the case for more 'other-regarding' actions in conjunction with self-regarding actions in business (Daly and Cobb 1989). The gist of this chapter is the consideration of how this new paradigm might become a prac- tical issue in human rights in the workplace. The stand we take on this issue depends very much on what we take to be the measure of humanity, that is on convictions about human nature, which is the subject of the next chapter.

9

ON HUMAN NATURE

Everything has a nature, and the virtue of everything
is the fulfilment of its nature.

Frederick Ferre, *Living and Value*, 2001, p 37.

We strive for organizational models that are more
congruent with human nature ... our traditional
organizations are not designed to provide for people's
higher order needs, self-respect and self-actualisation.

Bill O'Brien, President of Hanover Insurance, quoted in Senge,
The Fifth Discipline, 2000, p 140.

If the misery of our poor be caused not by the laws
of nature, but by our institutions, great is our sin.

Charles Darwin, *The Voyage of the Beagle*, 1860, p 497.

In this chapter we look more directly at what we mean by
human nature — with its implications for the fullness of life — and as well
its opposite. We face the question asked so long ago by Charles Darwin, in the
quotation that heads this chapter, written on his first encounter with slavery
in all its cruelty in Brazil.

Ideas of quality of life and what constitutes human flourishing are based
on convictions about human nature. That there is a human nature that all of
us share means that we all universally share the same human needs. This we
discussed in Chapter 2. This leads to the belief that all humans have certain
rights, which is the subject of Chapter 8. In between these chapters we have
asked: How fully a human flourishing does the workplace and its practices
permit, and how good a life in the workplace does human nature permit? In

other words there are constraints in the workplace on human nature, and there are constraints within human nature on what can be achieved. We should not settle for less than human possibilities allow, but we should avoid demands that exceed a realistic estimate of those possibilities.

Reinhold Niebuhr (1944) was emphatic that a civil society prospers best in an atmosphere that encourages neither an overly pessimistic nor an overly optimistic view of human nature. Utopias don't last. We know that from American experience, as well as elsewhere, of utopian societies established in the nineteenth century. These societies all flourished briefly then faded away. The earlier over-optimistic utopian spirit gave way to the harsher realities of human nature and commerce. All utopias have been tame because risk has been reduced at the cost of vitality. Get rid of any opposition is the catchcry of utopians. The opposite principle of toleration, on the other hand, is summed up in the words 'Let both grow together until the harvest' (Matthew 13:30).

Hence the story of the old man in India, who sat in the shade of a tree whose roots disappeared away into a swamp. He noticed that a scorpion had become entangled in the roots. He reached down to extricate the scorpion, which was struggling in an environment so unnatural for it. When he touched the scorpion it lashed his hand with its tail, stinging him painfully. His hand became swollen so he returned to the shade of the tree to recover. A young man standing by had witnessed the whole episode. He taunted the old man and said, 'Why help a scorpion to live when all it can do to you is harm?' The old man replied, 'Simply because it is in the nature of the scorpion to sting and it is my nature to save life wherever I find it'. Hence the quotation above that everything has a nature. That includes us.

What then is human nature?

Pavlov said: how like dog.

Hamlet said: how like a god.

Pascal said: the glory and scrapings of the universe.

The psychologist said: how like a rat.

The scientist said: how like a machine.

An appropriate behaviour is not established merely by conceiving the most ideal possible solution for a problem. It must deal with the realities of human nature as well as its ideal possibilities. As to these realities, there are strong differences of opinion. Perhaps the best we can do is to envisage the ideal possibilities within the limits set by human recalcitrance.

MECHANISTIC MAN

The Czech writer Karel Capek published a play called *R.U.R.* The title stood for Rossum's Universal Robots, which was the name of a fictional company that manufactured human-like machines designed to perform all hard, dull and dangerous work for people. The machines eventually grew to resent their jobs, and rebelled with disastrous results for their bosses. Capek called his machines 'robots' from the Czech word *robota* meaning 'forced labour'. Robot made its way into our language in 1923 when *R.U.R.* was translated into English. Is it our nature to be robots?

In his film *Modern Times*, Charlie Chaplin became a robot in the factory where he worked as an automaton or zombie. The reference to Nazi society was obvious. Or perhaps it was also a reference to Henry Ford's conveyor belt assembly line that was based on the 'scientific management' of Frederick Taylor. Taylor's view of human nature was that workers are primarily machines and are to be treated as such. His was the concept of mechanistic man. But if your only tool is a hammer, all problems look like nails. The robot, in any guise, is a caricature of what its is to be human, indeed to be anything from protons to people. We know too much about matter to be mechanists and materialists any more.

In earlier chapters of this book we have used *Homo economicus* for mechanistic man in commerce. Its guiding principle in classical economics is the proposition that human beings are primarily motivated by self-interest. That is our human nature. Adam Smith, the Scottish moral philosopher, is considered to be the father of economics and its principle of the motivating force of self-interest. However, he also recognised the fundamental human capacity for sympathy and 'other-regarding' behaviour, which his modern interpreters tend to ignore.

The principle of *Homo economicus* is illustrated by a simple but telling piece of research. Robert Frank asked some American university students at the beginning and end of a semester whether they would return a lost envelope with $100 in it. Students who had taken an economics course during the semester showed a greater shift away from returning the envelope than students who had taken an astronomy course (Singer 2002). Reinforcing that finding is a study by Roccas and Gandal (2002) comparing the values and motives of 199 economics students with 165 students of other subjects. The economics students were less interested in protecting the environment or helping the poor than students in other subjects. They were more interested in gaining power and influence, making money and having a good time.

Homo economicus abstracts from human feelings about what happens to others, from the sense of fairness and from judgments of relative value. It is an abstraction from the real person that leads to differences of behaviour between that posited of *Homo economicus* and that of real people. The assumption that rationality largely excludes other-regarding behaviour as an ethical ideal runs counter to the deep convictions of the Western understanding of human nature from Saint Augustine onwards through the Protestant reformation (Daly and Cobb 1989, p 95).

Another version of mechanistic man is found in technological managerialism. Albert Speer, the highly successful Nazi minister for armaments, is a classic example. He was described by Sebastian Haffner in 1944 as:

> The pure technician ... with no other original aim than to make his way in the world ... it is the lack of psychological and spiritual balance, and the ease with which he handles the terrifying technical and organizational machinery of our age which makes this slight type go extremely far nowadays ... The Hitlers and Himmlers we can rid ourselves of, but the Speers, whatever happens to this particular specimen, will long be with us (from Fest 2002, p 353).

Speer had neither the independence of judgement nor the moral conviction that would have enabled him to discriminate between the conflicting claimants in a Nazi society for his many talents.

A further example of mechanistic man is seen in the career of Edward Teller, who was one of the architects of the crash programme to build and test the world's first hydrogen bomb. During the development of that programme, Teller became involved in a permanent dispute with his rivals. He is said to have threatened to leave the project remarking 'If I can't work with the peacemakers, then I'll work with the fascists' (Fest 2002, p 392). Whatever the facts, Fest remarks that this episode illustrates the unscrupulousness with which some scientists are prepared to achieve their own plans without any moral reservations. Both Speer and Teller are classic examples of this separation of facts from values.

A scientific version of mechanistic man is the concept of genetic man. Under this conception, we are nothing but our genes, which determines what we are. The 'This is how I was made' attitude is genetic determinism. If my genes are for aggressiveness then I behave aggressively. I have no choice. This is a genetic version of the old theological doctrine of predestination espoused by Calvinists. Despite its promotion in 'evolutionary psychology' — the newest incarnation of 'sociobiology' — it is as insidious as it is wrong.

A modern version of genetic determinism is to be found in the human genome project. Here the human being is defined in bits of DNA, some of it good, some of it bad. The human genome consists of parts that can be replaced at will by genetic engineering. We are promised a future in which the bad bits will be replaced by good bits. Genomic medicine therefore sees the body as a machine that consists of parts that can be replaced. But this dream of perfect health is specious. New forms of disease will continue to emerge as bacteria and viruses evolve. Genes mutate and our environment changes. Thinking of the body primarily as a machine results in excessive reliance on surgery and drugs, and already partly accounts for the impersonal nature of some managed care. It isolates organs from bodies, diseases from patients, doctors from communities and turns physicians into technicians. Being human is more than having the right molecular composition. The face of the beloved is more than nucleotide bonds.

'You can't change human nature' is the cry of the biological determinist, and some committed capitalists. Of course you couldn't change human nature, if our nature were completely determined by the genes given us at our birth. With this kind of thinking, biological determinism becomes a social weapon. Because it is exculpatory, it has a wide appeal. If men dominate women, it is because they must. If employers exploit their workers, it is because evolution has built into us genes for entrepreneurial activity. If we kill each other in war, it is the force of our genes for territoriality, xenophobia, tribalism and aggression. Genetic determinism can even be used to defend the free market. It is said to account for why we do what we want to do, and why we sometimes behave like cavemen. The ethics of genetic determinism is the ethics of the jungle. Struggle for existence is its law of life. The trouble with this view is that there is a flaw in its understanding of the relation between the gene, organism and environment (see Birch 1999, pp 66-71).

Some behavioural characteristics such as aggression have been extensively studied by biologists. At one stage it was thought that the rare genetic abnormality of males carrying a second Y chromosome turned the carriers into super-males. Efforts were made to see if males possessing an extra Y chromosome had a higher level of 'male' hormones such as testosterone that might make them unusually aggressive and criminally inclined. Such proposals or claims are now discounted. There is a relationship between testosterone and aggression, but it is quite a complex and subtle one. We give this as an example of how human behaviour is not to be understood by the simple approach of biological determinism. The following account is the relation of testosterone and aggression as it has been unravelled by Sapolsky (1997).

Males account for less than 50 per cent of the population, yet for an incredibly disproportionate percentage of the violence in the community. Could this difference be due to the hormone testosterone? Both males and females produce testosterone, but males produce much more. Some males produce more testosterone than others. And some males are more aggressive than others. We might then ask: Are the highest testosterone levels found in the most aggressive individuals? Study after study has shown that testosterone levels predict nothing about who is going to be aggressive. In fact, different levels of aggressiveness drive the hormonal changes, rather than the other way round. For some reason or other, probably some stimulus in the environment, an individual becomes aggressive. This then causes the level of testosterone in the aggressor to rise. Furthermore, fluctuations in testosterone levels within one individual over time do not predict changes in the level of aggression in that individual. You need some testosterone around for normal aggressive behaviour. But from some 20 per cent of normal to twice normal levels its all the same. Only quite abnormal increases such as a quadrupling (the sort of increase generated in weight-lifters abusing anabolic steroids) increases aggression. The principle seems to be that testosterone doesn't cause aggression. It exaggerates the aggression already there.

The moral is that there isn't a single gene or a single hormone or a single nerve impulse that causes aggression. 'Testosterone equals aggression' is just no answer. The action of testosterone can only be understood in the context of environmental and social factors. This is an example of how fallacious it is to attribute specific behaviour to a specific biological determinant. Each of us has a capacity for aggression. Some become more aggressive than others and at times more aggressive than at other times. All sorts of social and environmental factors may cause these differences. But once aggression begins, it is driven further by the hormone testosterone. What then are we to do to reduce aggression? We can seek to understand the social and environmental circumstances that initiate aggressive behaviour and intervene there. This is an extremely important insight for a world so wracked with violence.

Another version of mechanistic man is environmental or cultural determinism. I am what I am by virtue of the environment I was brought up in, my home, school and society at large. Each of us is likened to a lump of formless clay waiting to be moulded by our environment. Extreme cultural determinists believe that the organism is born with John Locke's *tabula rasa* (blank tablet), on which culture and society can write anything. In truth our individual lives are the outcome of a great multiplicity of causal pathways that involve genes, our environment, and choices we make during our lives. Our human nature is simultaneously biologically and socially constructed (Birch 1999). In Chapter 2 we referred to the environment and culture of ancient Athens, with the remark that it is no accident that this environment gave to the world such people as Sophocles, Euripides, Pericles and Socrates. It would be absurd to suppose that the people of Athens had all the good genes and their neighbours none. It is reasonable to suppose that the cultural environment of Athens was favourable to the development of genius.

Man as machine, whether in the surgery or the corporation, needs a counterweight. An alternative view of human nature is that we are not given at birth unalterable qualities. It is true that I am born with blue eyes, and that this is determined by the genes I was given by my parents. But in less tangible qualities that have to do with our behaviour and attitudes, most of them are not completely genetically controlled (Ehrlich 2000). It looks more as though any one of us could be all sorts of person — aggressive or non-aggressive, cruel or kind, thoughtful or thoughtless. What makes us what we are is, to a large extent, choice together with the moulding effect of environment. We have a degree of freedom to choose. We can be changed. Every human being is ultimately responsible for the decisions he or she makes. Our genetic make-up, the moulding effect of environment and human choice permit a wide range of behaviour, from Ebenezer Scrooge before to Ebenezer Scrooge after; from Saul before to Paul after.

In all human motives there is a mixture of self-regard and creativity. One or other may become dominant or we may achieve a balance. The Chinese sage Kao Tzu compared human nature to a pool of water. It can be made to flow to the east or to the west, depending on where one makes a breach. Like water, human nature can flow either way (Singer 2002, p 4). Though humans are rooted in their biology they simultaneously tower above it. That is why humanness cannot be defined exclusively in genetic terms of 3.2 billion nucleotides arranged in a specific order in our cells (Birch 1999).

Charles Darwin's *The Origin of Species* published in 1859 led, years later, to what became known as Social Darwinism. This claimed that struggle for existence and natural selection were the harsh social laws of nature of humans and all species alike, a view which appealed to both Hitler and Mussolini to justify their conquests. It was Thomas Henry Huxley, the great protagonist of Darwin, who challenged this view in 1893 in his famous Romanes lecture in Oxford entitled 'Evolution and ethics'. The law of the jungle is not the law of civilisation. Aggressive, competitive, 'testosterone' values lead to conflict and exploitation, which is the law of the jungle.

Social or cultural evolution is not achieved by a struggle for existence in which the weak go to the wall. Nature may be indifferent to the suffering involved, but humans came of age when they ceased emulating nature. Social ethics concerns values and their justification in terms of what contributes most to the richness of life of all peoples and other creatures who share the Earth with us. A responsible society will be deeply opposed to weapons of mass destruction. A responsible society is judged, not by how it helps the fit to survive but almost the opposite — how it deals with marginalised and oppressed people in the world. This is what ethics is about. There may be no greater sin than indifference to social values. Hate is not the opposite of love, indifference is. So devastating is apathy or indifference that Dante reserved a particularly fierce circle of the Inferno for those guilty of it.

HUMAN BEINGS IN COMMUNITY

Central to an alternative to mechanistic man is the concept of the person characterised by intrinsic value, which we introduced in Chapters 1 and 2. Intrinsic value is the value the individual has quite independent of his or her usefulness to the community. What gives us intrinsic value is our capacity for feeling. Only feeling gives intrinsic value. Until more people widely recognise this principle we can easily become a society that devalues life. The Jewish philosopher Martin Buber championed the cause of the intrinsic value of the individual person. He made the distinction between the 'I/it' relation and the 'I/thou' relation. There are lot of 'its', or objects, in our environment such as rocks and computers. But to treat a human person as an 'it' is to devalue that person.

Intrinsic value is the value a person has for himself or herself in itself. Because I am a feeling subject I am valuable. There are other subjects in the living world that also have feelings which Buber did not pursue. We are not islands of feeling marooned in an unfeeling universe (see Birch 1993b). Intrinsic value, wherever it occurs, should be respected. Each one of us, as a centre of intrinsic value, is vulnerable to being harmed. An ethical principle is to respect and not to harm. Every life is a centre of possible fullness of life with an aim at rich integrity. Happiness is a satisfaction that arises from functioning well, fulfilling our capacities.

Ethical principles arose as a result of the threefold urge of what Whitehead (1929, p 8) called the urge '(i) to live, (ii) to live well, (iii) to live better. In fact the art of life is first to be alive, secondly to be alive in a satisfactory way, and thirdly to acquire an increase in satisfaction.' This quest is the basis for recognising what we call human rights (Chapter 8).

We each discover our intrinsic value in community. In this world there is no such thing as an individual person apart from his or her relationship to other people and to other entities in their environment. This changes the face of history. Jeremy Bentham did not understand this. For him only individuals had meaning the community had none (Bronowski and Mazlish 1960, p 440). Margaret Thatcher was of a similar mind when she claimed there was no such thing as society, there are only individuals and families. It was for Robert Owen to make the profound discovery for his time (early nineteenth century) that man has no nature independent of his 'social nature' (Bronowski and Mazlish 1960, p 471).

We are not thrown into the world willy-nilly like a bunch of marbles nor like lumps of unmoulded clay. We exist with capacities that are influenced both by the internal environment of our genes and the external environment of society and numerous other entities. It is as though we enter the world waiting to become fully human. That, some of us believe, can happen best in a democratic society.

The word democracy comes from the Greek *demos* (people) and *kratia* (authority), hence 'rule by the people'. A democratic society is built on the proposition that each individual is an end as well as a means, and should have equality of opportunity to develop his or her talents, his or her intrinsic value and fulfil his or her life in an open society. It is for each to experience one's own self-worth and the self-worth of others. Each action has two sides: its effects on us, and its effects on others who are our community. Life is caring. This is as relevant to organisations as to nations.

There should be no discrimination of particular groups in the democratic society. There should be freedom of expression and opportunity for persuasion that can change us. The structure of society and its organisations should be such as to bring these values to the top. This will happen to the extent to which the people have a deep belief in human nature that is fulfilling and not false. It does matter what we think about human nature.

The challenge to organisations as well as to states is the extent to which the principles of democracy are practised within them. At least some principles are imperative: the leader who leads will do so, not by coercion but by persuasion. He or she has every right to put before the organisation a vision of what needs to be done, but has no right to force anyone to believe in that vision. If there is a minority of dissenters it is their obligation to abide by the decisions of the majority while still retaining their right to seek to persuade others of their own convictions. At the basis of all this is the belief that organisations and societies should be so structured as to bring out the best in human nature in a learning community.

OUR COMMON HUMANITY

The phrase human nature implies that all humans share a common nature. This was an emphasis of the Enlightenment. Some people, perhaps many, find this a difficult concept today. Are the terrorists who deliberately flew two jets with their load of innocent passengers into the two trade towers in New York on 11 September 2001 the same human beings that the rest of us are? Some want to argue that they are different and lack something such as a humanity or humanness. They may have been motivated in large part by hate, yet they were very courageous, were doing it for a cause they believed in, knowing that their own fate was certain. They would appear not to have counted the cost either to themselves or the passengers in the ill-fated jet airliners. Were they humans like the rest of us? Our answer is that while there is one human nature, there are a hundred versions of it.

Were Hitler and his fanatical Nazi followers of the same human nature as the rest of us? Some people want to call them 'beasts' far removed from human. Others see beyond this slick response. Robert Antelme was a member of the French Resistance. Arrested in June 1944 he was sent to Buchenwald concentration camp, then to Gandersheim in a forced labour *kommando*. Antelme's (1992) book, *The Human Race*, tells of what he and his companions experienced through to his exodus from one camp, under the escort of distraught SS fleeing the approaching Allied armies, to arrival in Dachau and their final liberation. He was near death, but thanks to the intervention of François Mitterand, also then of the Resistance, he got back to France and survived. What is extraordinary about his story is that Antelme never ceased to be aware that the tormentor who sought to deprive his victim of his human quality was himself a human being. His book is written without hatred, a work of boundless compassion. His world and ours goes on awash in wickedness, arrogance, mediocrity and cruelty. Antelme shows us that the business of living may yet be accomplished with goodness, humility and nobility. Perhaps the meek really will inherit the Earth.

Primo Levi was an Italian Jew. On 23 February 1944 he arrived at the Auschwitz concentration camp with 649 others. Only he and two others survived. His first book was an account of his time in the camp before it was liberated by the Russian army. He called it *If This is a Man* because the whole purpose of the Nazi programme of extermination was to deny the humanity of the prisoners. He tells the story of an extraordinary football match at the horror camp between the SS guards and the Jewish *Sonderkommandos*. These were the prisoners forced to work in the crematoria as accomplices to the Nazi crimes. They had to administer the death-showers, push corpses into ovens after extracting gold from their teeth. Eventually their time too came when they suffered the same fate. Levi reports on an impromptu twilight football match between teams from the SS and the *Sonderkommandos*. There was much laughter from the players and onlookers alike. Levi was horrified when he heard of an account of this eerie event. He heard 'Satanic laughter' in this game played at 'the gates of hell'. It seemed to him to be the final triumph of Nazi over Jew. Inga Clendinnen (1998) disagrees with his judgement. She thinks it is possible to read the game differently, as men being allowed to recognise each other, however briefly, as fellow humans. They were discovering their common humanity. This could be a candle lit, however briefly, in one corner of the darkness that was Auschwitz.

Raimond Gaita (1999), as a youth, worked as a ward assistant in a psychiatric hospital. His patients were judged to be incurable, and appeared to have lost everything which gave meaning to life. One day a nun came to the ward and spoke to the patients. Everything about her contrasted with the behaviour of the clinicians. Even though they professed themselves equal to those whom they wanted to help, she revealed in her behaviour that in their hearts they did not believe this. The thought would occur to many people that it would be better that these patients had never been born. The nun had a different view of human life. 'Her behaviour' says Gaita (p 20), 'was striking, not for the virtues it expressed, or even the good it achieved, but for its power to reveal the full humanity of those whose affliction had made their humanity invisible ... the nun's love was unconditional'.

We should ask ourselves: Do we believe in our heart of hearts that the terrorists of September 11th 2001, the SS in Nazi Germany and the patients declared insane in a mental hospital share our common humanity? Or do we think there is not one human nature that everyone who belong to the species *Homo sapiens* shares, but that there are many human natures? This is the deep mystery of human nature: to account for the good and the bad in all of us. There are not just good people and bad people. There are people who are both good and bad — like all of us. Racism is a denial of a common humanity that all share. So is anti-Semitism, sexism and homophobia. These terms refer to categories of what some people want to call bad people, unlike themselves.

How do we discover the truth about human nature? There is a paradox here. Discovering our own self-hood at a deep enough level, the more we find our species-hood. This was a discovery made by Ralph Waldo Emerson and the New England Transcendentalists. While you learn what you are and how you are different from others, you learn at the same time what it means to be human like all other humans.

Acceptance of the idea of a common humanity has, as Stuart Rees (2002, p 2) argues, an impressive history:

> Socrates claimed that he was neither a citizen of Athens, nor of Greece but of the world. Arguments about global citizenship have been influenced by a vision of inclusiveness: the fruits of the world to be shared, no-one to be excluded ... Some belief in the indivisibility of peoples also carries the assumption that everyone feels pain, loss and grief, and everyone benefits from expressions of love, joy and compassion, those virtues experienced by people whatever their ethnic background, their culture or religion.

What we have in common should be recognised as more important than our differences.

The recognition of our common humanity has two consequences. There is the possibility of virtue, even greatness, in every one of us. There is also the possibility of evil in everyone of us. The subtitle of Hannah Arendt's book *Eichmann in Jerusalem* is *A report on the banality of evil*. Trying to find what she meant by her subtitle led to much controversy. One reading is that we are all Eichmanns; that there is an Eichmann, or at least elements of an Eichmann, in each one of us waiting only for the appropriate circumstances for its realisation (Bergen 1998).

The word 'banality' in Arndt's book suggests that evil hides under a cloak of ordinariness. Eichmann had a seemingly happy family, he did not appear to be a sadist, for much of his life he believed himself to be living by Kant's categorical moral imperative, yet his activities in the Third Reich were responsible for sending millions of fellow Germans and others to death camps. For him it was a logistical operation. And he was very efficient at it, even during wartime when transport and other facilities were so stretched. There was a job to be done and he did it. There is an Eichmann in every one of us. There is a weak being in every strong one. There is cowardice in every courage, there is unbelief in every faith, and hostility in every love. There is a non-Christian in every Christian, a Christian in every non-Christian. There is ambiguity in every life (Tillich 1963, p 127).

It may be only after the events that we truly become aware of our failures in not living up to our supposed belief in our common humanity. Pastor Martin Niemoller was arrested by the Gestapo in 1937 for opposing the Nazification of the Protestant churches. He spent the next seven years in concentration camps first a Sachsenhausen and then at Dachau until liberated by Allied troops. After the war he wrote:

First they came for the Jews and I did not speak out
because I was not a Jew; then they came for the
Communists and I did not speak out because I was not
a Communist; then they came for the unionists and I
did no speak out because I was not a union man. Then
they came for me — and there was no one left to speak
out for me (in Taylor and Shaw 1987, p 238).

CULTURAL CHANGE

Biologists talk about cultural evolution, by which they mean changes in society — be it of chimpanzee or human— brought about by learning. Much of
evolution is genetic and conforms to the laws that Darwin and his followers
discovered. But the differences between cave man of a hundred thousand
years ago and us is not genetic, but mainly cultural. These differences are
learned differences. They gave rise to the agricultural revolution, the industrial evolution and the information revolution. So today changes in our society are a consequence of learning and not genetics. What has to be learned is
passed down through our families, schools and universities.

The basic presumption of this chapter is that what we think about human
nature and how we act on that belief determines what sort of society or what
sort of corporation in that society we shall create. It is then a matter of individuals, corporations and governments becoming advocates of a new way of
doing things. Individuals may initiate change, as was the case with Mahatma
Gandhi's programme of non-violence and non-participation for India's independence. It started with grass-root individuals, hence his inspirational exhor-
tation, 'Be the change you wish to see in the world'. Sweeping cultural
change occurs when all sectors of society work together, though its origins
are often in grass-roots movements: the Ghandi-led movement for India's
independence, Poland's solidarity movement, South Africa's struggle against
apartheid, and the civil rights movement in the United States.

Change is more likely if all sectors of society are involved. During World
War II, the United States converted to a war economy virtually overnight by
tapping the energy of citizens, corporations and government. People recycled
metal, rubber and other materials. Automobile plants shifted from the production of cars to tanks and aeroplanes. Households sowed millions of Victory
Gardens and women replaced men in factories. This was a major cultural
change in American society, without which the war may not have been won.

Making a similar effort to build corporations and society serve humane goals
will require that individuals, corporations and governments become conscious
agents of change, building on each other's strengths. Public participation is often

catalysed by hitting on just the right word or phase that spells the difference between old and new: the 'ecologically sustainable society' or simply 'sustainability', 'zero population growth', 'biodiversity hotspots' or simply 'biodiversity'. These have all been powerful points of leverage in modern times. Or it could be a sentence in a great speech: Roosevelt's 'The only thing we have to fear is fear itself'; or Ben Chifley's 'the light on the hill' speech; or Martin Luther King's 'I have a dream' speech with its climactic statement 'Free at last'; or Churchill's 'I have nothing to offer but blood, toil, tears and sweat … Let us therefore brace ourselves to our duty and so bear ourselves that if the British Commonwealth and Empire last for a thousand years men will still say, this was their finest hour'.

Every step forward is confronted with constraints: fragmentation limits the influence of the civil society; the pursuit of profits reduces options for corporations; and competing interests tie the hands of governments. But collectively the three sectors — individuals, corporations and governments — are capable of wholesale cultural change that could create a civilisation worthy of being called human. It would be a just, egalitarian, participatory and ecologically sustainable society, which is virtually the title of a worldwide programme of the World Council of Churches begun in 1976 (Abrecht 1978).

Yet who does not feel the irresistible forces which drive individuals and corporations and nations into conflicts, internal and external; into arrogance and stupidity; into revolt and despair; into inhumanity and self-destruction? Each is involved in these conflicts and are driven to a greater or lesser degree by these negative forces that rule the world along with forces for good. While creativity is responsible for the conquest of nature, the organisation of societies and states, the execution of justice and the triumph of knowledge, it works alongside the terror of destructiveness in our personal lives and in the lives of nations. Little wonder that some are driven to cynicism and despair.

Life, personal and historical, is a creative and a destructive process in which freedom and destiny, chance and necessity, responsibility and tragedy are all mixed with each other in everything and in every moment. Tensions, ambiguities and conflicts make life what it is. Love is corrupted by greed. Greed feeds on power. Power corrupts and absolute power corrupts absolutely. There is a drive in everyone who has a human face to draw as much as possible of the world into oneself. It is turning towards ourselves and making ourselves the centre of our world and of ourselves. This realisation drives us to the necessity of a courage, which can accept life without being conquered by it. It is a courage, which enables people to accept the double-faced rulers of life, their fascination and their anxiety, their threat and their promise, even in their darkest hour.

As an example, Elsa Brandstrom, the daughter of a Swedish ambassador to Russia during World War I, became known as the Angel of Siberia. At the beginning of the war when she was 24 years old, she looked out the window of the Swedish Embassy in St Petersburg and saw German prisoners of war being driven through the streets on their way to Siberia. From that moment she could no longer endure the splendour of diplomatic life. She became a nurse and began visiting prison camps. There she saw unspeakable horrors and began, almost alone, the fight against cruelty — and she prevailed. She had to fight against the resistance and suspicion of the authorities — and she prevailed. She had to fight against the lawlessness of the prison guards — and she prevailed. She had to fight against cold, hunger, dirt and illness — and she prevailed. Whenever she appeared it was said that despair was conquered. She visited the hungry and gave them food. She saw the thirsty and gave them drink. She welcomed the stranger, clothed the naked and strengthened the sick. She fell ill and was imprisoned. After the war she initiated a great work for orphans of German and Russian prisoners of war. With the coming of the Nazis she, with her husband, were forced to leave Germany and go to the United States. There she became a helper of European refugees. Millions came to love her. On her deathbed she received a delegate from the king and people of Sweden representing people all over Europe assuring her that she would never be forgotten by those to whom she had given back the meaning of their lives. Her love was overwhelmingly manifest in the darkest hour of many thousands of people. Such is human nature (Tillich 1955, p 27).

The theme of this chapter is that truly civil individuals, corporations and societies are built on the following eight propositions about human nature:

- We are born with a capability for good and for evil. What we become depends initially upon our environment from the moment we are conceived.

- What we become depends not only on our environment but also on how we respond, for we have a degree of choice and are not solely determined by our genes and our environment. We can alter the determinants. In the end we are all moral agents.

- While much of what we are is determined by our genes and our environment we are not primarily mechanisms or robots. To be treated as such is to deny our humanity.

- We are social beings and are what we are by virtue of our relationships in a broader society.

- We learn through our culture to change, to trust or distrust, to be aggressive or non-aggressive, or to love or to hate. Our human nature can be directed to good or to evil ends.

- There is one common humanity to which all human beings belong. Our objective is the fulfilment of human flourishing. Only this is an adequate guide to public policy. We have to figure out what allows human beings to prosper and what policies to pursue. But the standard mix of utilitarianism and scientific materialism is not an adequate basis for guiding public policies.

- Every step in change has its constraints: fragmentation limits the influence of civil society; the pursuit of profits reduces options of corporations; competing interests tie the hands of governments.

- Ambiguity and conflict make life what it is: love is corrupted by greed, greed feeds on power, power feeds on further power. It is courage which enables us to accept the double-faced rules of life with their promise and their threat.

How then do organisations in a capitalistic environment learn to change their values to improve the quality of work and life? We begin that discussion in the next chapter, on the culture of organisations. It is our concept of what human nature is that determines the culture of corporations.

10

CULTURE

> The conduct of human affairs is entirely dominated by
> our recognition of foresight determining purpose, and
> purpose issuing in conduct ... so we speak of the policy
> of a statesman or of a business corporation.
>
> A N Whitehead, *The Function of Reason*, 1929, p 13.

A MORAL DILEMMA

The culture and policy of organisations has to do with moral values. In his book *How Are We to Live?* Peter Singer (1993) relates the following story. Two and a half thousand years ago, at the dawn of Western philosophical thinking, Socrates had the reputation of being the wisest man in the civilised world. An affluent youth, Glaucon, asked him the question: 'How are we to live?' This question is one of the primary concerns of Plato's *Republic*, a foundational work in the history of Western philosophy.

According to Plato, Glaucon tells the story of a shepherd who served the reigning King of Lydia. The shepherd was out with his flock one day when a storm broke and a chasm opened up in the ground. He went down into the chasm and found a golden ring, which he put on his finger. A few days later, while sitting and chatting with his fellow shepherds, he happened to fiddle with the ring and to his amazement discovered that when he turned the ring a certain way he became invisible to his companions. After he had made this discovery, he arranged to be the messenger, sent by the shepherds to the king to report on the state of the flocks. Arriving at the palace, he coveted the wealth, position and power that people had, and promptly used the ring to his own advantage. He seduced the queen, plotted with her against the king, killed him and so obtained the crown.

This story of Glaucon is used by Plato to portray a common view of human nature, the moral being that any one who possessed such a ring would abandon all ethical standards and would be quite rational to do so:

> no one, it is thought, would be of such adamantine nature as to abide in justice and have the strength to abstain from theft, and to keep his hands from the goods of others, when it would be in his power to steal anything he wished from the market place with impunity, to enter any house and have intercourse with whom he would, to kill or to set free whomsoever he pleased; in short, to walk among men as a god ... if any man who possessed this power we have described should nevertheless refuse to do anything unjust or to rob his fellows, all who knew of his conduct would think him the most miserable and foolish of men, though they would praise him to each other's faces, their fear of suffering injustice extorting that deceit from them (Plato, *The Republic*, book 2, p 360, as quoted by Singer 1993).

Glaucon challenged Socrates to show that this common opinion of human nature is mistaken. Furthermore, he argued that surely there are reasons for doing what is right rather than out of fear of being caught. Show us, he says, a wise ethical person who, unlike the shepherd who found the ring, would continue to do what is right.

Moving 2500 years ahead into the twenty-first century, is there such a leader in corporate organisations who would be wise and ethical, and continue to do what is right if the ring possessed the magic of unlimited wealth and power?

Karl Marx, according to Singer (1993), would have answered Glaucon's question by saying there is no satisfactory answer unless we change society. 'As long as we are living in a society in which economic production is geared to satisfy the interests of a particular class, there is bound to be a conflict between individual self-interest and the interests of society as a whole' (p 12). The shepherd then would be acting quite rationally if he used his magic ring to take what he pleased and kill anyone he chose.

It was Socrates' belief, of which Plato informs us, that no man would willingly choose falsehood over truth or evil over good. It is ignorance that makes a bad choice possible. The whole of Jeffersonian democratic theory is based on this conviction that full knowledge leads to right action (see Chapter 9). Little wonder that Jefferson, in his enthusiasm for the power of learning, founded two universities, one the University of Virginia and another one, west beyond the mountains in Kentucky, the University of Transylvania.

Fyodor Dostoyevsky, in his semi-autobiographical novel *Notes from the Underground* (1972), expresses a similar view of human evil as Socrates, that people act against their own best selves, because they do not know their best selves.

> Isn't there something that is dearer to almost every man than his own very best interests, some good which is more important and higher than any other good, and for the sake of which man is prepared, if necessary, to go against all laws — that is against reason, honour, peace and quiet, prosperity — only to attain that primary, best good which is dearer to him than all else? (p 11)

And he answers his own question: 'that something, the factor that has been omitted from all the calculations ... is the perverse insistence of human beings on their right, if they choose, to act against all their own best interests' (pp 10-11). They do this in ignorance of what is their own best interest.

According to Plato, Socrates after a lengthy dialogue, convinced the young Glaucon and his companions present, that whatever profit injustice might bring, only those who act rightly are really and truly happy. Citizens of a new society based on common ownership would find their own happiness in working for the good of all. But given the chance of obtaining a golden ring, can we truly live an ethical life and do what is right? Is it possible to resist greed and monetary gain in order to live a life, which is meaningful and non-exploitative? Plato firmly believed that it is possible. His faith was that if you really knew the good, you would do it.

CORPORATIONS AND QUALITY OF LIFE

Organisations today have that chance of developing culture that is concerned with doing what is right. Indeed, CEOs and senior executives have the opportunity to create a new future and to make their mark on the corporate and global scene. They are in a unique position to shape the foundations of the future, to be an example, lead by example, and alter the thinking and beliefs of Western society which at the present time are focused on individualism and selfishness.

This brings us to the question regarding quality of working life. Why should today's corporations be concerned with the quality of working life of their employees?

Two questions are asked by corporations today regarding quality of life. The first focuses on economics and the second questions the value of such a focus:

- How does focusing on or improving the quality of life increase profits for the company and shareholder wealth?

- If employees are willing to sacrifice their quality of life and work (thereby saying nothing in protest), then why not take advantage of this in the interests of the company?

The fundamental belief behind the premise of such questions is based on economics. Anyone who promises a solution, a key, a process, an answer, a model, a strategy which increases profits and the share price of a company's stock is put on a corporate pedestal or given vast incentives to come on board globally and implement such promises. For example, 're-engineering' in the early 1990s was one such model which was embraced globally by corporations as a solution involving shedding thousands of jobs and increasing profits. To this day re-engineering, in its many emergent forms, continues to be practised. However, it has been widely acknowledged (for instance by Downs 1996) that it has not delivered the desired results corporations were looking for — namely to substantially increase their profit margins, significantly improve their share prices, and enlarge their market share.

To challenge the economic model of a market economy is to challenge the 'gods', since it is a model that has been with us for the past 200 years. We measure a corporation's, or a person's success in the corporation, by the amount of money they make and how much they can spend. This includes beating competitors or buying them out and gaining market share. Success in real terms is rarely questioned. For example, companies are rarely questioned or measured on:

- How well does a company look after the well-being of its employees?

- Is a balanced lifestyle of its employees a company concern?

- Does the company encourage the personal development of character and maturity as part of its training and development?

- What other incentives are there to motivate employees other than monetary ones?

In terms of individuals, success is rarely measured in terms of their:

- depth, maturity and character

- ability to relate and communicate with a wide variety of people

- emotional intelligence and emotional management, rather than emotional outbursts

- being a true team player, rather than looking out for and promoting individual interests.

In both corporate and individual success, financial indicators are perceived to be the one clear measure of success. A study in the United States compared people with two sorts of beliefs. One group believed that happiness lay in the pursuit of external goals — wealth, fame and physical attractiveness. The other believed that happiness lay in the pursuit of intrinsic goals such as personal relationships and contribution to the community. Of the two, the group with the intrinsic goals was happiest, while the extrinsic goal-oriented individuals had shorter, more conflictive and competitive relationships that had a negative impact on their lives and the lives of others. The pursuit of money and fame led to a lower quality of life than to which the goals of community and internal relatedness contributed (Birch 1999, p 47; Eckersley 1999, pp 13–17).

A 1997 Coopers and Lybrand survey (Golan 1997) of over 1200 business students, from 30 of the world's leading universities across 10 countries including Australia, concluded that the overwhelming desire of these participants was to have a balanced lifestyle and a rewarding life outside of work. Long-term employment was low on the list compared with a high desire to invest in personal development and growth, and spend time with family, friends and relatives. Over 70 per cent disagreed with the idea that a career is more important than family and friends.

According to Golan (1997) other surveys by companies such as DuPont, Fel-Pro and William Mercer, found that when the work policy enables employees to have a quality of life outside their work environment they are less stressed, more productive and increase their commitment. Not only does this reduce the turnover of staff and retain corporate memory, it eliminates other hidden costs, rarely discussed or examined — such as recruitment and training, induction of new employees and reduced productivity in the initial months of employment. Such costs are estimated to be between one and a half to two times each new employee's salary. Employees who have work-family conflict are more likely to quit their jobs (43 per cent) compared with those who do not have such conflicts (14 per cent). A lack of balance in the lives of employees was why four out of ten managers had their jobs terminated, voluntarily resigned, or were given poor performance reviews (Golan 1997).

By satisfying employee needs, organisations can be more productive and profitable. By acknowledging the balance between work and home, and the personal and social networks outside work, organisations are more likely to attract and retain good, committed employees. The danger for many organisations that encourage longer working hours and compensation structures that focus primarily on financial rewards, is that they tend to lose their best staff to competing organisations offering higher salaries. So they often have a high turnover of staff rather than a high degree of commitment. By focusing on the soft issues (such as family and quality of life) they gain the upper hand in attracting the right people, with the right skills, at the right price. Job satisfaction, in the long term, is a greater competitive advantage than only offering financial rewards.

Apart from job commitment, there is also growing evidence, some of which is given in Chapters 1 and 2, to indicate that increasing the quality of life of the employee increases the overall productivity and effectiveness of the employee.

THE CULTURE OF ORGANISATIONS

The culture of an organisation is understood to embrace shared meanings and values of people in the organisation. So organisational culture affects attitudes, behaviour and performance of employees. A study by Kabanoff (1992) of 88 organisations in Australia recognised three main types of culture into which the sample could be categorised:

- elitist (22 organisations)
- leader-focused (21 organisations)
- collegiate (15 organisations).

Of the remaining 30 organisations, 14 had some collegiate qualities, while 16 did not fit any category. Elitist cultures are the least integrated and most differentiated amongst the types Kabanoff identified. In such a culture, power, resources and rewards are focused at the apex of the organisation. In this type of culture, economic performance is valued more highly than interpersonal relationships. The values that this culture reinforces strongly include reward, authority, equity and performance. This is a mechanistic culture with little time for quality of life. Examples of elitist culture are found in the banking, insurance and transport sectors.

The leader-focused culture has an unequal distribution of power, rewards and resources. Such a culture 'seeks to build integration though creating a system of leadership and teamwork throughout the organisation by having a loyal cadre of leaders below the apex who are delegated some of the elite's power' (Kabanoff 1992, p 21). A leader-focused culture strongly espouses values which include authority, leadership, affiliation, commitment, teamwork, equity, and reward for performance. It depends heavily on an omniscient leader who knows who to reward and how to reward loyal followers. It is a culture often lacking a commitment to quality of life. Examples of the leader-focused culture are found in industrial and retail sectors.

Collegiate cultures are concerned with everyone having a voice in the decision-making processes, especially those who might be affected by a change. In contrast to large corporations, where decisions are usually made at the senior levels of the organisation and where those affected by such decisions are rarely consulted, collegiate cultures base their model on well-evolved democratic principles. Little is known of such cultures, though their structure suggests that they allow much room for considerations of the quality of life of employees.

Collegiate culture is the rarest type among Australian corporations, and more likely to be found in academic institutions and some government departments. Other examples are non-profit non-government volunteer organisations whose mission is looking after the needs of the community. The rewards in such a culture are the satisfaction of doing good (and, in the case of religious orders of nuns and brothers, possible rewards in a hereafter).

CHANGING THE CULTURE

In large organisations, features such as values, norms and accepted codes of behaviour are generally deeply entrenched. Their culture tends to be self-perpetuating and protective. Therefore innovative ideas are slow to be implemented and attitudes are difficult to shift. According to Peters and Waterman (1982), the most successful companies at the time of their study had very strong cultures traditionally difficult to transform in the short term. Yet they may be in deep need of change. Part of the difficulty of transformation are the intangible hurdles — such as power, politics, turf-protection — competing within internal divisions of the company rather than competing with the external competition. Higher authority is far removed from the front line, middle managers are weak, supervision and communication are weak. The size of these organisations makes it difficult to change swiftly and easily. They suffer from cultural immobility, a besetting defect of many organisations.

In addition to these intangible hurdles, downsizing strategies have severely reduced resources such as money, equipment and technology. It has limited support for conducting research, testing and follow-up. Teams are often reduced so there are fewer members to contribute knowledge, experience and creativity. Hence, what is generally left over is a deflated and unenthusiastic group of individuals who constantly worry about the security of their jobs. In such companies, success is generally measured by cost-cutting measures and profit margins with little focus on anything else such as quality of life.

Old and powerful bureaucracies perceive change as turmoil rather than liberation. Adhering to the stability of the present systems and rules is often preferred to the emancipation that change could bring. Change threatens power bases and control mechanisms. Thus many corporate cultures are generally driven by power and authority, with an emphasis on reward for performance.

With the emphasis on profits, power and internal competition, there is little room for organisations to think about issues such as quality of life. The internal cultures of organisations are such that they destroy aspects that could enhance quality of life. They do this subtly by:

- increasing the guilt of those who work more reasonable hours compared to their colleagues, thus promoting long hours of work

- implying that those who do less hours are not producing high quality work or questioning their loyalty and commitment

- rewarding quantity (lengthy, verbose material) rather than quality (succinct, clear, transparent material)

- promoting poor managers of people to higher levels of authority

- tolerating poor work practices such as 'turf protection' and scapegoat mentality

- encouraging secrecy instead of transparency by sanctioning poor communication practices

- tolerating and allowing poor behaviour and conduct to flourish

- focusing on problems, blame and punishment rather than finding solutions

- downsizing and rationalising divisions, departments and branches, and thus being totally unaware of the increasing the workload of those who survived the 'axe'

- ignoring the 'corporate dead wood' that is often hidden in the organisation, and protecting it from the downsizing axe

- increasing the workload without taking into account the increased stress levels of staff

- encouraging cultures that punish creativity and risk

- showing or giving little support from the senior echelons in the organisation

- promoting bureaucracy and red tape rather than cutting through it

- rewarding those at the apex of the organisation rather than distributing the profits more equably throughout the organisation

- putting profits and shareholders before employees who create the profits.

This list is by no means exhaustive, yet it serves to highlight the plight of employees in large organisations. How can such cultures change? Is it the responsibility of the leadership of the organisation? Or do we leave such change to time in the hope that some day such cultures will be transformed? Too many CEOs see cultural change as a project they can delegate to their 'human resources' director or a consulting firm. On the contrary, there must be an involvement that includes the CEO and a range of leaders and managers below. The organisation with all its human potential must be committed.

When Louis Gerstner was recruited in the early 1990s to rescue IBM, he emphasised the personal dimension of change when he declared: 'Changing a culture is not something you do by writing memos. You've got to appeal to people's emotions. They've got to buy in with their hearts and their beliefs but not just their minds' (Gardner 1997, p 144). Armed with his new story of identity he toured the country and told his employees 'I'm one of us now'. Some of the processes of the 'how' of change are discussed in Chapter 11.

ORGANISATIONAL CHANGE THAT FAILED TO DEAL WITH QUALITY OF LIFE

The history of Apple Computer illustrates the case of what happens when a firm, the success of which largely derived from its employees, later failed to put people first. Founded in 1976 in a garage, Apple became a leader in the computer field. The company built a cult-like commitment among its employees. Apple was more than a company; it was an innovator of user-friendly personal computers. When it took actions that resulted in the loss of that dedicated work force, its business leadership was irreparably harmed. A succession of downsizing initiatives, because of substantial competitive stress and loss of profits, led to a remaining work force that had its spirit broken. This led to a further downward spiral (Pfeffer 1998, pp 25-28).

A study by Lee (1995) analysed the unsuccessful attempt at organisational change of the electric power division of the company AlliedSignal. This aerospace company embarked on change that primarily focused on the non-organic elements of the change process (for example structures and formal strategies), and failed to incorporate elements such as people, culture, politics and communication. Lee concludes that the reason for the failure to change was the lack of real support from senior management and the stress on non-organic factors.

The following examples come from a large financial institution in Australia studied by Paul (2000). He gave this corporation the pseudonym ALFINA. It had undergone major organisational restructure, which changed its finances from being in the red to being in the black, taking it from near death to being a winner on a number of fronts. The changes included large-scale downsizing, selling most of its overseas networks and interests, selling its vast holdings in gold, and the sale of substantial assets and other enterprises. The examples below from ALFINA all show a negative approach to quality of life. It may well be asked how typical these examples are of ALFINA? Of the total of 150 staff interviewed at all levels of the organisation by Paul (2000), only one was positive about the quality of life in the company, which indicates the critical relationship between culture and quality of life in large-scale organisational change.

The first example involves Pam negotiating a job contract as an ALFINA executive (Neill 1997). She thought she had heard all the right noises before she left a senior management role in the United States. She communicated to the senior management that she was keen to work for an organisation that consulted all levels of its organisation, rather than one which handed down information from the top and where the boss was seen as the infallible, almighty leader with a seven-figure pay package. She felt strongly that man-aging people was as important as the bottom line. She also made it very clear that she would not work 12-hour days because she had a young daughter and a life outside work. ALFINA's management fully supported and nodded vig-orously to such a perspective.

Eight months later Pam left, causing front-page headlines in the news, just as ALFINA was making a name in the business world as a corporation which proactively sought and promoted women. Six of its most senior women left within six months, with one taking legal action.

The frustration and disappointment of Pam's encounter with ALFINA's 'command and control' management style, its single-minded focus on 'just stick to the figures', and its passive, apathetic resistance to creativity and inno-vation was clearly evident. The solemn promise of a family-friendly week was quickly transmuted into 12-hour days. 'Once you are an integral part of that kind of culture, it is difficult to work less hours as you are the odd one out, if you don't conform to the same working hours.' If you do work less hours, you are seen to be slack, uncommitted and don't have enough work to do, or worse, you are doing a second-rate job, hence you are able to leave earlier. So any work you delegate, people think you should do it yourself, since you have so much time on your hands.

While ALFINA's managers think they do a great job and receive a glow-ing commendation from their bosses, the same managers would be devastat-ed to learn how the staff rated their managerial and people skills. If executive share options focused not just on the bottom line, but also on their people management skills and the way they deal with the human aspects of change, there would quickly be a very different style of management and overall organisational perspective. Senior management is oblivious and blind to the kind of management practices in place. So long as they are obeyed and the profits show an improvement, they are happy, as they still get their bonuses and salary.

Pam found that the culture in Australia, compared with working for a similar US corporation, was not people-focused at all, either from a staff or customer point of view. It was quite archaic. She judged the culture to be dominated by ambitious men who want the top jobs, and by a certain type of woman who advocates this kind of ambitious, egotistic management culture in order to get ahead. Managers at all levels know that they only get rewarded if they make money; the rest does not matter — and that is reinforced in both overt and subtle ways over and over again. The internal culture has not changed, despite the rhetoric and carefully crafted stories presented to the media (Neill 1997).

The second example is Tom, a senior manager at ALFINA. He said in an interview:

> Stress is the greatest enemy of the staff around here. Senior managers do not get time to look at stress, yet alone address it. And the rest of us learn to hide it or, if you take that lady over there, she is about to quit because of the level of stress. There are many like her, but the real reasons for leaving are never communicated to senior management. They are not seriously interested, or even concerned. As long as the job of the person leaving is covered and there is minimal interruption to the productivity, no one bothers. That's just the nature of work. I find it difficult to motivate my staff when I know that no one cares upstairs. Why should I encourage them to stay? And what is the point of motivating them to give their best, when there is not even a simple 'thank you' from the chief? (Paul 2000).

Lastly comes Bill, a senior manager at ALFINA. In an interview he said:

> Staff and managers at [ALFINA] often work longer than 10-hour days. Staff tend to work over 10 hours and managers are often working longer than 12 hours; most work 14 hours. I don't want to work more than 8 hours and I don't mind a lower wage. The sad part is the high unemployment rate in Australia, and we want

to increase the workload of those who are already screaming for help because of the hours they work. And yet we [management] refuse to give others a chance to work. If only we could reduce our working week to 40 hours, then there would be enough vacancies to help the morale in the community and increase our own levels of productivity. Often my staff tell me they don't want to come to work because they feel like a rat on a treadmill, and they are no better than factory workers on an assembly line (Paul 2000).

TABLE 10.1 Division of the day by staff at ALFINA

Activity	Hours	
	Staff	Managers
Work	>10	>12
Sleep	< 8	< 8
Commuting to work		
(average 1 hour or more train/bus journey)	> 1	> 1
Time left	5	3

SOURCE Paul, 'Communicating complex change', 2000.

The number of hours of work shown in Table 10.1 leaves barely time to eat an unhurried lunch, prepare dinner, eat or leisurely spend time with the family, shop, domestic chores and odd jobs. There is even less time for rest and relaxation, let alone anything like reading, watching TV, scanning the net, responding to e-mails and snail mails, going to the movies or an opera, or dining out with family or friends. Most staff are also studying at university in an attempt to get that higher-paid job, which leaves even less personal or family time. So the only thing that they can compromise on is sleep. They can't cut down on work for fear losing their jobs. Tiredness quickly turns to depression and depression turns to acute mental and emotional problems, which may end in suicide or long-term therapy. As (Macken 1997) argues, more time spent at work does not increase productivity.

For the most part the examples above are of organisational change that failed to look after the quality of life of employees. Unfortunately such cases are far too common. In some of the examples it is known that failure to take account of quality of working life during change led to a further decline in profits.

These examples show that organisational culture plays a dominant role in change. It is probably the essential ingredient, which determines the quality, longevity and pervasiveness of change. Culture also plays a key role in how much employees enjoy working in and for the organisation.

WHO ARE THE BEST EMPLOYERS TO WORK FOR?

This question was asked of 165 companies in Australia and 20 000 of their employees (Fox 2002). The question could have been: What companies have the best culture? The brief answer from this study is: Those organisations that manage to combine a healthy bottom line of profits together with a culture that emphasises quality of life of employees. Some 700 organisations were invited to participate in the study; 165 accepted. Data was obtained from three sources. A random selection of employees answered a questionnaire about their satisfaction with 15 key variables of work, along with their intellectual and emotional commitment to the organisation. Second, the organisation was asked to provide data on its 'people practices'. Third the CEOs completed a questionnaire on their 'people practices'.

Those organisations that came out on top excel in leadership, communication, respect and responsibility for their employees. They regard these values of their culture as paramount. The leadership is visible and focuses on employees, giving them a sense of working together. And the leaders know their staff, communicating with them about 30 times a year compared with about 8 times in the less successful companies. Important for the employees also were flexible work practices and their work/life balance. The survey highlights the battle between rhetoric and action. While more and more companies proclaim their credentials as good workplaces where happy employees mean better results, they lag behind in putting a new culture into place. That can take from five to seven years to achieve and requires patient effort. Lots of organisations try for a couple of years but that is not enough. In the successful organisations, 64 per cent of employees were passionate about the achievement of business goals, while only 40 per cent said so in the less successful organisations.

Top of the list, in this study, of best companies in Australia with more than 1000 staff were Flight Centre, followed by Macquarie Bank. Top of the list of best companies with fewer than 1000 staff were Cisco Systems, followed by Nokia Australia. The judges said that each company had a firm eye on the bottom line of profit as well as on the people factor. Well represented in the top 20 organisations is the IT sector. Notable as absent from the top 20 organisations are the big retail banks and legal firms. Only a small number of best companies came from the areas of manufacturing, consulting and accounting.

In another Australian study, the Corporate Research Foundation (2002) assembled a team of 17 of Australia's leading business journalists who nominated companies they believed deserved the title of Best Companies to Work for in Australia. They nominated over 500 companies and invited them to participate in the study. Some declined. They ended up with a total of 29 companies which they assessed worthy, judged on their attitude to employees and as well rates of pay and career prospects. Flight Centre figured again. Otherwise the two lists were quite different, probably indicating the subjective nature of judgments involved. The Corporate Research Foundation, for example, gave high assessments to some companies that hardly promised a balanced lifestyle for their staff. Maybe the main value of such studies is to alert the business world to its responsibilities.

In his search for the elements that constitute a culture that would lead to high peak performance of staff, Katzenbach (2000) identified five sorts of 'pathways':

- mission, values and pride
- process and metrics
- entrepreneurial spirit
- individual achievement
- recognition and celebration.

In each one, a balance was maintained between enterprise performance and employee fulfilment. Corporations that were characterised by peak performance of staff might incorporate more than one pathway, but usually with an emphasis on one in particular.

'Mission, values and pride' is a pathway characterised by value-driven leadership, team opportunities and often a rich history (for instance family companies). Founded in 1902, 3M is an example. It is notable for giving its staff opportunity to exercise initiative. This is, of course, very important in an organisation that depends upon perpetual innovation of products over a huge range. Everyone wants to make a difference and to be proud of the company.

The 'process and metrics' pathway involves making clear measures for business priorities, performance transparency and a broad distribution of leadership. Avon, which makes a wide range of cosmetics, is an example. Quality and cost are basic considerations that involve constant measuring of quality of goods. The staff have pride in their work and a sense of group support.

The 'entrepreneurial spirit' pathway shows high risk and high reward, significant employee ownership, and distributed leadership. Hambrecht and Quist, of Silicon Valley, is an example. This pathway is associated with growth companies in health care, high technology, investment banking and professional services. Staff have a passion for their work in a volatile and often high-pressure environment. A special sort of zest and attitude is needed. The leaders are said to have magnetic qualities that fit the culture.

The 'individual achievement' pathway has highly ambitious individuals predominating in the work force. It offers attractive earnings without significant risk, performance transparency and widespread opportunity. McKinsey, a top management consulting firm, is an example. It fundamentally offers an achievement environment that operates under intense time pressures that favour individual performance. The employee finds recognition of achievement and an atmosphere of freedom of choice that favours personal growth. The firm claims to hire the best and to expect the best.

The 'recognition and celebration' pathway stresses the performance of the average worker and recognises their true value. Marriott is an example. It chooses to be the employer of choice in the industry by seeking to have a peak-performance work force. The employee is celebrated, as is his/her relationship with guests. Each employee becomes familiar with Marriott's ten rules for success, which stress that every moment and experience is something to celebrate. Be happy and your guest will be happy.

Katzenbach uses the term 'balanced pathway' in this study to mean whatever combination of pathways makes sense to the organisation. Most organisations find that more than one is needed. Whatever combination is chosen the role of magnetic leaders is paramount.

LEADERSHIP

Any discussion of culture involves leadership, since leaders (which include directors of boards, CEOs and senior executives) all have a say in how corporate cultures evolve. Jan Carlzon (CEO of Scandinavian Airlines), Jack Welch (CEO of General Electric), Ricardo Semler (CEO of Semco) are examples of individuals, whom we have discussed, who shaped and changed their company cultures.

Australia has its particular brand of leaders. In its early agricultural phase Massey Harris led the way in innovation of agricultural machinery such as the wheat harvester. The old agricultural machinery of Europe did not fit the new continent. The wheat harvester and the stump-jump plough did. The application in Australia of modern science to agriculture, secondary industry and now the information age has been dependent upon the leadership of great heads of the CSIRO from its early days such as David Rivett, A E V Richardson, and Ian Clunies Ross. There have been notable entrepreneurs in commercial enterprises in Australia, such as Sidney Myer of the Myer Emporium, Dick Dusseldorp of Lend Lease, Maurice Mawby and Rod Carnegie of Rio Tinto, and Frank Lowy of Westfield.

Richard Walsh (2002) interviewed 'nine of the most successful Australian CEOs of recent times'. They were successful in the sense of presiding over highly profitable, large enterprises. There was little unanimity in their responses, except for an emphasis on passionate enthusiasm, and some concern for the quality and well-being of their employees and the satisfaction of their customers. So it could be said that in terms of the triple bottom line, profits and growth came first, social responsibility a somewhat muted second and environmental concerns a neglected third.

Abraham Lincoln is said to have had a plaque on his desk which read 'The buck stops here', meaning that he was willing to take on the challenge, the responsibility or the blame of anything in his administration that went against the ideals of his leadership. (The term is derived from poker where 'passing the buck' means passing without bidding, that is evading one's responsibility.) A leader can't responsibly pass the buck.

Now for the bad news. All is not well on the leadership front. In addition to ethical failure (as discussed in Chapter 9) there is lack of confidence in leaders. A survey of 6000 executives in 14 countries in 2001 found that the level of confidence in leaders had declined since a similar survey in 1999. The survey concluded that most executives don't have much confidence in the ability of their bosses to successfully manage the business. Australian executives need mentors, says Bernice Dover of the company Development Dimensions International. She added that 'if leaders do not convey a clear image of the organization's goals in a compelling way, employees are likely to lose faith in the organization' (Dover 2002, p 7).

Leadership attracts people and inspires them to generate incredible effort for a common cause — willingness to go beyond the call of duty for the achievement of a bigger goal and fulfilment of a vision. Leaders, in this sense, are few in number in most organisations. Instead, leadership positions are filled by managers who merely fulfil their job description. So long as organisations are content to maintain the status quo, managers are sufficient to run the company. If however, organisations are to keep pace with and be ahead of their competitors, then they must be prepared to undergo real change, with decisive, strong, example-led leadership at the helm and also in the boiler-room.

The psychologist Abraham Maslow considered the following (abbreviated) list as unique characteristics of distinguished leaders:

• They accept other people as they are and accept their own limitations.

• They are problem-centred rather than self-centred.

• Their appreciation of people and things is fresh rather than stereotyped.

- Their values and attitudes are democratic.

- They do not confuse means with ends.

- They have a great fund of creativeness.

- They resist conformity to the prevailing culture.

- They transcend the environment rather than just coping with it.

There is nothing Machiavellian about this list. It may even appear to be starry eyed. Yet it is to a considerable extent confirmed by Jim Collins' (2001) study of 28 US companies to find out what sort of leadership could turn a good company into a great one (even when good and great in this study were measured by profits). Collins came to the conclusion that leaders who turned good into great have a paradoxical blend of humility and professional will. 'Professional will' here means a stoic resolve, almost fanatical commitment to make the company great. They are, he said, more like Lincoln and Socrates than Patton or Caesar. A parallel study was made (Hubbard et al 2002) of what were deemed the top 11 organisations in Australia. Nine elements were shared by these leading companies, including leadership of a team rather than a single leader, rapid adaptation, and clear strategy that also recognised fuzzy areas that had to be explored.

Leaders are responsible for the strategic direction or big picture of the company, since they make the crucial decisions regarding communication, corporate strategy, culture, values, vision, human resources systems, techno-logical innovation and organisational structure. They bring these into align-ment. As a result of making such decisions, leaders can bring about change, which embraces quality of life in the organisation.

Thus leaders are often called upon to present a vision, to lead the way, to go where no-one has gone before in terms of radical change. They don't let the world squeeze them into its mould. Conformity can be acceptance of corruption. The alternative to conformity involves a three-fold response; to exercise judgment, to offer resistance when necessary and to effect a transfor-mation. The non-conformist must be prepared to risk opposition, even ostracism, as well as the possibility of being wrong.

But a leader is not going to risk this if he or she fears the consequences of making a mistake. When James Strong was appointed CEO of Qantas from outside he said it was, for Qantas, like a body transplant. Every part of the body tries to resist the new organ. But by patience, planning and convincing people, he won through (Walsh 2000, p 80). Albert Einstein said 'Great spir-its have always encountered violent opposition from mediocre minds'. The mediocre mind is often unwilling to take risks. He who risks and fails can be forgiven; he who never risks and never fails is a failure in his whole person.

The articulation of a clear and valid vision can reduce uncertainty and can energise and motivate change, encouraging stakeholders to resolve conflicts, increase co-operation and actively support the change process. Unless change is fully supported and committed to by the senior levels of the organisation, the effort to change is marginal in its achievements (Cummings et al 1991).

THE RELATIONSHIP BETWEEN ORGANISATIONAL CULTURE AND QUALITY OF WORKING LIFE IN AUSTRALIA

The issue of quality of working life in Australia has not yet reached breaking point because people are willing to work the long hours with little reward. They will continue to be so used. Generally, there is little time to enjoy any serious time with family, recreation and a balanced lifestyle. The question is: Are all these people giving their best to their teams and to the company?

At 'ALFINA' and similar large organisations, working longer hours is interpreted by management that one is dedicated to the job and is conscientious. Long hours are expected as other viable alternatives cost more. Refusal to complete the job outside of working hours may result in being dismissed.

Companies such as ALFINA are communicating that quality of life is not an important factor when embarking on large-scale change. Nor is quality of life for the most part a considered factor after change initiatives have been implemented. However, focusing on improving the quality of life of employees could improve productivity and, therefore, increase profits. A deep, pervasive change could contribute to a happier work force. It must profoundly affect the foundation of the organisation's beliefs, values, expectations, norms, aspects of organisational life which are taken for granted, and those things which contribute to the culture and everyday life of the organisation and permeate the innermost qualities of the human mind and spirit (Kilmann 1991). Sadly however, the critical elements of the organisation which affect change — such as people, culture, communication and relationships — are often less visible and overlooked. They exist in abstractions, rather than as concrete entities which can be manipulated or controlled.

Although corporations, senior executives and academics can see that the rhetoric of 'change' per se involves an aggregate of broad inter-related facets (such as profits, processes, products, stakeholders, shareholders, communities) coupled with a host of internal organisational concerns (such as power, politics, culture and quality of life), there is little to suggest that the change has moved convincingly beyond rhetoric. What is discussed in the literature in terms of improving the quality of life, in practical terms, is all but absent. People are looking toward CEOs and senior executives to provide inspiration; instead they are governed by desperation. Fear keeps almost everyone glued to two roles — looking after their jobs, and trying to survive.

The thesis of this chapter, and indeed of this book, is a call to CEOs and senior executives to make a difference; make a difference by being concerned about the quality of life in their organisations, and then doing something radical about it. Set a new frontier in leadership rather than merely managing the corporation. Don't make excuses, instead find the courage to create the change. Lead by example rather than merely parroting the rhetoric. The higher evolution of our communities lies in the domain of corporations, since most of the waking hours of individuals are spent in that domain.

On the flip-side, we give evidence how companies have greatly benefited from employees who are energised by their work rather than emotionally exhausted, being creative rather than being mediocre, working at their peak potential rather contributing in their stress, giving their best efforts instead of conserving their meagre resources. By focusing on enhancing the well-being and the quality of life of their employees, companies stand to reap not just improved performance levels, but greater profit margins and outstanding service levels within the community in which they operate.

In a world lacking outstanding, memorable and noble leaders who are paragons of virtue, honesty and integrity, there is a great opportunity for making a mark on the global corporate landscape. It may only take one company, one CEO, one committed team of senior executives, to focus on making a success of improving the quality of life of their employees before others follow.

If quality of life were a focus, then the outcome could be that employees could not wait to come to work, nor would they want to leave, they would talk about it to others. The media would be swarming like bees to the honeypot to understand this new work ethic, and the evening news would be reporting new levels of innovation, creativity and profits. Universities would be teaching about such a company as a model, books would be written, consulting companies would be changing their tune and promoting such a model, other corporations would come seeking for wisdom. Customers would be happier, indeed they would be leaving the competitors and joining such a company. The share price would rise and shareholders would be satisfied. However, as Dostoyevsky (1972, p 10) argued:

> A man does evil only because he does not know his real interests. If he is enlightened and his eyes are opened to his own best ... interests, man will cease to do evil and at once become virtuous and noble, because when he ... understands what will really benefit him he will see his own best interest in virtue ... it is well known that no man can knowingly act against his own best interests.

'Sleepers, wake!' urged Barry Jones (1990) — thus quoting the title of J S Bach's wake up Cantata No 140. He appealed for a revolution to change our perception of work and our relationships to work in Australia. Where that could lead us is the subject of the next chapter.

11

BRAVE NEW WORLD

Be the change you want to see in the world.
Mahatma Gandhi

It is not a matter of knowing all the answers. Lunatic
asylums are full of people who know all the answers.
It is a matter of asking the right questions and then
working together, no matter how long it takes, to find
and agree on the best answers.
Sir Brian Urquhart, 'Between sovereignty and globalisation',
2000, p 14.

The business world is myopic and repressive when it recognises only one of the two human values; intrinsic value and instrumental value.
(The intrinsic value of individuals is value which is quite independent of the
individual's usefulness. Instrumental value is the usefulness of the individual
to others, including the organisations they serve.) The organisation that
recognises both sorts of value is more generous, more compassionate and
more humane. When conditions in the workplace are unfavourable — such
as excessive hours of work, associated stress, a sense of insecurity, or lack of
concern for time for family and recreation and other creative pursuits —
there is a downside to quality of life in both sorts of value. But an organisation's efficiency and profitability increase when the quality of life of its
employees improves. It does matter when morale and expectation are low,
even when profits are the bottom line.

PROFITS, MEANING AND EFFICIENCY

In the same direction as ours, but with a somewhat different approach,
Lynda Gratton (2000) reports on analyses of a variety of British organisa-

tions to show how profits and efficiency depend on what she calls 'meaning' and 'soul'. 'Meaning' is the extent to which the explicit goals of the organisation fit with the overall meaning employees have in their lives, including the role of family and other extra-organisation pursuits. It includes the conviction that they are making a personal contribution to something which is meaningful. 'Soul' refers to emotional aspects of life such as commitment, trust, justice, hopes, dreams and compassion. She speaks of the soul of an organisation as measured by the extent to which these values are appreciated and inspired.

Her objective is 'putting people at the heart of corporate purpose', which is the subtitle of her book. She organises a broad strategy that covers a shared vision in the organisation, performance objectives, recruitment, resistance to change, rewards, recognition, giving a voice to employees, opportunities for retraining and renewed inspiration, pride, and multi-disciplinary task-forces to assess the overall programme. Concerning voice, for example, her study of five organisations revealed that only an average of 10 per cent of their employees felt that senior management were well informed about what people at lower levels think and do.

Her concerns are not new. The American transcendentalist poet and essayist Ralph Waldo Emerson said 'A wise employer should educate his workers and should generally seek to raise the level of their good sense, vision and quality of life' (Pfeffer 1998, p 171). This statement, and Emerson's essay 'Compensation', from which it comes, influenced none other than Henry Ford. Ford had introduced the mass production of cars adopting F W Taylor's principles of 'scientific management'. Most famous of his innovations was the moving conveyor belt. Each worker performed only a few movements over and over. However, the boredom for the workers was such that there was much absenteeism and a high turnover.

Not particularly known for his generosity or love of the working man, Henry Ford nevertheless took bold action to keep his factory operating. He reduced working hours and doubled the pay. He instituted the so-called $5 a day wage. This was, in part, because of the economics of the situation, but also because of the influence of Emerson's essay about quality of life. As a result of Ford's changes absenteeism and turnover of staff dropped. The *Wall Street Journal*, at the time, accused Ford of a blunder that would soon return to plague him and the industry he represented. In his 'naïve wish' for social improvement, the journal claimed that Ford had injected 'spiritual principles into a field where they do not belong'. Henry Ford liked to present his $5 a day as a hard-headed matter of efficient engineering with 'no charity in any way involved'. Be that as it may, Ford's action turned out to make brilliant business sense. More people wanted jobs in Ford, and those hired tended to stay longer in the job (Pfeffer 1998, pp 171-72).

ENHANCING THE QUALITY OF LIFE OF EMPLOYEES

Pfeffer (1998, ch 3) lists seven practices that he considers enhances the quality of life of the employee:

- employment security
- selective hiring of new personnel
- self-managed teams
- decentralising of decision-making
- employee co-determination in management
- extensive training
- rewarding good performance.

We can broaden the word 'training' to have a current meaning of learning as in the learning organisation. To this list can be added flexibility of working hours to enable better relations between work and home, and physical conditions in the workplace. The value of these items tends to be underestimated by many organisations. We now consider two of them, which we have not discussed in general terms in previous chapters: the learning organisation, and a sense of place.

THE LEARNING ORGANISATION

'Dare to know!' was the slogan of the Enlightenment (Kant 1783). It could also be the slogan of the learning organisation of today. We have already indicated the importance of an up-to-date learning process, particularly in avoiding accidents and disasters (Chapter 6). We now look at its importance more generally for organisations.

Peter Drucker (2002) compares a successful knowledge-based business to a successful department in a university or to a successful symphony orchestra. What makes a great university department is that it attracts and develops outstanding teachers and scholars, and makes it possible for them to do outstanding teaching and research. A great orchestra is one whose members are enabled to perform at their peak. Successful conductors work closely with individuals and with groups of instrumentalists. It is the people skills of the conductor that makes the difference, as the following quotation emphasises:

> Executives will need to learn what the effective depart-
> mental head in the university or the successful conduc-
> tor of the symphony orchestra have long known: the
> key to greatness is to look for people's potential and
> spend time developing it. To build an outstanding uni-
> versity department requires spending time with the
> promising young post-docs and younger staff until they
> excel in their work. To build a world-class orchestra
> requires rehearsing the same passage in the symphony
> again and again until the first clarinet plays it the way
> the conductor hears it (Drucker 2002, p 49).

Such is the picture of the learning organisation — like a thriving university department or a world-class orchestra. If Peter Drucker had known the
Sydney Opera House, home of the Sydney Symphony Orchestra, he might
well have added the importance also of change of place from one that was initially unfriendly to its operators and clients to one that is its pride (see below).

The modern business requires a well-prepared and adaptable labour
force. It has to become a learning organisation. There are many changing circumstances that lead to the need to learn to adapt. Business needs to adapt as
we move from a relatively closed economy protected by tariff barriers to a
more global economy. Or an overseas company setting up in Australia needs
to learn of new work practices and culture. Or an organisation may have
become set in ways that are inefficient or lacking in concern for the quality
of life in the workplace. Field and Ford (1999) emphasise moving from 'us vs
them' to 'all of us' — all of us, managers and employees working together
rather than adversarial relationships. We explore some of these situations
below. One of the techniques is to replace the traditional role of supervisor
with teams which will question the status quo and make ongoing improvements. Learning time will need to be allocated within working hours so that
there is continual learning in the workplace. The same applies to training skills
for a particular job (Field and Ford 1999).

Learning new ways to enhance quality of life and productiveness in the
workplace is a process of education. But what do we mean by education?
What is called a general education is important not so much for the facts it
teaches as for the frame of adaptable and creative mind it forms. General education is multi-dimensional because what we call intelligence is multi-dimensional. There is factual intelligence, analytic intelligence, numerate
intelligence, emotional intelligence and many others (see Handy 1998,
pp 211-213). Emotional intelligence, for example, involves self-control, self-
motivation and self-awareness. Of the top 50 companies in the United States,
40 are said to be now focussing on the social and emotional needs of their

employees. These companies are driven by profitability not philanthropy. Some employ special mentors or guides (Margo 2002). There is even a Machiavellian intelligence, which is the selective use of cunning, co-operation and deceit to manipulate others (Ehrlich 2000). It seems to exist in some animals and no doubt in some humans. It is as well to know that it exists and how it operates so that we can better understand and deal with it: Machiavelli dealt with how people behave in organisations, not how they ought to behave; we need to understand both.

From the quest and need for continual learning comes the spirit of the learning organisation, as promoted by Senge (2000). The term 'learning organisation' applies particularly to the idea that any organisation should con-tinually monitor its position in relation to the three bottom lines. More par-ticularly, in practice it has been seen to have particular importance to the bottom line of profits. The learning process involves forever improving the product or service and, secondly, learning from mistakes identified early in the history of the corporation. To do this, the most important task of business is to develop talent.

It is not easy to get an organisation going. Of every ten start-up compa-nies in the United States, one half disappear within the first five years, only four survive into their tenth year, and only three into their fifteenth (Senge 2000, p 117). 'Learning disabilities … are fatal in organisations' says Senge (in Meen and Keough 2002, p 1). He goes on to say that because of them, few corporations live even half as long as a person. Most die before they reach the age of 40. The organisation that survives is the one that learns from its mis-takes and identifies what is going wrong before it is too late.

That is easier said than done. It has been said that it needs the ability to see the totality of the Gordian knot and to be able to identify the right end to pull (Meen and Keough 2002, p 3). The learning organisation is one that unsnarls the knot, and continually expands its capacity to create its future. It does this not only from the top down but from the bottom up as well. The top does not just mean the CEO, but a partnership of senior executives who share the commitment to building a new type of organisation. That takes time. The CEO of the highly successful American engineering firm Emerson spends 60 per cent of his time meeting heads of divisions to discuss and chal-lenge their plans (Anon 2002a).

Time and again organisations have failed to see the future coming. There is much that we can learn from the major military blunders of the twentieth century says Elkington (2001, p 200). Think of the Russians before Hitler launched Operation Barbarossa in 1941; the Americans at Pearl Harbour the same year; the British in Singapore in 1942; the Germans before D-day in 1944; the British before the Argentine invasion of the Falkland Islands in 1982. In each case evidence was there but no conclusions were drawn from it.

What follows are two examples of failure of corporations to learn, and one that was successful. The electronics company WonderTech was founded in the mid-1960s. It had virtually complete control of its market niche. It had a meteoric rise, yet after its first three years it never sustained its rapid growth. Eventually it declined into bankruptcy. WonderTech's managers were unable to see the reasons for their own decline. Only after sorting out all possible factors it turned out that top management had paid little attention to the time customers had to wait to get their products, even though there was a history of longer waits as the production grew. 'WonderTech's managers had fallen prey to the classic learning disability of being unable to detect cause and effect which were separated in time' (Senge 2000, p 119).

WonderTech was an organisation that sold a product. There are also many examples of growth followed by decline in industries that provide services. Schools let the quality of their courses slip. Hospitals with a reputation for patient care lose their favoured qualities as old facilities are not upgraded and the staff becomes increasingly overworked. Their quality of life declines along with that of the institution. People Express Airlines was founded in 1980 to provide low-cost, high-quality airline service in the eastern United States. It grew in five years to be the nation's fifth largest carrier. Yet despite its spectacular success, in 1986 People Express was taken over by Texas Air Corporation, having lost US$133 million in the fist six months of 1986 alone. It was not at all obvious what was happening. Much of the airlines' success had been attributed to deeply discounted fares and friendly, no-frills service. But customers began to complain that service was not what it once was. By its last year of operation, People Express had become such a dismal experience that it was nicknamed 'People Distress'. It now seems that the company's reputation and ability to serve brought demand that outstripped its ability to serve.

People Express drove growth, through its aggressive addition to its fleet and flight schedule, but it was unable to maintain its reputation for service. No-one seemed to learn from this mistake until it was too late. Had it been able to maintain high-quality service with low fares, it would have been hard to beat (Senge 2000).

One outstanding example of an organisation that anticipated successfully an uncertain future, by a very deliberate learning process, is Royal Dutch/Shell. In 1972, a year before OPEC and the onset of the energy crisis, the executives realised there were discontinuities in the future world oil market. While Shell's planners did not predict OPEC exactly, they foresaw the types of changes OPEC would eventually bring. Yet attempts to impress upon Shell's managers the radical shifts needed led to no more than a third of Shell decision centres acting on these insights. However, they faced their failure to convey this to Shell's managers in more than the hundred of its companies operating across the world. They realised Shell's task was then to help managers rethink their worldview. After a great deal of promoting a new learning process, many managers still remained sceptical. Their old habits were good enough. But they weren't. Eventually the exercise began to unfreeze the mind-set of managers around the world and incubate a new worldview.

When the OPEC oil embargo started in the northern winter of 1973-74, Shell responded differently from the other oil companies. The net result was spectacular. In 1970 Shell had been considered the weakest of the seven large companies. By 1979 it was probably the strongest. This was largely due to managers, at the behest of the top planners, overcoming an irrelevant mind-set and replacing it with a new and relevant one. This involved a huge learning process (Senge 2000). (Unfortunately, this part of the Shell story stands in strong contrast to its failure to learn in its oil explorations in Nigeria, which are discussed in Chapter 8.)

At another level of learning is technical training for particular jobs. How this is done varies. For example, the amount of training given to newly hired workers in automobile assembly plants around the world varies greatly. The hours of training in the first six months for new workers in Japanese auto-assembly plants exceed all others, having an average of 364 hours. Plants in the United States and Australia have the lowest: 42 hours and 40 hours respectively. Studies of automobile assembly plants in the United States consistently provide evidence of inadequate levels of training. There could be a number of possible explanations for these differences, however Pfeffer (1998) argues that the differences are primarily due to the different views of people held by firms in different countries. Japanese-owned plants train a lot because they rely on flexible production, whereas plants in the United States and Australia follow traditional practices and philosophies of mass production.

People used to learn and then earn; now many learn as they earn. Work is often the best environment for learning and training. This is why some businesspeople, especially those without an academic background, look askance at new university graduates. In a learning organisation, people learn to create and sustain learning, particularly in relation to change within the organisation. The purpose is that its members will continue to be curious and adaptable to new ideas and continue to learn together from one another. It is a process of fully developing the talents of the members of the organisation in a changing scene. There are various ways of going about this which are discussed by authors such as Burzon and Moore (1999) and Senge (2000).

Bill Ford is notable in Australia for his use of learning teams, in a variety of organisations, that enabled them to re-create their present and their future. Notable examples of his work are with ICI, Lend Lease, Kent Breweries, the Sydney Opera House and the Benevolent Society of New South Wales (Field and Ford 1999; Michaux 2002). We shall give just one example from this list, the Sydney Opera House (Sydney Opera House Trust 2000).

In addition to being an architectural icon, the Sydney Opera House is one of the world's busiest performing arts centres with some 88 000 people visiting it each week. But it was one of the most notoriously divided workplaces in Australia, racked by industrial disputes. Bill Ford worked closely with the CEO to establish learning teams. These have played a vital role in transforming industrial relations, customer services, strategies to broaden the organisation's market such as disabled access and children's programmes, and other activities. The renewal was achieved with a group called the Concept Team, made up of people from all levels of the organisation. The programme is therefore not driven from the top down, but by people working at every level. It has gained the involvement and commitment of the entire work force. There is a diverse wealth of talent among the people who work at the Sydney Opera House. Teamwork has harnessed their expertise and skills to their full potential.

At the same time the Opera House prepared a new enterprise development agreement called 'Relationships, Empowerment and Leadership'. For this purpose 11 teams involving 89 people were established. They made valuable recommendations on improved communication, identifying shared values, recognising changing focus of the house's business, making strategic partnerships work, and feeding issues into the building plan from an artistic, commercial and building perspective. (One high priority is improved access for people with disabilities.) More than 100 staff have been involved in the programme overall. There is now a sense that the Sydney Opera House is a place where individuals are empowered to make a contribution to the organisation. There is a new focus on personal growth, initiative and excellence of performance. According to the Sydney Opera House Trust's annual report (2000) 'the transition to a learning organisation has produced a more cohesive and rewarding work culture at the House. It has also produced tangible commercial benefits' (p 20).

Another notable Australian example of a learning organisation with which Bill Ford had some involvement was the Sydney Olympic Games in 2000. This has been described as 'the world's largest peacetime event' (Webb 2001, p 3). The games involved a A$3.2 billion construction project; a A$136 million cleaning up of what was previously a toxic waste dump at Homebush Bay; the assembly of a work force of about 200 000 people for staging the games, a third of them volunteers; a public transport system that would enable the games to be largely car-free; feeding (not just 5000 people for one meal but) 500 000 people each day for 16 days; high-tech facilities for the media that were to occupy a space equivalent to eight football fields; and security that involved 5000 police on site, 4500 contract security personnel and 2000 security volunteers.

All this involved a huge collaborative effort between government, private enterprise and unions. One of the operators spoke of the achievement in the workplace of trust, fairness, respect, empowerment and openness (Webb 2001, p 67). The overall aim was to find out how the ideals of the triple bottom line of people, environment and the economy could be achieved. The people involved had to have a high sense of purpose, their environment had to be safe. The games were committed to be the 'green' games with products recycled, and as much solar energy as possible. The total economic cost had to be within the limits set by the organisers.

The whole project was very much a learning one, from before construction to the last day of the games, and beyond to the Paralympic Games. The work force first had to be trained. More than 44 000 people attended 52 orientation sessions in the capital cities, and 82 000 people participated in venue training. Collaborative effort during construction meant that the huge Showgrounds Dome became unique in being built on the ground and then jacked up, thus reducing greatly the risk of working high up. When the seating of the aquatic centre had to be increased from 4000 to 16 000 by the construction of a temporary 12 000-seat stand, something went wrong. What was important was how the stakeholders in the project dealt with the problem. Workers, unions and contractors collaborated in finding a solution. The construction of the 110 000-seat main stadium was an extraordinary task in terms of management of people, time and tools. In all the building projects, collaboration and sharing of experience — between the design consultants and contractors, and all the way down to work force levels, often in teams — led to a learning collaboration. All in all the 2000 Olympic Games project established a workplace culture that was 'the moral equivalent of war' in terms of collaboration and pride.

A SENSE OF PLACE

People are uniquely different from capital and technology, though many organisations act as though they are to be considered in the same way. Humans do not exist to serve production systems and service systems. The systems exist to serve humans. The challenge is to understand the human side of organisations. People are not simple, uniform entities that thrive in a box. Buildings that are alternatively solar ovens or refrigerators, with discomfort and energy bills to match, are coming to be seen as unacceptable. What people want is a sense of place, be it in the home or the office. The right sense of place owes much to correct design.

Hawken, Lovins and Lovins (1999) provide many examples of how the physical environment of the workplace is important for health and well-being. One of the key innovations in this area is 'superwindows'. They typically combine two or three invisible thin coatings (which let light pass through but reflect heat) with heavy gas fillings such as krypton to block the flow of heat and noise. They not only make for more comfortable buildings, but in the long run are (in the United States) said to be less expensive to install and run. Hawkins, Lovins and Lovins (1999) give many more examples of what they call 'green development' that provides comfort, variety and aesthetics with lower costs. They claim that for the past 60 years 'business schools have been teaching the myth that only management — not working conditions — can substantially affect employee productivity ... working conditions also matter, and have been too long neglected' (p 90).

In Australia, the large 1920s office of Fairfax newspapers in Sydney occupied a triangular block between two main streets. It outgrew its main use and so was redesigned as a high-tech banking building. Apart from what turned out to be an unsuitable design, the people in it had no need to be in the heart of the city. It failed despite the fortune spent on refurbishing the building. Instead, the bank rebuilt and refurbished an existing structure for its banking systems in an outer suburb close to a railway station and convenient for people who were to work there. It was a great success. Another example of a building that became a hallmark of a good place in which to work is the North Sydney campus of MLC. An existing building was redesigned with much involvement of staff and architects. Architects who didn't listen to suggestions of staff were sacked and others were appointed. The final involvement of staff and architects turned into a great success story. People were glad to be there (personal communication Professor Bill Ford). In another instance, Lend Lease set up 'work area teams' to develop the community-style design of Darling Park in Sydney. It is a landmark community of business designed to be beautiful for workers and visitors (Michaux 2002).

Juan Arena, the chief executive of Spanish bank Bankinter, hated his original Madrid offices: 'all the dark wood panelling and heavy drapes so [he] moved the firm to a modern open plan space that fits with the open-necked atmosphere of the company. ... It has been one of the most fascinating experiences of my professional life' (Reeves 2001, p 50).

Slow City is the name of a project launched in Italy for those searching for a tranquil *dolce vita*. So far 32 cities have joined the programme which improves the quality of life of workers, inhabitants and visitors (Natanson 2002). The aim is the preservation of the traditional and distinctive quality of life in Italy's smaller towns. It challenges the urban 'American' model that has invaded some of Italy's cities. Slow City is a place to be enjoyed. Pedestrian areas are enlarged. Squares and parks are made greener. Alarms and other noises that disturb the peace are banned. Neon signs and posters are taken down. In contrast to fast food, it encourages 'slow food' which promotes leisurely eating in a relaxed atmosphere. The mayors of these cities are not opposed to progress, they simply want to preserve a traditional way of life.

'Think Big' was the sales gimmick of Detriot's monster tail-finned cars. In contrast, Hitler is said to have enlisted Ferdinand Porsche to design a 'people's car' to look like a beetle. The Volkswagon rolled off the assembly line in the early 1940s only to be converted to wartime use. In the late 1950s, influenced by a ground-breaking 'Think Small' advertising campaign, Americans started buying the Volkswagon in large numbers. It even became a hippie icon, to star in the movie *The Love Bug* (Patton 2002). 'Think Small' and 'Slow City' epitomise the human desire to have an appropriate speed and appropriate size, and an appropriate sense of place to human needs.

PROGRESS AND RETROGRESS

We need only go back 200 years before the industrial revolution when, at least according to one modern scholar, most people lived in a such a state of perpetual hunger that they suffered from hallucinations (Barzun 2000, p 112). The Western world of today presents quite a different picture, largely due to the industrial revolution. But the happy state of affairs does not exist in much of the developing world. There is little progress there. Each year, in recent decades in the developing world, 10 million people have died of hunger and up to about one billion people have been unable to obtain sufficient food to have enough energy to carry on normal activities. It is as though they lived in medieval times. We have a long way to go (Ehrlich et al 1995, p 162).

We have already discussed in Chapter 2 how modern people perceive their quality of life in subjective terms. For some it is getting better, but not for others. In this section we are considering progress in what has happened to the quality of working life in the modern world.

Dunphy (2000, pp 255-58) indicates the nature of progress in a two-dimensional matrix (Figure 11.1). The two dimensions are ecological sustainability and human sustainability — (the latter refering to progress in quality of life) — and the four quadrants reflect degrees of these qualities. The goal is to move from quadrant 1 (low sustainability in both) to quadrant 4 (high in both). Dunphy (2000) suggests the kind of change appropriate for moving from one step to the next. In some cases an incremental change is appropriate, in others a more rapid change is called for. Likewise, in terms of style of change in management, in some cases a collaborative or consultative management is appropriate, in other cases the change can be more directive.

FIGURE 11.1   The four categories of ecological sustainability and human sustainability

Quadrant 3 The people-concerned corporation	**Quadrant 4** The sustainable corporation
Quadrant 1 The unsustainable corporation	**Quadrant 2** The ecologically concerned corporation

Human sustainability (vertical axis: High / Low)

Low — High

Ecological sustainability

SOURCE After Dunphy, 'Implementing the sustainable corporation', 2000, p 256.

Quadrant 1 exists because of the misuse of knowledge. The achievements of humanity turn against humanity itself. Quadrant 4 exists only in so far as organisations consciously work with zeal for a triple bottom line. It is well to remember that each of these quadrants is a feature of the modern world. This is because progress is modern in the sense that the industrial revolution, which was a new organisation of production, is little more than 300 years old.

In the past century in Australia there has clearly been progress. Workers are better paid, work shorter hours, retire in good health, have safer workplaces and more interesting work. There is a social safety net to assist those who lose their jobs and for those unable to finance their old age (Richardson 1998). However, if we take the last 20 years, the story is somewhat different. It can be argued that on the average there has not been progress, but retrogression.

Comparing the present to 20 years ago, the following negative comparisons can be made:

- There has been a fall in the amount of paid employment per person of working age. Much work is unpaid and this is not voluntary (eg longer hours).

- There is a growing pool of older men who have been forced out of the work force.

- There has been a large rise in unemployment and under-employment, with an especially damaging growth in long-term unemployment.

- There has been a rise in both excessive hours and insufficient hours.

- People feel less secure in their jobs.

- There has been a growth in the proportion of people who are employed on a casual basis.

- The transition from education to employment has become more difficult for young people, with many being forced to accept part-time work, and more being unemployed.

- The value of the average male real wage has increased by 8 per cent. But for the 30 per cent of lowest paid men, it has fallen, since there has been a rapid growth in lower paid jobs for men. (Richardson 1998, p 218)

The negative side is also apparent in the comprehensive survey by Morehead et al (1997), which showed that Australian employees were generally dissatisfied with their work in many respects. The survey, targeted over 37 000 workplaces, indicated that employees lacked trust in management, disliked the long working hours per day, and felt that appreciation for their work was rarely acknowledged in comparison with the senior ranks of the organisation.

However there have been advances as well in the last 20 years:

- Real wages have risen on average by 8 per cent for men and 17 per cent for women.

- The work force is better educated, and is likely to become even more so as new entrants are more educated than their older fellow workers.

- Working time lost to industrial disputes has fallen dramatically.

- Inflation caused by wage increases in excess of average increases in labour productivity has almost (up to the present) disappeared. (Richardson 1998, p 219)

Richardson (1998) concludes that, in her opinion, when all items are taken into account there has not, on the average, been progress. Others may want to draw a different conclusion about the net balance in the positives and negatives in the above two lists. However, what is not controversial is that over the past 20 years women have gained relative to men. Despite the existing inequalities between men and women (discussed in Chapter 5), there have been advances for women in the Australian workplace in the past 20 years:

- Women work a higher proportion of total paid hours.

- They have a greater proportion of jobs, including full-time jobs.

- They have higher pay.

- Women are more educated.

- They have an increasing share of the good jobs, especially as managers professionals and para-professionals.

We have given various examples of a positive concern and action of organisations about the quality of life of their staff in this book. Some of them are Lend Lease (Chapter 1), Merck, Walt Disney, Unilever, Semco, Flight Centre, Scandinavian Airline Systems, Virgin-Blue (Aust), Johnson and Johnson (Chapter 2), Paronat (France) (Chapter 4), SAAB, Volvo, (Chapter 7), Berri, Xerox, ATT (Chapter 8), Avon, Marriott, IBM, Macquarie Bank, Cisco, Hambrecht and Quist (Chapter 10), Sydney Opera House (Chapter 11). There are still too many organisations that recognise only one bottom line-profits.

TEN CORE PRINCIPLES FOR INCREASING QUALITY OF LIFE IN THE WORKPLACE

We summarise our recommendations in the form of ten core principles, which we present as a way to increase quality of life in the workplace. There are additional desirable principles for quality of life in the workplace, which we have discussed, but what follows are what we consider to be core principles:

1   Work is meant for people not people for work. Organisations must recognise the employee as more than a maximiser of profits, and as one who has emotions, values, hopes and a need for a meaning in life.

2   Eight hours for stress-free work, eight hours for rest and eight hours for recreation for five days of the week with no overtime. This is the objective. Organisations should give particular attention to reducing stress in the most stressful professions such as air-traffic controllers, medical doctors (especially their first year in hospital), police and the law.

3   Women are equal with men. This involves the recognition of equality of women, especially at higher levels, both in terms of numbers and attitudes and pay. Organisations must work against dominantly male culture and instead value and manage diversity.

4   A flexi-week and flexi-day. This involves the flexibility of working hours in terms of which days of the week are for work, the hours of starting and finishing, and allowances for emergency needs — all aimed at a better balance between work, home, extracurricular activities and leisure.

5   Security of employment. Contracts should include not only adequate pay but also a clause for security of employment.

6   A learning organisation that rewards good performance. This applies particularly in relation to organisational change.

7   Self-managed teams and decentralised decision-making. The participation of the worker in decisions about work.

8   Improved physical conditions of work. Organisations should incorporate of latest technical developments, and strive, in consultation with all staff, to achieve a sense of place.

9   The health of the worker is paramount. This involves the conceptual shift of accepting the World Health Organisation's definition of health as a state of physical and mental well-being, not just the absence of injury and disease.

10   Stress management programmes that primarily deal with removing the causes of stress in the work environment. Preventing the causes of stress must have priority over dealing with the symptoms.

None of these principles is particularly new. Yet it seems singularly difficult, even when recognising their importance, to put them into practice, particularly as a whole. A piecemeal approach is almost certain to fail. The ten principles are like the pillars of a Grecian temple. Remove just one pillar and the whole edifice is threatened. We can easily become overwhelmed by the task of change and rest on our laurels, such as they are. That is to be pessimistic, and pessimism only serves to maintain the status quo.

No doubt each organisation will need to work out its own salvation in relation to each one of these ten principles, and do so without compromising to existing negative values in the organisation. In quite a number of examples we have given in this book, an organisation faced what seemed to be a hopeless situation but one which was eventually overcome. It is difficult to hope when all seems to be against hope. That was the situation in South Africa in the early days of activism against apartheid. What helped many in that situation was the oft repeated affirmation: 'Hope is believing in spite of the evidence and watching the evidence change'. It did change. And so it can in organisations. To take the ten core principles seriously would be a major step toward a brave new world.

CONCLUSION

The purpose of the successful corporation is not just to make profits. It is to be found in its existence as a community of people who are endeavouring to fulfil their basic needs in the service of society. Profit is one measure of the life of a corporation. It is not the only bottom line. The quality of life and human values are essential ingredients in the corporation as well. We have to find a mutuality between 'work' and a person's belief and purpose.

The driving energy of humans comes from their Promethean spirit, their dominant will and their intellectual daring. It is this spirit that has enabled humanity to work the miracles of the industrial age and the information age now upon us. Our task is to use this same spirit to free ourselves from present constraints and work out a richer future that will make central the quality of human life and our positive relation to our environment.

This won't just happen. It is a costly enterprise. Are we prepared to identify its demands, count the cost and decide if we have the capacity to manage change in whatever working life we are part of? As an ancient management precept says: 'For which of us, intending to build a tower, does not sit down first, and count the cost whether we have sufficient to finish it?' (Luke 14:28). Even so there is an ambiguity here. The tower, once seemingly completed, has to be renewed from the ground up again and again.

To change the metaphor: managing change is like riding a bicycle. If your bicycle is stationary, you fall over. You can only keep upright by constantly moving forward.

O brave new world
That has such people in't
William Shakespeare, *The Tempest*, V: i.

~

REFERENCES

Abrecht, P. (1978). *Faith Science and the Future*. Philadelphia: Fortress Press.

ACTU (1998). A report on the Australian Council of Trade Unions National Occupational Health and Safety Unit Survey on stress at work. Melbourne: ACTU OHS Unit.

—— (1999). Working people want a balanced secure working life. http://www.actu.asn.au.

Adamson, J. (2002). Dads and the tug of work. *Sydney Morning Herald*, section 7, 4-5 May, p 1.

Anon (1986) Report. Centre for Woman Cooperative Limited.

—— (1998). Improving quality of life improves quality of work. http://www.news.harvard.edu/gazette/1998/02.26/Studyimproving Q.html.

—— (2000a). Emerging-market indicators: Quality of life. *The Economist*, 356:8177, p 104.

—— (2000b). The quality of working life: 1999 survey of managers' changing experiences. *Report of the Institute of Management Services*. March.

—— (2000b). Why honesty is the best policy. *The Economist*, supp, 362:8263, 9 March, p 7.

—— (2000c). Pressure drives heads to drink. *Times Education Supplement News*, 14 July. http://www.nswtf.org.au/world/2000816_longhours.html.

—— (2002). Back to Basics. *The Economist*, supp, 362:8263, 9 March, p 4.

Antelme, R. (1992). *The Human Race*. Marlboro Vermont: The Marlboro Press.

Armstrong, K. (2001). *The Battle for God: Fundamentalism in Judaism, Christianity and Islam*. London: HarperCollins.

Bachelard, M. (2001). Job time row is academic. *The Australian*, 24 November, p 9.

Barzun, J. (2000). *From Dawn to Decadence: Five hundred years of Western cultural life, 1500 to the present*. New York: HarperCollins.

Beder, S. (2000). *Selling the Work Ethic: From puritan pulpit to corporate PR*. Carlton North, Victoria: Scribe Publications.

Bergen, B.J. (1998). *The Banality of Evil: Hannah Arendt and 'The Final Solution'*. Boston: Rowan and Littlefield.

Biggs, S. and K.F. Horgan. (1999). *Time On, Time Out: Flexible work solutions to keep your life in balance*. Sydney: Allen & Unwin.

Birch, C. (1993a). *Confronting the Future: Australia and the world the next 100 years*. Melbourne: Penguin.

—— (1993b). *Regaining Compassion: For humanity and nature*. Sydney: UNSWP.

—— (1999). *Biology and the Riddle of Life*. Sydney: UNSWP.

Birch, C. and L. Vischer (1997). *Living with the Animals*. Geneva: Risk Book Series of the World Council of Churches.

Birch, D. and M. Glazebrook (2000). Doing Business. In S. Rees and S. Wright (eds). *Human Rights, Corporate Responsibility: A dialogue*. Sydney: Pluto Press, pp 41–52.

Bix, A.S. (2000). *Inventing Ourselves out of Jobs? America's debate over technological unemployment 1929-1981*. Baltimore: John Hopkins University Press.

Blainey, G. (1994). *A Shorter History of Australia*. Sydney: Random House Publishers.

Blake, D. (2001). *Skroo the Rules: What the world's most productive workplace does differently*. Melbourne: Information Australia.

Boyden, S., S. Dovers and M. Shirlow (1990). *Our Biosphere under Threat: Ecological realities and Australia's opportunities*. Oxford University Press.

Brack, G. (1998). Shorter hours won't mean jobs. *Sydney Morning Herald*, 13 November, p 19.

Bronowski, J. (1973). *The Ascent of Man*. London: British Broadcasting Corporation.

Bronowski, J. and B. Mazlish (1960). *The Western Intellectual Tradition: From Leonardo to Hegel*. London: Hutchinson.

Brundtland, G.H. (2000). Investment in health yields higher growth. *The Australian*, 18 October, p 13.

Buchanan, J. and S. Bearfield (1997). Reforming working time: alternatives to unemployment, casualisation and excessive hours. Melbourne: Brotherhood of St Laurence.

—— (1998). *Australia at Work: Just managing?* Sydney: Prentice Hall.

Burke, K. (2001). Homework for adults booming. *Sydney Morning Herald*, 29 May, p 2.

Burzon, N. and J. Moore (1999). *Reconnecting with People*. London: Crisp Publications.

Callus, R. and R.D. Lansbury (eds) (2002). *Working Futures: The changing nature of work and employment relations in Australia*. Sydney: The Federation Press.

Carlzon, J. (1987). *Moments of Truth: New strategies for today's customer-driven economy*. New York: Harper and Row.

Catalano, A. (1993). Working overtime at keeping a job. *Sydney Morning Herald*, Agenda, 12 November, p 9.

Clanchy, M. (1997). Insensitive staff-cutting can undermine the loyalty of those who stay. *Business Review Weekly*, 15 September, pp 70-72.

Clark, Manning (ed Michael Cathcart) (1995). *History of Australia*. Abridged from six volumes. Melbourne: Penguin.

Clendinnen, I. (1998). *Reading the Holocaust*. Melbourne: Text Publishing.

Cobb, C., T. Halstead and J. Rowe (1995). *The Genuine Progress Indicator: Summary of data and methodology*. San Francisco: Redefining Progress.

Collins, J. (2001). *Good to Great: Why some companies make the leap and others don't*. London: Random House.

Comcare Australia (1995). *Annual Report 1994-95*. Canberra: Commonwealth of Australia.

—— (1999). *Annual Report 1998-99*. Canberra: Commonwealth of Australia.

Connell, Bob (2000). Global trends tilt the scales against women. *University of Sydney News*, 32:18, 19 October, p 4.

Cooper, D. (1997). Life in the balance. *Weekend Australian*, 20-21 December, p 51.

Corporate Research Foundation (2002). *The Best Companies to Work for in Australia*. Sydney: Allen & Unwin.

Corporations and Human Rights (2002). www.GlobalIssues.org/TradeRelated/Corporations/ Human Rights.asp.

Covey, S.R. (1989). *The 7 Habits of Highly Effective People*. New York: Business Library.

Cox, E. (1998). Measuring social capital as part of progress and well-being. In R. Eckersley. *Measuring Progress: Is life getting better?* Melbourne: CSIRO Publishing, pp 157-67.

Cummings, T., A. Mohrman and I. Mitroff (1991). The actors in large-scale change. In Mohrman et al. *Large-Scale Organizational Change*. San Francisco: Jossey-Bass Publishers.

Curtis, L. (1938). *Civitas Dei: The Commonwealth of God*. London: Macmillan.

Daily, G. and K. Ellison (2002). *The New Economy of Nature: The quest to make conservation profitable*. Washington: Island Press.

Daly, H.E. and J.B. Cobb (1989). *For the Common Good: Directing the economy toward community, the environment and a sustainable future*. Boston: Beacon.

Darwin, C. (1860). *The Voyage of the Beagle*. New York: Doubleday edition, 1962.

De Geus, A. (1997). *The Living Company: Habits for survival in a turbulent business environment*. Boston: Harvard Business School Press.

De Heus, P. and R.F.W. Diekstra (1999). Do teachers burn out more easily? A comparison of teachers with other social professions on work stress and burnout symptoms. In R. Vandenberghe and A.M. Huberman (1999). *Understanding and Preventing Teacher Burnout: A sourcebook of International Research and Practice*. Cambridge University Press, pp 269-84.

Denniss, R. (2001). Measuring employment in the 21st century: New measures of underemployment and overwork. *Discussion paper 36*. Canberra: The Australia Institute.

Diesendorf, M. (2000). Sustainability and sustainable development. In D. Dunphy, J. Benvenise, A Griffiths and P Sutton (eds) (2000) *Sustainability*. Sydney: Allen & Unwin, pp 19-27.

Diesendorf, M. and C. Hamilton (eds) (1997). *Human Ecology, Human Economy: Ideas for an ecologically sustainable future*. Sydney: Allen & Unwin.

Dinham, S. (1997). Teaching and Teachers' families. *Australian Educational Researcher*, no 24, pp 59-87.

Dinham, S. (2001). Middle managers under pressure. *Independent Education*, March, pp 29-31.

Dinham, S. and C .Scott (1996). *The Teacher 2000 Project: A study of teacher satisfaction, motivation and health*. University of Western Sydney, Nepean: Faculty of Education publication.

Doherty, L. (2002). Pressure turns the boss into a bully. *Sydney Morning Herald*, 5 January, p 3.

Donaghy, B. (1995). Distress signals. *Sydney Morning Herald*, 30 September, Employment, p 27A.

Donaldson, T. (1982). *Corporations and Morality*. Englewood Cliffs NJ: Prentice Hall.

Donnelly, J. (1989). *Universal Human Rights in Theory and Practice*. Ithaca NY: Cornell University Press.

Doogue, G. (2002). The life and times of us. *Sydney Morning Herald*, Good Weekend, 25 May, p 49.

Dostoyevsky, F. (1972). *Notes from the Underground*. London: Penguin Books.

Dover, B. (2002). Take me to a leader. *HR Monthly*, February, p 7.

Downs, A. (1996). *Corporate Executions: The ugly truth about downsizing – how corporate greed is shattering lives, companies and communities*. New York: Amacon, Division of the American Management Association.

Drucker, P.F. (2002). Future Firm. *Financial Review*, Boss, 8 March, pp 44-49.

Duffield, C. (2000). Multinational corporations and workers' rights. In S. Rees and S. Wright (2000) (eds). *Human Rights, Corporate Responsibility: A dialogue*. Sydney: Pluto Press, pp 191-209.

Dunphy, D. (2000). Implementing the Sustainable Corporation. In D. Dunphy, J. Beneviste, A. Griffiths and P. Sutton (eds) (2000). *Sustainability: The corporate strategy of the 21st century*. Sydney: Allen & Unwin, pp 12-73.

Dunphy, D. and J. Benveniste (2000). An introduction to the sustainable corporation. In D. Dunphy, J. Beneviste, A. Griffiths and P. Sutton (eds) (2000). *Sustainability: The corporate strategy of the 21st century*. Sydney: Allen & Unwin.

Dunphy, D., J. Beneviste, A. Griffiths and P. Sutton (eds) (2000). *Sustainability: The corporate strategy of the 21st century*. Sydney: Allen & Unwin.

Dunphy, D. and Stace (2002). Changing forms of organisation and management. In R. Callus and R.D. Lansbury (eds) (2002). *Working Futures: The changing nature of work and employment relations in Australia*. Sydney: The Federation Press, pp 206-21.

Dusevic, T. (1997). The lost weekend. *Sydney Morning Herald*, Good Weekend, 5 April, pp 13-19.

Eckersley, R. (1998a). Perspectives on progress. In R. Eckersley (ed.) *Measuring Progress: Is life getting better?* Canberra: CSIRO Publishing, pp 3-34.

—— (1998b). Redefining progress: shaping the future of human needs. *Family Matters*, no 51, pp 6-12.

—— (1999). Quality of Life in Australia: an analysis of public perceptions. *Discussion paper 23*. The Australia Institute.

Edgar, D. (1998). In memory of old what's his name. *Weekend Australian*, Review, 19-20 September, p 29.

Ehrlich, P.R. (2000). *Human Natures: Genes, cultures and the human prospect*. Washington: Island Press.

Ehrlich, P.R., A.H. Ehrlich and G .Daily (1995). *The Stork and the Plow: The equity answer to the human dilemma*. New York: Grosset/Putman.

Elkington, J. (1997). *Cannibals with Forks: The triple bottom line of the 21st century business*. Gabrioa Island, BC, Canada: New Society.

—— (2001). *The Chrysalis Economy: How citizen CEO's and corporations can fuse values and value creation*. Oxford: Capstone/AJ Wiley.

European Union (1993). *The Working Time Directive*. http://europa.eu.int/eur-lex/en/lif/dat/1993/ en-393L014.html.

Feldman, G. (2002). Work Stress. *New Scientist*, 2324, 5 January, p 11.

Ferre, F. (2001). *Living and Value: Towards a constructive postmodern ethics*. New York: State University of New York Press.

Fest, J. (2002). *Speer: The final verdict*. London: Phoenix Press.

Field, L. and B. Ford (1999). *Managing Organisational Learning: From rhetoric to reality*. Melbourne: Addison Wesley Longman.

Fitz-enz, J. (1990). *Human Value Management: The value-adding human resource management strategy for the 1990s*. San Francisco: Jossey-Bass.

Fox, C. (2002). The best employers: What makes a winner. *Australian Financial Review*. 1 February, pp 78-79.

Frank, H. (1999). *Luxury Fever: Why money fails to satisfy in an era of excess*. New York: Free Press.

Freeman, T. (1998). Distress signals. *Sydney Morning Herald*, 26 September, pp 1-2.

French, H. (2002). Reshaping global governance. In C. Flavin, H. French and G. Gardner (eds) *State of the World*, pp 174-98.

Frost, P. and S. Robinson (1999). The toxic handler. *Harvard Business Review*, July-August, pp 97-106.

Gabriel, P. and M.-R. Liimatainen (2000). *Mental health in the workplace*. Geneva: International Labour Office.

Gaita, R. (1999). *A Common Humanity: Thinking about love and truth and justice*. Melbourne: Text Publishing.

Galbraith, J.K. (1996). *The Good Society: The humane agenda*. Boston: Houghton Mifflin.

Gardner, H. (1997). *Leading Minds: An anatomy of leadership*. London: HarperCollins.

Gardner, H., M. Csikszentmihalyi and W. Damon (2001). *Good Work: When excellence and ethics meet*. New York: Basic Books.

Gardner, J.W. (1991). Personal renewal. *McKinsey Quarterly*, no 2, pp 71-81.

Garten, J.E. (2001). *The Mind of the CEO*. New York: Basic Books.

Gates, J. (2001) Ways to reduce workplace accidents. http://www.emporia.edu/bed/jour/jour22h/gates.htm

Gettler, L. (2002). Good reputation index: Australia's 100 biggest companies and how they rate. *Sydney Morning Herald/Age*, special, 28 October, pp 1-19.

Gittins, R. (1997). The boss cracks the whip. *Sydney Morning Herald*, 9 April, p 17.

Golan, P. (1997). 'Careers don't always come first.' *Australian Financial Review*, 5 August, p 17.

—— (1997a). Juggling career and kids; a man's role is rarely recognised. *Sydney Morning Herald*, 11 March, p 15.

—— (1997b). Unhappy homes a work hazard. *The Australian*, 23 July, p 13.

—— (2000). Human resources, capabilities and sustainability. in D Dunphy, J Beneviste, A. Griffiths and P. Sutton (eds). *Sustainability: The corporate strategy of the 21st century*. Sydney: Allen & Unwin, pp 55-77.

Goodman, S. (2001). French unions walk out of talks over 35-hour week. *Nature*, 411:6838, p 622.

Gough, K. and M. Price (2002). Workers win right to knock back overtime. *The Australian*, 24 July, p 3.

Grameen Bank (2000). www.citechco.net/grameen/bank/

—— (2001). www.rdc.com.au/grameen/

Gratton, L. (2000). *Living Strategy: Putting people at the heart of corporate purpose*. Sydney: Pearson Education Australia.

Green, R. (2000). Globalisation, trade, policy and labour standards. In S. Rees and S. Wright (eds) *Human Rights, Corporate Responsibility: A dialogue*. Sydney: Pluto Press, pp 143-57.

H and S (2001). Home Pages. Counting the cost of accidents. http://www.healthandsafety.co.uk/finhse.htm

Hadfield, P. (2001). If you think you're overworked, think again. *New Scientist*, 172:2320, 8 December, p 15.

Hamilton C. (2002). Over-consumption in Australia: the rise of the middle-class battler. *Discussion paper no 49*. The Australia Institute.

—— (2003). *Growth Fetish*. Sydney: Allen & Unwin.

Hamilton, C. and E. Mail (2003). Downshifting in Australia: A sea-change in the pursuit of happiness. *Discussion paper no 50*. The Australia Institute.

Hamilton, C. and H. Saddler. (1997). The genuine progress indicator for Australia: A new index of change in well-being in Australia. *Discussion paper no 14*. Canberra: The Australia Institute.

Hancock, K. (2002). Work in an Ungolden Age. In R. Callus and R.D. Lansbury (eds). *Working*

Futures: The changing nature of work and employment relations in Australia. Sydney: The Federation Press, pp 6-26.

Handy, C. (1998). *The Hungry Spirit: Beyond capitalism — a quest for purpose in the modern world.* London: Arrow Books.

Harris, M. (1998). Executives manage to bury stress. *Sydney Morning Herald*, 4 August, p 1.

Hartman, L.P. (1998). *Perspectives in Business Ethics.* New York: McGraw Hill.

Hartmann, N. (1932). *Ethics: Moral values*, vol 2. New York: Allen and Unwin.

Harvey, C. (2001). Savvy women still losing corporate race. *The Australian*, 15 August, p 3.

Harris, T. (2002). Women still can't break the glass ceiling. *The Australian*, 27 November, p 1.

Havel, V. (2002). A farewell to politics. *New York Review of Books*, 46:16, 24 October, p 4.

Hawken, P., A.B. Lovins and L.H. Lovins. (1999). *Natural Capitalism: The next industrial revolution.* London: Earthscan.

Head, B. (2002). Corporate plays. *Financial Review*, Boss, 6:3, pp 51-52.

Hewett, J. (1997). Virtual work. *Sydney Morning Herald*, 19 August, p 11.

Holliday, C.O., S. Schmidheiny and P. Watts (2002). *Walking the Talk: The business case for sustainable development.* San Fransisco: Berrett-Koehler.

Hopkins, A. (1999). The lessons of the Moura Coal Mine. In C. Mayhew and C.L. Peterson (eds). *Occupational Health and Safety in Australia.* Sydney: Allen & Unwin, pp 140-57.

Horin, A. (2001). Women go it alone when glass ceiling won't shatter. *Sydney Morning Herald*, 15 August, p 15.

Horin, A. and V. Wilson (2001). A nation of work, all stress and no play. *Sydney Morning Herald*, 5 September, p 3.

Horin, J. (1997). All work and no pay. *Sydney Morning Herald*, Spectrum, 27 December, p 6.

Horne, D. (2001). *Looking for Leadership: Australia in the Howard years.* Viking: Ringwood Victoria.

Hornery, A. (1997). Pity the boss: He's working harder. *Sydney Morning Herald*, 20 February, p 32.

Hubbard, G., D. Samuel, S. Heap and G. Cocks (2002). *The First XI: Winning organisations in Australia.* Milton: John Wiley and Sons.

Hughes, J. (1988). Absent men find new way home. *The Australian*, 26 August, p 3.

Hulbert, A. (2000). Unfinished business. *New York Times Book Review*, 17 December, p 28.

Human Capital (2002a). Virgin values. *Human Capital*, December, p 10.

—— (2002b). Paid maternity leave: a not so immaculate conception. *Human Capital*, December, pp 22-25.

Hunnicutt, B. (1996). Take my job please. *New York Times Book Review*, 19 January, p 4.

Hutton, W. (2002). The European Lecture of the Cheltenham Festival in the United Kingdom. *Background Briefing.* Australian Broadcasting Corporation Radio National, 15 December.

Inter Press Service (2001) Review 2000: Rights.www.oneworld.org/ips2/dec00/01_46_003.html

Jacobson, G. (2000). Women still seen as inferior: Judge. *Sydney Morning Herald*, 15 July, p 3.

James, W. (1917). *Selected Papers on Philosophy.* London: J.M. Dent, Everymans Library.

Jamieson House Employment Group (1996). Redistributing Work: Solutions to the paradox of overwork and unemployment in Australia. *Discussion paper, no 7.* Canberra: The Australia Institute.

Janke, T. (2000). Our culture/our future: Indigenous cultural and intellectual property rights. In S. Rees and S. Wright (eds). *Human Rights, Corporate Responsibility: A dialogue.* Sydney: Pluto Press, pp 69-88.

Jones, B. (1990). *Sleepers, Wake!: Technology and the future of work.* Melbourne: Oxford University Press.

Kabanoff, B. (1992). An exploration of the organisational culture in Australia, with a closer look at the banking sector. *CCC paper 023.* Sydney: The Centre for Corporate Change, Australian Graduate School of Management, University of New South Wales.

Katzenbach, J.R. (2000). *Peak Performance: Aligning the hearts and minds of your employees.* Boston: Harvard Business School Press.

Kazin, M. (1996). Quitting time. *New York Times Book Review*, 22 December, p 9.

Kelly, P. (2001). Labor's thinking cap. *The Weekend Australian*, 19-20 May, p 29.

Kemp, K. (2001). Charles Ives: The unanswered question. *Sydney Symphony Australia programme.* Sydney. May.

Keynes, J.M. (1930). Economic possibilities for our grandchildren. In *Essays in Persuasion, Collected Works*, vol 9. Cambridge: Cambridge University Press.

Kilmann, R. (1991. A completely integrated program for organizational change. In Mohrman et al (eds). *Large-Scale Organizational Change*. San Francisco: Jossey-Bass.

Knowles, R. (ed.) (2000). *Ethical Investment*. Sydney: A Choice Book.

Kodz, J., B. Kersley, M.T. Strebler and S. O'Regan (1998). Breaking the long hours culture. *Report no 352*. London: Institute of Employment Studies.

Kriakov, I. (2000). The movement toward shorter working hours might have begun. http://www.geocities/com/SouthBeach/Cove/6831/work.html

Lagan, A. (2000) *Why Ethics Matter: Business ethics for business people*. Melbourne: Information Australia.

Landes, D. and R. Landes (2001). She devils. *The Australian*, 10 October, p 31.

Larriera, A. (1996). Have women lost the battle? *Sydney Morning Herald*, Agenda, 16 December, p 11.

Lawson, M. (1996). Sign of the times as executives tick up longer hours. *The Australian Financial Review*, 8 November, p 17.

Lecky, S. (1998). The failure of slash and earn. *Sydney Morning Herald*, 4 July, p 83.

Lee, H. (1995). *A case study of the unsuccessful organizational change at electric power division of allied signal company*. Unpublished doctoral dissertation. Walden University, USA.

Lee, M.D. and S.M. MacDermid (1998). Improvising new careers: Accommodation, elaboration and transformation. West Lafayette: The Center for Families, Purdue University.

Lehmkuhl, L. (1999). Health effects of long work hours. http://www.web.net/32hours/Health%.20v2.htm

Lewontin, R.C. (1991). *Biology as Ideology: The doctrine of DNA*. New York: HarperCollins.

—— (2000). *The Triple Helix: Gene organism and environment*. Cambridge MA: Harvard University Press.

Loane, S. (1997). The importance of being family friendly. *Sydney Morning Herald*, Employment, 5 July, pp 1-2.

Longstaff, S. (1997). *Hard Cases, Tough Choices: Exploring the ethical landscape of business*. Sydney: Pan Macmillan.

Mackay, H. (1997). *Generations: Baby boomers, their parents and their children*. Sydney: Pan Macmillan.

—— (1999). *Turning Point: Australians choosing their future*. Sydney: Pan Macmillan

Macken, D. (1997). Executive retreats. *Sydney Morning Herald*, Spectrum, 3 May, p 4.

Macken, J. (1997). Australia's new energy crisis: Too much work, not enough sleep. *The Australian Financial Review*, Weekend Edition, 3-4 January, pp 2-3.

Margo, J. (1998). How to survive the corporate king hit. *The Weekend Australian*, 5-6 September, p 51.

—— (2002). A less emotional way to better business. *The Australian Financial Review*, 7 February, p 51.

Mayhew, C. (1999). Occupational violence: a case study of the Taxi industry. In C. Mayhew and C.L. Peterson (1999). *Occupational Health and Safety in Australia*. Sydney: Allen & Unwin, pp 127-39.

Mayhew, C. and C.L. Peterson (1999). *Occupational Health and Safety in Australia*. Sydney: Allen & Unwin.

McCallum, R. (2000). *Employer Controls over Private Life*. Sydney: UNSWP.

McKenna, E.P. (1997). *When Work Doesn't Work Anymore: Women, work, and identity*. Sydney: Hodder and Stoughton.

McNeill, J.R. (2000). *Something New under the Sun: An environmental history of the twentieth-century world*. New York: WW Norton.

Meen, D.E. and M. Keough (2002). Creating the learning organisation. *The McKinsey Quarterly*, 13 March, pp 1-11.

Merson, J. (2001). *Stress: The causes, the costs and the cures*. Sydney: ABC Books.

Michaux, A. (2002). The learning organisation: Is it achievable in a human services context? Unpublished paper. ACWA Conference, 2 September.

Moodie, AM (1997). Businesses are more family friendly: Study. *The Australian Financial Review*, 31 October, p 50.

Morehead, A., M. Steele, M. Alexander, K. Stephen and L. Duffin (1997). *Changes at Work: The 1995 Australian workplace industrial relations survey*. Melbourne: Addison-Wesley Longman.

Morrison, A.M., R.P. White and E. van Velsor (1992). *Breaking the Glass Ceiling*. New York: Addison-Wesley.

Moynihan, R. (2002). Dangerous liaisons. *Australian Financial Review Magazine*, March, pp 49-54.

Myers, D. and E. Diener (1996). The pursuit of happiness. *Scientific American*, 71(1), pp 40-43.

Natanson, P. (2002). *At a Snail's Pace*. http://abcnews.go.com/sections/world/DailyNews/slowcities000724.html

National Occupational Health and Safety Commission (NOHSC: 2000). *Data on OHS in Australia: the overall scene*. Sydney: NOHSC.

Neill, R. (1997). Boardroom backlash. *The Australian Weekend Review*, 19-20 April, pp 5-6.

Niebuhr, U.M. (ed.) (1974). *Justice and Mercy*. New York: Harper and Row.

Niebuhr, R. (1944). *The Children of Light and the Children of Darkness*. New York: Charles Scribner's Sons.

—— (1949). *Faith and History: A comparison of Christian and modern views of history*. New York: Scribner's Sons.

Nierenberg, D. (2002). Correcting gender myopia: Gender equity, women's welfare, and the environment. *Paper 161*. Washington: World Watch Institute.

Nussbaum, M. (1993). Non-relative virtues: An Aristototelian approach. In M. Nussbaum and Amartya Sen (eds). *The Quality of Life*. Oxford: Clarendon Press.

Nussbaum. M. and Amartya Sen (eds) (1993). *The Quality of Life*. Oxford: Clarendon Press.

Olson, M.H. and P. Toyne (2000). Guiding principles: The way ahead. In D. Dunphy, J. Benveniste, A. Griffiths and P. Sutton (eds). *Sustainability*. Sydney: Allen and Unwin, pp 236-49.

Oppenheimer, M. (2002). Commentary. In R. Callus and R.D. Lansbury (eds). *Working Futures: The changing nature of work and employment relations in Australia*. Sydney: The Federation Press, pp 39-45.

Pagan Westphal (2002). Opinion interview. *New Scientist*, no 2324, 5 January.

Patton, P. (2002). *Bug: The strange mutations of the world's most famous automobile*. New York: Simon and Schuster.

Paul, D. (2000). *Communicating complex change: An explorative, ethnomethodological case-study of communication and its role in large scale organisational change*. Doctoral dissertation. Sydney: Macquarie University.

Pescott-Allen, R. (2001). *The Wellbing of Nations: A country-by-country index of quality of life and the environment*. Washington: Island Press.

Peters, T. (1999). *Reinventing Work: The brand YOU*. New York: Robert A Knopf.

Peters, T. and R. Waterman (1982). *In Search of Excellence*. New York: Harper and Row.

Petrie, D. (1998a). Hey dad, remember me? *Sydney Morning Herald*, Good Weekend, 27 June, pp 26-30.

—— (1998b). *Father Time: Making time for your children*. Sydney: Macmillan.

Pfeffer, J. (1998). *The Human Equation: Building profits by putting people first*. Boston: Harvard Business School Press.

Pincus, L.B. (1998). Tee-shirt and tears: Third world suppliers to first world markets. In L. Pincus. *Hartmen in Business Ethics*. Singapore: McGraw Hill, pp 763-64.

Pocock, B. (2001). *Having a Life: Work, family, fairness and community in 2000*. Adelaide: Centre for Labour Research, University of Adelaide.

Pocock, B. (2002). The Exhausted Australian? *Discussion Paper no 33*. Canberra: Australia Institute, pp 10-11.

Polanyi, M. (1957). *The Great Transformation*. Boston: Beacon.

Pratt, K. (1998). Work/life: Middle managers and off-site workers get less satisfaction. *Macquarie University News*, no 300, June, pp 3-4.

Preston, R.H. (2000a). The ethical legacy of John Maynard Keynes. In R.J. Elford and I.S. Markham (eds). *The Middle Way: Theology, politics and economics in the later thought of R H Preston*. London: SCM, pp 239-56.

—— (2000b). 'Laborem exercens': Pope John Paul II on work. In R.J. Elford and I.S. Markham (eds). *The Middle Way: Theology, politics and economics in the later thought of R H Preston*. London: SCM, pp 167-79.

Pusey, M. (1998). Incomes, standards of living and quality of life. In R. Eckersley (1998). *Measuring Progress: Is life getting better?* Melbourne: CSIRO Publishing, pp 183-97.

Putnam, R.D. (2001). *Bowling Alone: The collapse and revival of American Community*. New York: Simon & Schuster/Touchstone.

Randerson, J. (2002). Public mislead over fire-safe cigarettes. *New Scientist*, 176:2374/5, pp 6-7.

Rasmussen, L.L. (1996). Why the moral center will not hold. *New York Union Seminary News*, Winter/Spring, pp 15-17.

Read, V. (2000). Technologies and processes for human sustainability. In D. Dunphy, J. Beneviste, A. Griffiths and P. Sutton (eds). *Sustainability: The corporate strategy of the 21st century*. Sydney: Allen & Unwin, pp 78-102.

Rees, S. (2002). Recovering humanity: The means of peace with justice. Lecture, Tasmanian Peace Trust.

Rees, S. and S. Wright (eds) (2000). *Human Rights, Corporate Responsibility: A dialogue*. Sydney: Pluto Press.

Reeves, R. (2001). *Happy Mondays: Putting the pleasure back into work*. London: Pearson Education.

Richardson, S. (1998). Progress in the workplace. In R. Eckersley. *Measuring Progress: Is life getting better?* Melbourne: CSIRO Publishing, pp 201-21.

Robinson, D. and C. Sidoti (2000). The status of human rights in Australia. In S. Rees and S. Wright (eds). *Human Rights, Corporate Responsibility: A dialogue*. Sydney: Pluto Press, pp 24-40.

Robinson, J. (2000). What you need is more vacation. *Time*, 12 June, p 69.

Robinson, P. (2001). Australians buck world trend and work even harder. *Sydney Morning Herald*, 8 October, p 5.

Roccas, S. and N. Gandal (2002). Greed by degrees. *New Scientist*, 176(2373), p 26.

Sachs, A. (1995). Eco-justice: Linking human rights and the environment. *Worldwatch paper 127*.

Salin, M. (2001). *European Agency for Safety and Health at Work*. Press release. 12 March.

Salzman, A. (1990). The new meaning of success. *US News & World Report*, 17 September, p 57.

Sapolsky, R.M. (1994). *Why Zebras Don't Get Ulcers: A guide to stress, stress related diseases and coping*. New York: WH Freeman.

—— (1998). *The Trouble with Testosterone: And other essays on the biology of the human predicament*. New York: Simon and Schuster.

Semler, R. (1994). *Maverick: The success story behind the world's most unusual workplace*. London: Arrow Publications.

—— (2003). *The Seven-Day Weekend*. London: Random House.

Senge, P.M. (2000). *The Fifth Discipline: The art and practice of the learning organization*. Sydney: Random House.

Sennett, R. (1998). *The Corrosion of Character: The personal consequence of work in the new capitalism*. New York: WW Norton.

Sharp, M. (1995). Clampdown on 'excessive' claims for leave. *Sydney Morning Herald*, 7 July, p 4.

Sheehan, M., P. McCarthy. M. Barker and M. Henderson (2002). Mean testing. *HR Monthly*, February, pp 34-36.

Sinclair, A. (2002). Endnote. *Financial Review*, Boss, 5:3, p 66.

Singer, P. (1993). *How Are We To Live? Ethics in an age of self-interest*. Melbourne: Text Publishing Company.

—— (2001). *Writings on an Ethical Life*. London: HarperCollins.

—— (2002). My better nature. *Sydney Morning Herald*, Spectrum, 2-3 March, pp 4-5.

Smith, P.H. (2001). *Quaker Business Ethics: A plumb line guide to practical applications in business and industry*. Wilton CT: Diamond Library Publishers.

Sonnenberg, F. (1993). *Managing with a Conscience: How to improve performance through integrity, trust and commitment*. New York: McGraw Hill.

Sorros, J.C. and A.M. Sorros (1992). Social support and teacher burnout. *Journal Educational Administration*, no 30, pp 55-68.

Stainback, M. and K.M. Donato (1998). Going to work but never leaving home. *Population Today*, 26(9), September, p 3.

Suzuki, D. (2000). Second Annual Transformation lecture. *The University of Sydney News*, 32(4), p 1.

Suzuki, D. and H. Dressel (1999). *Naked Ape to Superspecies: A personal perspective on humanity and the global eco-crisis*. New York: Allen & Unwin.

Sydney Opera House Trust (2000). *Annual Report: Making the house zing*.

Taylor, B.B. (2001). Physics and faith: the luminous web. In R.L. Hermann (ed.). *Expanding Humanity's Vision of God*. Philadelphia: Templeton Foundation Press, pp 23–40.

Taylor, J. and W. Shaw (1987). *The Third Reich Almanac*. New York: Pharos Books.

Tillich, P (1955). *The New Being*. New York: Charles Scribner's Sons.

—— (1963). *The Eternal Now*. London: SCM Press.

—— (1968). The person in a technical society. In W. Gibson (ed.) *Social Ethics: Issues in ethics and society*. London: SCM, pp 120–42.

Tuettemann, E. and K.F. Punch (1992). Psychological distress in secondary teachers: Research findings and their implications. *Journal of Educational Administration*, no 3, pp 43–53.

—— (1996). Reducing teacher stress: The effects of support in the work environment. *Research in Education*, no 56, pp 63–72.

Turner, R. (2002). Everybody's beautiful. *Australian Financial Review*, Boss, vol 3, November, p 15.

United Nations Development Programme (UNDP: 1996). *Human Development Report 1996*. Oxford: Oxford University Press.

Urquhart, B. (2000). Between sovereignty and globalisation: Dag Hammarskjold Lecture. *Development Dialogue*, 2000:1, pp 7–14.

Verrender, I. (1997). Bludgers no more. *Sydney Morning Herald*, Spectrum, 1 October, p 1.

Vincent, P. (2002). Ill-gotten pains. *Sydney Morning Herald*, My Career, 23–24 March, p 1.

Wade, M. (2001). Few join fight for human rights. 'Good Reputation', *Sydney Morning Herald*, 22 October, p 12.

Walsh, R. (2002). *Executive Material: Nine of Australia's top CEO's in conversation with Richard Walsh*. Sydney: Allen and Unwin.

Wajcman, J. (1999). *Managing like a Man: Women and men in corporate management*. Sydney: Allen & Unwin.

Walker, T. (2002). Howard and Co focus on the big picture. *Australian Financial Review*, 7 June, p 16.

World Commission on Environment and Development (WCED: 1987). *Our Common Future*. Oxford University Press.

Wearing, A.J. and B. Headey (1998). Who enjoys life and why: Measuring subjective well-being. In R. Eckersely (ed.). *Measuring Progress: Is life getting better?* Melbourne: CSIRO Publishing, pp 169–82.

Webb, T. (2001). *The Collaborative Games: The story behind he spectacle*. Sydney: Pluto Press.

Welch, J. (2001). *Jack: What I've learned leading a great company and great people*. London: Headline Book Publishing.

Westphal, P. (2002). Opinion. Interview, *New Scientist*, no 2324, 5 January.

Wetham, P. and L. Wetham (2000). *Hard to be Holy: Unravelling the roles and relationships of church leaders*. Adelaide: Openbook Publishers.

Whitehead, A.N. (1929). *The Function of Reason*. Boston: Beacon.

—— (1938). *Science and the Modern World*. London: Penguin Books.

Winefield, T. (2001). The Higher Education Workplace Stress Survey. www.nteu.org.au/whatsnew/newmediarel/mr30marchØ1.html

Wooden, M. (2002). The changing labour market and its impact on work and employment relations. In R. Callus and R.D. Lansbury (eds). *Working Futures: The changing nature of work and employment relations in Australia*. Sydney: The Federation Press, pp 51–69.

Woods, J.D. (1993). *The Corporate Closet: The professional lives of gay men in America*. New York: Free Press.

World Health Organisation Quality of Life Group. (WHOQOL: 1995). The World Health Organisation Quality of Life Assessment. WHO Paper. *Social Science Medicine*, no 41, pp 1403–1409.

Worrall, L. and C. Cooper. (1999). *The Quality of Working Life*. London: Institute of Management, Public Affairs Department.

Yankelovich, D. (1981). New rules of American life: Searching for self-fulfilment in a world turned upside-down. *Psychology Today*, 15 (4), pp 35-91.

Yencken, D. and L. Porter (2001). *A Just and Sustainable Australia*. Sydney: The Australian Council of Social Service.

INDEX

THE ETHICS OF ECONOMIC RATIONALISM
John Wright

Does economic rationalism work to maximise human happiness?
Does inequality matter?
Does the free market maximise individual liberties?

These are some of the challenging issues philosopher John Wright confronts in this timely book, in which he tackles economic rationalism from a moral perspective and weighs up the validity of its moral defences. For anyone who has questioned the desirability and moral costs of the continuing imposition of economic-rationalist policies by governments of all political persuasions and at all levels, *The Ethics of Economic Rationalism* will be essential reading.

ISBN 0-86840-661-9

GLOBALISATION: AUSTRALIAN IMPACTS
Christopher Sheil (ed.)

In *Globalisation:Australian Impacts* eighteen of Australia's most provocative thinkers write about the meaning and effects of globalisation in their own particular field. Each chapter assesses the present state of play in relation to an area or issue that is critical to Australian society and public policy, such as welfare, the media, democracy and the environment. *Globalisation* is a diverse and detailed critical analysis of the effects of the major forces defining our time, and will generate debate about our nation's future directions and prospects.

ISBN 0-86840-794-1